Six Billion Plus

Human Geography in the New Millennium
Issues and Applications

SERIES EDITOR
Barney Warf, Florida State University

Human geography is increasingly focused on real-world problems. Applying geographic concepts to current global concerns, this series focuses on the urgent issues confronting us as we move into the new century. Designed for university-level geography and related multidisciplinary courses such as area studies, global issues, and development, these textbooks are richly illustrated and include suggestions for linking to related Internet resources. The series aims to help students to better understand, integrate, and apply common themes and linkages in the social and physical sciences and in the humanities, and, by doing so, to become more effective problem solvers in the challenging world they will face.

TITLES IN THE SERIES

Six Billion Plus

World Population in the Twenty-first Century

Second Edition

K. Bruce Newbold

ROWMAN & LITTLEFIELD PUBLISHERS, INC.
Lanham • Boulder • New York • Toronto • Oxford

ROWMAN & LITTLEFIELD PUBLISHERS, INC.

Published in the United States of America
by Rowman & Littlefield Publishers, Inc.
A wholly owned subsidiary of The Rowman & Littlefield Publishing Group, Inc.
4501 Forbes Boulevard, Suite 200, Lanham, Maryland 20706
www.rowmanlittlefield.com

P.O. Box 317, Oxford OX2 9RU, UK

British Library Cataloguing in Publication Information Available

Library of Congress Cataloguing-in-Publication Data

Newbold, K. Bruce, 1964–
    Six billion plus : world population in the twenty-first century / K. Bruce
Newbold—2nd ed.
        p.   cm. — (Human geography in the new millennium)
    Sub-title on 2002 ed.: Population issues in the twenty-first century.
    Includes bibliographical references and index.
    ISBN-13: 978-0-7425-3928-0 (cloth : alk. paper)
    ISBN-10: 0-7425-3928-8 (cloth : alk. paper)
    ISBN-13: 978-0-7425-3929-7 (pbk. : alk. paper)
    ISBN-10: 0-7425-3929-6 (pbk. : alk. paper)
    1. Population forecasting.   2. Population geography.   3. Population—
Environmental aspects.   4. Public health—Forecasting.   5. Social prediction.
6. Twenty-first century—Forecasts.   I. Title.   II. Series.
HB849.53.N484 2007 (2006)
363.9—dc22

                                                        2005037851

Printed in the United States of America

To Blake and James

Contents

Contents

List of Figures and Tables

FIGURES

TABLES

Acknowledgments

I gratefully acknowledge the editorial assistance of David Grzicic (first edition) and Adrienne Witherspoon (second edition), both of whom put in the numerous hours needed to complete these manuscripts. I would also like to acknowledge the cartographic assistance of Ric Hamilton, School of Geography and Earth Sciences, McMaster University.

Introduction

The World of Child
Six Billion

THE LIFE AND DEATH OF CHILD SIX BILLION

October 1999 saw the birth of child six billion. While some marked the event, it was not necessarily greeted with enthusiasm. After all, the latest billion people had been added to the world's population in just fourteen years, with an additional eighty-two million souls being added each year. Not all agree that population growth is a problem, but there is consensus that the world's population cannot continue to grow indefinitely as it places increasing pressure on the earth's resources and the ability of states to govern. It is little wonder that fears of resource scarcity, environmental degradation, and ethnic, religious, or racial conflicts due to rapid population growth often dominate discussions of national and international security around the globe.

The world and future that child six billion inherits will likely depend on where he was born. Although he may have been born in one of the developed countries of North America, Europe, Japan, Australia, or New Zealand, it is more likely that he was born in one of the economically developing countries, where over 80 percent of the world's population lives and where 98 percent of the world's population growth is now occurring. Put in another perspective, of the 130 million children born in 2002, only 13 million were born in the developed, industrialized countries,[1] leading the Population Reference Bureau to conclude that the twenty-first century will feature a major transformation of the world's population.[2] Child six billion likely faces a rather bleak future if he was born in the **developing**

1

world, where health, war, famine, disease, resource scarcity, and environmental degradation are, more often than not, rules rather than exceptions.

In fact, his simply surviving infancy and childhood is uncertain. Although we have made large gains in **life expectancy** and mortality reduction in the past century, there are still widespread disparities. In developed countries, the **infant mortality rate** (IMR), which is the number of deaths of infants younger than one year of age per one thousand births, was six, compared to a world average of fifty-four in 2005.[3] The hardships are scarcely over if child six billion survives his first year of life. Life expectancy at birth, which measures the number of years an individual is expected to live, averaged seventy-six years in developed countries but only sixty-five in developing countries. In the developing world, the **child mortality rate** (CMR), which is the number of deaths of children under five per thousand, is eighty-five, compared to only ten in the **developed world.** Some of the poorest indicators are found in sub-Saharan Africa, where the IMR is 94, individuals can expect to live an average of forty-eight years from birth, and the CMR is 153. But one does not have to travel far to see these conditions: Haiti is the poorest country in the Americas and Caribbean, reflected in an IMR of 80, a life of expectancy of fifty-two years, and some 11.2 percent of children dying before the age of five.

To some degree, these variations reflect long-term factors, including development and the ability of governments to support health care initiatives. Poverty reinforces poor health by limiting adequate nutritional intake, as well as access to medicines, sanitation, and shelter. War, **refugee** movements, and simple geographic interaction across space perpetuate poor health and disease, but the high rates of mortality in sub-Saharan Africa and elsewhere also increasingly reflect the rise of infectious diseases, primarily **HIV/AIDS.** The African continent has been particularly hard hit by this epidemic, with an estimated 64 percent of the world's HIV/AIDS population living in sub-Saharan Africa. According to recent reports, the infection rate now approaches one in four among adults in many places.[4] Yet, the epidemic is only a portion of larger health problems and issues in the developing world. Although large improvements in the health of the general population and infant survival rates have been recorded within the past fifty years, infectious and parasitic diseases, including measles, malaria, and cholera, remain the leading causes of death in the developing world. Rapid population growth makes it difficult for governments not only to keep up with the demand for new health care resources but to maintain what is already present. Poverty, particularly at the household level, has clear implications for health and life expectancy since it is often associated with illiteracy, poor nutrition, poor sanitation, unsafe drinking water, and crowding, creating an environment that promotes illness.

Health issues aside, the world that child six billion inherits will likely be one scarred by war, resource scarcity, or environmental degradation. Clearly, the collective impact of six billion people on the world's environment and resources is large and increases as the population continues to place additional demands on resources, whether for basic survival or advanced consumer durables. Although this comment may seem relatively straightforward, there is much disagreement over the association between population, resource, and environmental issues. In reality, the benefits and costs of population growth occupy some middle ground between these different perspectives. Moreover, it is reasonable to assume that many of the stresses of rapid population growth are closely linked to poverty, educational attainment, health, and the status of women. Rapid population growth will stress forest and agricultural land, potentially leading to the loss of cropland through overgrazing and land degradation, limiting access to safe drinking water, and threatening water resources. This is not to say that population growth is solely responsible for these problems as they are facilitated by poor conservation practices or lax environmental regulations and pollution. Likewise, environmental degradation is a function not only of the number of people but of how much they consume and how their consumption alters the environment and existing political systems.

It is also reasonable to assume that national and international conflicts will increasingly reflect environmental scarcity.[5] While not yet a significant factor in the generation of violence, resource scarcity contributes to political instability. For those living in a developed country, it is easy to forget that the well-being of a majority of the world's population remains tied to local natural resources for food, energy, and income. Consequently, conflicts stemming from scarcities of cropland, water, and forests in the developing world may become increasingly common in the near future, affecting the developed world through trade and economic linkages, humanitarian involvement, and migrant or refugee flows.

It is important to realize from this line of argument the multiple interconnections between population and other concerns; for instance, it underlies many resource or environmental issues. There is a large potential for violence related to resource-scarcity and population issues, and local ethnic conflict or civil strife surrounding access and control of resources is a likely outcome of resource scarcity.[6] The reality is that the new face of war will often be a struggle for power and resources within a country or group of countries, often between opposing groups and ideologies. The uprising of Zapatista insurgents in Chiapas, Mexico, in the late 1990s was caused by rapid population growth, inequities in land distribution, and changes in laws governing access to the land. The violence in Chiapas further destabilized Mexico's government and economy, and the resulting devaluation of Mexico's peso caused deep-seated concern within America's financial markets. Ongoing conflict in Afghanistan between warlords, the elected government, and pro-Taliban forces represents ethnic and religious tensions between groups, and there is potential for the conflict to spread to Pakistan and other neighbors that share similar ethnicities and religious and ideological goals.[7] In Indonesia and Fiji, conflict reflects a history of forced migrations (Indians to Fiji under British rule and Muslim Indonesians out of Java) and the failure of subsequent governments to erase differences between the groups.[8] More recently, violence in Darfur, a region in western Sudan, reflects issues of racial and religious identity, competition for natural resources, and the role of the government.[9] Alternatively, the new face of war will be one against terrorism, in light of the events of September 11, 2001.[10]

Although less likely, violence relating to resource scarcity and population growth may also include large-scale violence created by the growing gap between haves and have-nots, which can be defined at the international, national, and regional levels. Although such conflict is typically cast with the developed pitted against the developing world, conflict between these two groups is less likely than regional conflicts within or between developing nations. The Middle East provides a ready example of the linkage between population, resource scarcity, and the potential for conflict in the form of water rights or other resources, including oil, gas, and minerals.[11]

In the past, population pressures could be relieved through voluntary emigration, just as North America and Oceania were settled at a time of rapid population growth within Europe. For child six billion, however, legal immigration options are scarce. Most developed countries tightly control immigration, often restricting entry to those who qualify under specific labor programs or "family preference" or "family reunification" guidelines. Most developed countries also actively promote the entry of individuals who are able to invest in the host country or who embody the education or skills demanded by developed countries. Yet, there is also a subtle but rising tide of anti-immigrant sentiment, particularly in European countries. Unlike Australia, Canada, New Zealand, or the United States, all of which partially see themselves as "nations of immigrants," European concerns with immigration and national identity have increased, provoking strong right-wing responses. Despite their immigration histories, the United States and Canada are not all that dissimilar, with occasional calls to limit **immigrant** intake.

While the movement of legal immigrants is not inconsequential, **illegal immigrants** and refugees dominate the international movement of people. For those seeking a better life elsewhere, illegal immigration may be a desperate option, but their only one. The risky and potentially deadly methods some use to enter countries, including paying smugglers, traveling through the Channel Tunnel between France and Britain in the undercarriage of trains,[12] or living in cargo crates for weeks on end while being smuggled in tractor-trailers or aboard ships, evidences their desperation. The smuggling of human cargo, with Chinese "snakeheads" or Mexican "coyotes" assisting individuals in entering a country illegally, has boomed, even though it usually comes with a steep price that indentures the individual for years to come. Some reports indicate that snakeheads are now charging upward of US$65,000 to smuggle a person into the United States or Canada and provide him or her with fake identification.[13] The price is also paid in loss of life, as exemplified by the high-profile death of nineteen illegal immigrants due to suffocation, heat, and thirst in the back of a locked tractor-trailer unit in Texas in May 2003.[14]

Exemplified by the saga of Mariel Cubans, Indochinese boat people, and victims of recent events in Afghanistan, Rwanda, Darfur, and Kosovo, refugees and displaced populations have become increasingly visible. Defined by the United Nations, refugees are people who are outside their country of nationality and are unable to return owing to fear of persecution for reason of race, religion, nationality, or association with a social or political group.[15] Major refugee-producing countries by mid-2004 included Afghanistan, Iraq, Sierra Leone, Somalia, and Sudan (Darfur). Overall, the United Nations High Commission on Refugees (**UNHCR**) estimated that there were more than seventeen million refugees and **asylum seekers** worldwide in 2004.[16] It is unlikely that child six billion will grow to see these numbers decline and, in fact, may become a refugee himself as ethnic, religious, environmental, or political conflicts increase. Refugees also face a world that increasingly rejects them as governments fear the economic, political, and social instability brought by the arrival of refugees, and Western governments react to the terrorist attacks of September 11, 2001 by tightening refugee admission policies. Instead, those who are displaced are likely to become **internally displaced persons** (IDPs), individuals who are forced to relocate within their own countries. By mid-2004, they were estimated to total over twenty-five million. This group is not protected by international law and has little access to assistance.

TRENDS IN POPULATION GROWTH

How did we get to six billion? How quickly is the population growing? Where or when does population growth end? In order to answer these questions, we must look at historical and current trends associated with population growth. For much of humanity's history, population growth was slow. High birth rates were offset by high death rates from famine, war, and epidemics. It is estimated, for example, that the bubonic plague reduced the populations of Europe and China by one-third in the four-teenth century.[17] Beginning in the 1600s, the world's population started to grow as life expectancy slowly increased with improvements in commerce, food production, and nutrition. Even by 1800, the world's population was only one billion, but the nineteenth century would bring a surge in population growth, particularly in what we now refer to as the developed countries. From 1800 to 1900, the population of Europe doubled, and North America's population multiplied by twelve, fueled by European immigration.[18] The populations of developing countries grew more slowly, but they already held the bulk of the world's population. By 1900, world population was approximately 1.7 billion, increasing to 2 billion by 1930. The mid-twentieth century saw unprecedented population growth, with the world's population reaching three billion by 1960, growing to four billion by 1974. The fifth billion was reached just twelve years later, and by mid-2005, the total population was 6.48 billion.

The explosion in the size and number of **urban** areas globally has accompanied the world's population explosion. Currently, approximately 47 percent of the world's population lives in urban areas. While the developing world lags behind the developed world in the proportion urbanized (41 percent to 76 percent, respectively), the urban population in the developing world is expected to grow rapidly in the coming decades, with upwards of 61 percent of the world's population living in urban areas by 2030.[19] Placing urban growth in another perspective, the number of cities in the developing world with populations in excess of one million will jump from 345 in 2000 to 480 by 2015. The number of **megacities** (cities with populations in excess of ten million) has also grown from eight in 1985 to eighteen in 2000, and is projected to grow to twenty-two by 2015. Most of these new megacities will be in the developing world, and megacities will be home to an increasing proportion of the world's population. The growth of urban areas, driven by **natural increase**,[20] net rural-to-urban migration, and urban reclassification, provides the raw ingredients for conflict.

The **population explosion** in Western countries during the 1800s marked the beginning of the shift from high to low **mortality** and high to low fertility known to demographers as the **demographic transition** and formalized by the demographic transition theory. Although the concept of demographic transition can be roughly applied to all countries, with a decline in mortality rates followed by an eventual decline in **fertility rates**, each transition's timing, pace, and triggers will vary. Within the developed world, these shifts in mortality and fertility occurred in the later parts of the nineteenth and early twentieth centuries, with major health improvements leading to a decline in infant mortality rates and increased life expectancy. Fertility rates were somewhat slower to change since social and behavioral change defining the desired family size tend to be slower, but they fell rapidly after 1900 as more children survived to adulthood, marriage patterns changed, women moved into the paid workforce, and parents placed greater value on the education their children received. In the United States, the **total fertility rate** (TFR), which is the average number of children a woman will have given prevailing birth rates, dropped from an average of four or five children in 1900 to approximately two children per woman by the 1930s. Canadian and European rates followed a similar pattern.

The most important determinants of population growth are the pretransition fertility rate along with the time lag between the decline in mortality and fertility. Even as mortality and fertility rates in the developed world stabilized, and low and stable rates of population growth were realized, much of Africa, Asia, and Latin America were still experiencing relatively high mortality and fertility levels. Since World War II, rapid population growth has largely occurred in the developing world when mortality rates were reduced dramatically with the introduction of modern medicines, including antibiotics and immunizations. As countries in the developing world started their demographic transition, they frequently had higher levels of birth and death rates than those observed in developed countries a century earlier, with fertility rates in many countries continuing to average more than six children per woman. Fertility reduction in the developing world was also slower than that experienced in the developed world (i.e., the lag between the declines in mortality and fertility was longer), and it varied across countries as a result of differences in social, cultural, and religious expectations; literacy rates; female participation in the work force; family and economic considerations; and the availability and acceptability of family-planning programs. Rates of natural increase (the birth rate minus the death rate, indicating the annual rate of population growth) remain high in much of the developing world.

At the dawn of the twenty-first century, there was some evidence that the developing world was finally transitioning from high to low fertility, evidenced by a 2005 TFR of 3.0 (3.5 if China is excluded), a rate that is considerably lower than that observed just a quarter of a century earlier.[21] With the expectation that fertility rates will continue to decline, some analysts have concluded that the risk of population growth has been greatly diminished.[22] Indeed, some authors have suggested that the new problem is a population *deficit* and an **aging** of the world's population,[23] and others have suggested that the threat of world population growth is now more regional than global and of consequence only in countries such as Pakistan and India. While the world's population growth rate peaked in the 1960s and started to decline slowly thereafter as fertility levels started to fall, the population is still rapidly expanding. But the perspective of population decline is a Western-centered one, and the threat of an aging population is overblown.[24] In part, for example, the arguments ignore growth rates and the potential for growth through **population momentum** in the developing world. In effect, to say that it is a regional problem allows the Western world

Introduction

to wash its hands of the problem, but only at its peril, particularly given greater likelihoods of unstable governments or resource scarcities in the developing world. The current fertility rate of 3.0 in the developing world translates to a growth rate of 1.5 percent (1.8 percent excluding China). This allows the population of the developing world to double in approximately forty-six years (thirty-eight years if China is excluded), assuming growth continues at its current rates. Even though fertility rates have dropped to 2.5 in Asia and 2.6 in Latin America and the Caribbean, they remain stubbornly high in Africa, with a 2005 TFR of 5.1. Moreover, in countries where fertility rates have dropped quickly, the young age structure of the population will ensure growth for the next two to three decades. Put another way, a huge proportion of the world's population has not started having children. Instead, these individuals *are* children. Consequently, a total world population of 7.9 billion by 2025 cannot be avoided, and most projections place world population between 7.3 and 10.7 billion by 2050, with nearly all of this growth occurring in the developing world (see table I.1).[25] So, while

Table I.1. Current Population Statistics by Selected World Regions, 2005

	Population Mid-2005 (millions)	Total Fertility Rate	Natural Increase (annual %)	Doubling Time (years)	Projected Population 2025 (millions)
World	6,477	2.7	1.2	58	7,952
North America	329	2.0	0.6	115	386
Central America	147	2.8	2.0	35	188
South America	373	2.5	1.5	46	467
Caribbean	39	2.6	1.1	63	47
Oceania	33	2.1	1.0	69	41
Northern Europe	96	1.7	0.2	345	102
Western Europe	186	1.6	0.1	690	190
Eastern Europe	297	1.3	−0.4	—	272
Southern Europe	151	1.3	0.1	690	152
Asia (excluding China)	2,617	3.0	1.6	43	3,283
Asia (including China)	3,921	2.5	1.3	53	4,759
Western Asia	214	3.6	2.0	35	303
South Central Asia	1,615	3.2	1.8	38	2,053
Southeast Asia	557	2.7	1.5	46	695
East Asia	1,535	1.6	0.5	138	1,708
Sub-Saharan Africa	752	5.6	2.4	29	1,148
Northern Africa	194	3.3	2.0	35	262
Western Africa	264	5.9	2.5	28	404
Eastern Africa	281	5.7	2.5	28	440
Middle Africa	112	6.3	2.8	25	189
Southern Africa	54	2.9	0.7	99	54

Source: Population Reference Bureau, *World Population Data Sheet*, 2005.

population growth is indeed slowing, we must still feed, clothe, and shelter a growing population, a task we are not certain the world can accomplish.

The certainty of continued growth is grounded in three assumptions. First, improvements in life expectancy (reduced mortality) will contribute to population growth as individuals survive longer. Longer life expectancies increase a child's likelihood of surviving infancy and childhood and completing his or her reproductive years. Second, the age structure of a population is key to its expected future growth; populations with a greater number of individuals in their childbearing years tend to grow faster, irrespective of the fertility rate. Women may have fewer children than in the past, but there are more women having children today. Excluding China, which has seen a shift in its age structure associated with its one-child policy, 32 percent of the population in the developing world is less than fifteen years old. In sub-Saharan Africa, 44 percent of the population is aged less than fifteen years. In comparison, only 17 percent of the population in the developed world is less than fifteen years old, a proportion that continues to decline. The young age profile of the developing world means that these members of this population have yet to enter their reproductive years. Even if fertility rates decline, population momentum will ensure sustained population growth. Third, most demographers expect that fertility rates will eventually decline below the **replacement fertility level**, ending the population explosion. Yet, fertility rates continue to remain above replacement in many regions of the world. Declines have been noted, but it is unknown whether we can expect further declines in fertility, with recent surveys in both Bangladesh and Egypt pointing to the danger of assuming that fertility will drop below the level needed to replace the population. Despite early successes in reducing fertility in Bangladesh, with fertility rates dropping from over 6 children per woman in the early 1970s to 3.0 in 2005, fertility rates have remained relatively unchanged through the 1990s. Similarly, Egypt's birth rate has remained greater than 3.0 since 1993. This trend is far from isolated, with Argentina's birth rate remaining at about 3 children for nearly fifty years, although by 2005 it had fallen to 2.4.[26]

As of mid-2005, the world's population was estimated at 6.477 billion. With approximately 130,000 births per year, the world's growth rate is currently 1.2 percent per year, meaning it will take approximately fifty-eight years to double the current population, assuming a constant rate of natural increase. **Doubling times** are shorter in much of Africa, averaging just thirty years. Within developed countries and given a growth rate of 0.1 percent, it will take an estimated 809 years for the population to double. While the world is unlikely to see a population of thirteen billion, pronounced differences in population growth and structure separate the developed and developing worlds, resulting in an unevenly distributed population across the globe. The geographic distribution is becoming more

Introduction

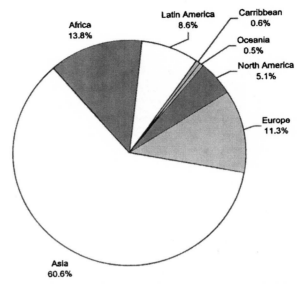

Figure I.1. World Population Distribution by Major Region, 2005. *Source:* **Population Reference Bureau, World Data Sheet, 2005.**

unbalanced. Rapid population growth in the second half of the twentieth century has meant that the share of the world's population residing in the developing world climbed from 68 to 81 percent. Regionally, North America and Europe represent only 16 percent of the current population (see figure I.1). According to UN projections, the percentage residing in the developing world will grow to 86 percent by 2050.

These averages tend to hide more local patterns of mortality, fertility, and growth rates. Demographers refer to a TFR of 2.1 as replacement fertility, or the number of children needed to replace their parents' generation exactly, accounting for premature death. While many developing countries in Asia still have above replacement TFRs, China, South Korea, Taiwan, and Thailand have fertility levels lower than replacement. China is, in fact, an important exception. With a population of 1.3 billion in mid-2005 and an annual growth rate of 0.6 percent, China is the world's most populous country. Despite fertility levels exceeding 7.0 recorded as recently as the 1950s, its fertility rate has plunged to below replacement level. This low level of population growth has been largely attributed to its restrictive one-child policy, which has artificially lowered fertility levels. India, too, has attempted fertility control policies but has had much less success. Although it has a smaller population (1.103 billion), India is growing at a rate of 1.7 percent, meaning it will surpass China's population by the middle of the twenty-first century. Progress in fertility reduction is echoed in improved measures of life expectancy and infant mortality. In other parts of Asia, such as Iraq and Pakistan, there has been little decrease in fertility. In Africa, the transition to a lower fertility regime is just beginning. Total fertility rates exceed 6.0 in countries like Burundi, Congo, Niger, Sierra Leone, and Somalia, and there is little evidence that a downward shift in fertility is about to occur. Throughout much of Africa, infant mortality rates remain high (eighty-eight per one thousand), and life expectancies are short (fifty-two years). In contrast, most developed countries are experiencing slow population growth rates (or even population decline), long life expectancies, and low infant mortality rates.

GEOGRAPHIC PERSPECTIVES AND DIRECTIONS

Despite attempts to cull some sense of order from population theories, such as the demographic transition theory, the role of space within the study of population has frequently been misplaced. Transition theory, for example, has been soundly criticized for its Western-centered insights into fertility decline. More importantly, it did not recognize the role of place and culture, and the model provided a weak explanation at best when applied to the different social, political, and economic circumstances of Asia, Africa, or Latin America. By effectively discounting the role of space and place, transition theory can make only modest claims to explaining demographic processes.[27]

The diversity of populations as a subject makes such generalizations difficult. Although the study of population is interdisciplinary in scope, with contributions by sociologists, economists, and anthropologists, the geographic perspective is especially valuable. Geography, by its nature, offers an integrative framework through which to view population (or other) issues. The disciplinary concerns of geography—space, regional variations, diffusion, place, and their role in human and natural processes—provide this unique framework for looking at population issues. Space is not a unique concern to geography, and geographers do not deal exclusively with space, but it is understanding spatial processes, such as the diffusion of ideas associated with small families or birth control techniques, that is of interest. Whether we are interested in population issues related to fertility or immigration, spatial processes are implied as states and their governments alter the demographic makeup of nations through policies related to, for example, immigration or families. Similarly, economic systems will determine fertility behavior, and the mortality of populations and environmental crises related to pollution, deforestation, and water scarcity provide examples of the linkage between regions. These are also dynamic processes, changing over time and across the landscape, and a geographical approach enables the explanation of past, present, and future relationships and patterns.

The geographic literature dealing with population issues has a relatively short, but rich, history. Initially defined in the 1950s, population geography dealt with the geographic character of places.[28] In its infancy, population geography was content to describe the location of a population and its characteristics and to explain the spatial configuration of these numbers. The field of population geography has since grown to draw upon a multiplicity of methods and theoretical approaches. Most writers and researchers now place population within a broader context, recognizing the importance of place and drawing upon the diverse insights provided by geography and related social science disciplines. The diversity of conceptual approaches provided by geography provides a framework through which to view complex phenomena. Economic and cultural geography provide insight into fertility choices, which may reflect the economic needs of the family, including a trade-off between viewing children as labor, or "pensions," and the ability to provide a more limited number with an education, or the larger cultural expectations of society. Similarly, political, social, and cultural geography provide insight into the potential for conflict by bridging disparate issues, enabling us to recognize the interrelationships between resources, environment, politics, and policy within the realm of population geography.

CHAPTER STRUCTURES AND AIMS

What does the twenty-first century hold for child six billion and his contemporaries? Will the population explosion result in a scarcity of resources or resource degradation? Why does fertility and mortality vary over time and space? What is responsible for large-scale population movements? While an understanding of demographic issues, such as changes in death rates or declines in fertility, may simply be motivated by a need to know, these issues cannot be viewed in isolation. Instead, they must be linked to broader issues that shape the economic, political, and cultural environments around us. They must also be put into geographical perspective. Although its effect is often overlooked, population growth in the developing world directly and indirectly influences the developed world daily through such avenues as immigration, trade and economic decisions, and disease patterns.

The primary purpose of this book is to uncover, illustrate, and understand population issues from a geographical perspective. The book relies on a mix of historical and contemporary perspectives and issues to ground the discussion and illuminate potential problems or issues that are only now emerging, with the intent of stimulating the reader to inquire and read further. The book will provide an overview of the themes of fertility, mortality, population movement, HIV/AIDS, and resource conflict within the geographical perspective, revealing the interdependencies inherent within the study of population. In large part, the book represents a synthesis of perspectives, approaches, and current literature, viewed from the geographical perspective. It is also meant to provide an international outlook, rather than relying on the experiences of the United States alone, which would provide far too narrow a perspective of population issues. Rather than providing a how-to on the mechanics of population research, each chapter identifies and focuses on salient trends and specific issues relevant to its theme,[29] then concludes with a discussion of relevant emergent themes and issues.

Chapter 1 assesses current fertility trends and issues in the developing and developed world. The chapter discusses fertility behavior as it is linked to a broad variety of social, cultural, and economic issues at the micro (individual) level, along with broader macro issues (i.e., nationalism, economics, aging). The other end of our life spectrum is captured in chapter 2, which discusses two major issues in **mortality** and **morbidity**. First, it focuses on the reemergence of infectious and parasitic diseases as challenges to population health in both the developed and developing worlds. Second, it considers notions of equity, discrimination, and marginalization within modern society by looking at the mortality experiences of African Americans in the United States, Aboriginals in Canada, and males in Russia. Building on these issues, chapter 3 focuses on the HIV/AIDS crisis in Africa, the emerging crisis in other world regions, and the demographic, social, and economic implications of this disease. The demographic toll that this epidemic is extracting from countries in Africa endangers their future economic development and national security. As such, it can be seen as a case study of infectious disease.

Chapters 4 and 5 explore the inherently geographical, but complicated, issues of immigration and refugee movements. Chapter 4 provides a brief historical overview of international migration before focusing on national immigration policies and the conflicting demographic and economic benefits and costs of immigration. Drawn from a largely Western perspective, the discussion addresses the emerging anti-immigrant sentiments found within Western countries. Chapter 5 focuses on refugee movements and the internally displaced population, the processes that generate these movements, and the responses of other countries. Both chapters examine the geographical patterns of movement within these groups, the reasons for movement, and government policies.

Chapters 6 and 7 focus on the linkages between population growth, resource scarcity, economic development, environmental degradation, and the potential for conflict. Although the linkages between population change and broader issues are apparent in most chapters, the intent is to draw together ideas from previous chapters and evaluate their relationships with broader socioeconomic and sociopolitical issues. In particular, these chapters are meant to gaze further into the twenty-first century, distilling possible relationships. In particular, chapter 6 focuses on the linkages between population growth, resource scarcity, and economic opportunities, with reference to conflicting viewpoints. Chapter 7 draws on current examples of national and international conflict and reveals their linkages to population issues. The chapter will also consider where (and why) it is likely that conflicts will increasingly find their roots in population issues. Finally, the conclusion distills the preceding discussion into five demographic forces that will shape the world.

NOTES

1. "Global Population Profile: 2002," at www.census.gov/ipc/www/wp02 .html (accessed May 20, 2005). See also LandScan 2003, which is a worldwide population database and is offered for free through the Oak Ridge National Laboratory.

2. *World Population Data Sheet* (Washington, DC: Population Reference Bureau, 2005). Unless otherwise noted, population statistics throughout this book are drawn from this source.

3. Following UN classification, the developed world includes Europe, North America, Australia, Japan, and New Zealand. The developing world includes all countries and regions outside the developed world.

4. UNAIDS, "AIDS Epidemic Update 2004," www.unaids.org/wad2004/ report.html (accessed June 14, 2005).

5. Thomas F. Homer-Dixon, *Environment, Scarcity, and Violence* (Princeton, NJ: Princeton University Press, 1999).

6. Homer-Dixon, *Environment*.

7. See Roger W. Stump, *Boundaries of Faith* (Lanham, MD: Rowman & Littlefield, 2000), for a discussion of the Taliban, their religious movement, and their implications for the region.

8. Jana Mason, *Shadow Plays: The Crisis of Refugees and IDPs in Indonesia* (Washington, DC: U.S. Committee for Refugees, 2001).

9. An overview of the crisis can be found at www.crisisgroup.org/home/ index.cfm?id=3060&l=1 or www.cbc.ca/correspondent/feature_050130.html (accessed June 2, 2005).

10. Susan L. Cutter, Douglas B. Richardson, and Thomas J. Wilbanks, *The Geographical Dimensions of Terrorism* (New York: Routledge, 2003).

11. Hussein Amery and Aaron T. Wolf, eds., *Water in the Middle East: A Geography of Conflict* (Austin: University of Texas Press, 2000).

12. Suzanne Daley, "Channel Tunnel's Risks Defied for a Dream of Life in Britain," *New York Times*, March 15, 2001, 15A.

13. Tom Fennell, "The Smuggler's Slaves," *Macleans* 113, no. 5 (2000): 14–19.

14. Ralph Blumenthal, "Immigrant-Smuggling Case against Driver Goes to Jury," *New York Times*, March 19, 2005, 11A.

15. Kathleen Newland, "Refugees: The New International Politics of Displacement," in *Perspectives on Population*, ed. Scott W. Menard and Elizabeth W. Moen, 314–21 (New York: Oxford University Press, 1987).

16. See the UN High Commission on Refugees website at www.unhcr.ch (accessed June 28, 2005).

17. Alene Gelbard, Carl Haub, and Mary M. Kent, "World Population beyond Six Billion," *Population Bulletin* 54, no. 1 (March 1999). See also Lori S. Ashford, Carl Haub, Mary M. Kent, and Nancy V. Yinger, "Transitions in World Population," *Population Bulletin* 59, no. 1 (March 2004), and Massimo Livi-Bacci, *A Concise History of World Population*, 3rd ed. (Oxford: Blackwell, 2001).

18. Gelbard, Haub, and Kent, "World Population."

19. United Nations, *World Urbanization Prospects: The 2003 Revision* (New York: United Nations, 2000), at www.un.org/esa/population/publications/wup2003/WUP2003Report.pdf (accessed June 14, 2005).

20. Fertility rates tend, on average, to be lower in urban areas in the developing world but remain greater than replacement in many cases.

21. China is frequently excluded from population indicators because its one-child policy has dramatically altered its demographic future and sets it apart from other developing nations.

22. See, for example, Barbara Crossett, "How to Fix a Crowded World: Add People," *New York Times, Week in Review*, November 2, 1997, 1; Ben Wattenberg, "The Population Explosion Is Over," *New York Times Magazine*, November 23, 1997, 60–63; Lori Ashford, "New Population Policies: Advancing Women's Health and Rights," *Population Bulletin* 56, no. 1 (March 2001).

23. Phillip Longman, *The Empty Cradle: How Falling Birthrates Threaten World Prosperity* (New York: Basic Books, 2004). See also *World Population Ageing: 1950–2050* (New York: United Nations, 2002).

24. In the Canadian context, the total dependency rate, or the proportion of dependents (aged 0–14 and 65+) in the population relative to the working-age population (15–64) was greater at the height of the baby boom than it is projected to be in the future. See http://socserv.socsci.mcmaster.ca/sedap for a series of research articles related to aging across countries (accessed February 3, 2006).

25. Recent Population Reference Bureau projections place total world population at nearly nine billion in 2050. See "Transitions in World Population," *Population Bulletin* 59, no. 1 (March 2004).

26. Carl Haub, "Flat Birth Rates in Bangladesh and Egypt Challenge Demographers' Projections," *Population Today* 28, no. 7 (October 2000): 4.

27. Michael S. Teitelbaum, "Relevance of Demographic Transition Theory for Developing Countries," in *Perspectives on Population*, ed. Scott W. Menard and Elizabeth W. Moen, 29–37 (New York: Oxford University Press, 1987).

28. Population geography first rose to prominence as a field of study in geography with Glenn T. Trewartha's call for its increased study at the 1953 Association of American Geographers annual meeting. The text is reprinted in Glen T. Trewartha,

"A Case for Population Geography," *Annals of the Association of American Geographers* 43 (1953): 71–97. See also Wilbur Zelinsky, *A Prologue to Population Geography* (Englewood Cliffs, NJ: Prentice Hall, 1966).

29. The book cannot hope to cover all aspects of each theme. Indeed, entire books can be, and are, written pertaining to refugees, immigrants, HIV/AIDS, and so forth. Undoubtedly, this book will neglect issues that some readers will interpret as important. Hopefully, the references and other lateral insights will be sufficient to direct the reader to appropriate resources. For instance, John Weeks' text, *Population: An Introduction to Concepts and Issues*, 7th ed. (Belmont, CA: Wadsworth, 1999), provides excellent coverage of measurement and data sources for a range of population issues.

1

✌

Fertility and State Policy

"THE STATE HAS NO PLACE IN THE NATION'S BEDROOMS"

The demographic transition is frequently used as a template to mark the shift from high to low mortality and fertility, along with the consequent population explosion as life expectancy and mortality rates improve. This shift in fertility regimes occurred throughout much of North America and Europe in the nineteenth and early twentieth centuries. In North America, the transition to modern fertility patterns, marked by stable and slow population growth, was essentially completed by the 1930s. In Canada, the French-speaking province of Quebec was an exception, with a total fertility rate (TFR) in excess of 4.0 during this time and a slower decline in fertility levels than elsewhere in the country. In other countries, the transition occurred much later, with many developing countries not experiencing mortality declines until the 1950s and still waiting for TFRs to decline.

Over the past century, worldwide improvements to mortality have been striking. Despite remaining variations in the mortality experience across space, its reduction has been achieved through improvements in sanitation, nutrition, and health care. Understanding and controlling fertility have been more problematic, reflecting its biological and social components. Worldwide, large variations in fertility rates are observed, ranging from a high of 8.0 in Niger to a low of just 1.2 in Poland and the Czech Republic, two of several countries facing a population decline (see figure 1.1).[1] Several other European countries, including Russia, Germany, Italy, and Spain, also have fertility rates that are well below the "replacement" level of 2.1

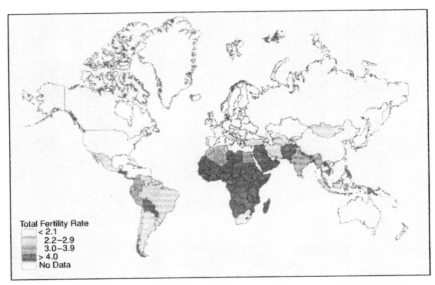

Figure 1.1.   World Variations in Total Fertility Rates, 2004. *Source:* **Population Reference Bureau, World Data Sheet, 2004.**

children, which is the number of children needed to replace the current generation exactly. Clearly, there is large variation in fertility behavior.

Fertility behavior is generally perceived to be a personal, private affair, with the United Nations affirming the right of couples to determine the number and spacing of children. As minister of justice in Prime Minister Lester B. Pearson's cabinet, Pierre Elliott Trudeau made his now famous statement that "the State has no place in the nation's bedrooms" in reference to changes to Canada's criminal code.[2] Despite his claims, most governments, including Canada's, have either an explicit or implicit presence within the bedroom, feeling that it is legitimate to intervene in individual fertility decisions. In countries where governments deem fertility too high, programs encourage lower fertility rates through family-planning programs that educate men and women about the benefits of smaller families and increase accessibility to and use of contraceptive devices. More stringent fertility programs, including China's one-child policy, have also been implemented in order to reduce fertility. At the opposite end of the spectrum, governments, including many Western European governments, may view fertility as being too low. Anxiety over an expanding elderly population and a smaller labor force capable of supporting the elderly has prompted concerns regarding the survival of social programs and a loss of economic or political power or both. In both cases, other policies such as access to legal abortion, child tax credits, or day care services indirectly influence fertility behavior.

Although the demographic transition theory has been widely applied, it has also been criticized extensively because of its Western-centric biases and its failure to account for myriad variations such as higher fertility levels, alternative forces associated with the decline in mortality, and social and cultural issues.[3] The failure of the demographic transition theory to explain differences in demographic events across countries has meant that its two key components (mortality and fertility) typically receive individual focus. This chapter looks at fertility, its determinants, and policymakers' ability to influence it. Complicating matters, however, is the fact that there is little agreement on what constitutes a desirable rate of population growth. Is it sufficient simply to replace the current generation? What are the political, economic, and social implications of below-replacement fertility? Can societies with below-replacement fertility, such as many European countries, survive politically and grow economically? In such countries, governments may actively promote fertility through **pronatalist** policies, typically by providing financial incentives to couples. Yet, how can governments speak of needing to increase fertility when there is an abundance of it elsewhere that could be used to augment growth in the developed world through immigration? Elsewhere, countries with rapid population growth will attempt to reduce fertility and slow population growth, with China's experiment at fertility control being the most widely known. Using both historical and current examples from the developed and the developing worlds, this chapter illustrates both the potential and shortcomings of fertility policy. The outcomes of both pronatalist or **antinatalist** policies are difficult to assess since fertility policies are often confounded by the unanticipated outcomes or effect of other policies. Every aspect of society influences fertility behavior. In turn, fertility and childbearing impact all of society. The interconnections are both minute and large, straddling political, economic, and social ideologies, meaning that the control of fertility behavior and the design and implementation of fertility policies are difficult tasks. Of interest too is the apparent paradox of concurrent fertility promotion and reduction.

WHAT DETERMINES FERTILITY?

Characteristic of preindustrial societies, survival in prerevolutionary Russia was difficult. Life expectancy was just over thirty years. Infant death rates might have reached upwards of 30 percent of all live births, and 50 percent of all children died by the age of five. In response to such high death rates, families were large; cultural practices, including early marriage before the age of twenty, reinforced the family structure, and any form of birth control was a criminal offence.[4] To remain single was a disgrace, and divorce was a sin. Within forty years of the revolution, fertility rates had declined to levels comparable with most Western societies.

While social, economic, and environmental considerations necessitated large families in prerevolutionary Russia, the Hutterites, a devoutly religious group found in the United States and Canada, value large families and in the early 1900s had a recorded average of eleven children.[5] Even at its peak, the fertility of this group fell far below the biological maximum, defined by **fecundity**, or the physiological ability of individuals to have children. Less evident are the social dimensions that work to keep fertility below its maximum level, including the roles played by economic issues, the government, and other institutions in altering fertility behavior. Similarly, cultural values regarding family size and the social roles of men and women alter fertility and the timing of fertility reduction. In many African states, for example, women enter into sexual unions at younger ages, and contraceptive use remains low, but families average six or seven children, far below the maximum. Cultural practices, including breast-feeding, abstinence from intercourse after birth, and indigenous birth control techniques, help to keep fertility below its maximum.

We can look at the experiences of Russia, the Hutterites, and other countries to generalize about the determinants of fertility. On an abstract level, demographer John Bongaarts identified four variables that explain nearly all of the variation in fertility levels across populations.[6] These include the proportion of the population that is married or in a sexual union, the proportion using contraceptives, the proportion of women who are infertile, and the incidence of abortion. First, in all societies, marriage has clearly promoted fertility. The longer women wait to enter sexual unions, the lower the fertility rate. Conversely, where women marry at a young age, fertility rates tend to be higher due to increased chances of pregnancy. Cultural values and practices relating to sexual activity, childbearing outside of marriage or union, and contraceptive use have an impact on fertility decisions as well. In the past, the age at entry into marriage and the age at entry into a sexual union were the same, but due to the increasing availability of modern birth control techniques and acceptance of premarital intercourse, this is no longer the case. Celibacy, abstinence, be it voluntary or involuntary (i.e., due to impotence), and frequency of intercourse within a union will either eliminate or alter the risk of pregnancy.

Second, contraceptive use and abortion are the key determinants of fertility in most developed countries. The "reproductive revolution," signaled by the availability and development of modern and effective family-planning methods such as the birth control pill, made it easier to avoid pregnancy. Increased access to methods of birth control and the desire to limit family size helped fertility reduction, and when these tactics have been used in developing countries, fertility decline has been much more rapid than that developed countries experienced during their **fertility transition.** Despite the reproductive revolution, contraceptive use varies dramatically over space and echoes variations in fertility levels. Among women in sexual unions and of reproductive age in the United States and Canada, for example, the rate of modern contraceptive usage is 69 percent.[7] Somewhat lower levels of use are observed in Europe, particularly in Eastern Europe, where contraceptive use rates are approximately 42 percent.

In the developing world, contraceptive use lags behind usage rates found elsewhere, but family-planning programs have had a strong influence on fertility by raising the awareness of means of, as well as the need for, contraception and control. Contraceptive use is lower in Asia, Latin America, and Africa as well, with less than 10 percent in the later using modern birth control methods in some areas. Instead, the regulation of fertility largely lies with traditional methods (i.e., withdrawal), and the low incidence of contraceptive use is attributed to religious beliefs or societal values. Various governments have also decried the use of birth control methods as an unwanted intrusion of lax Western morals, even in the face of the HIV/AIDS epidemic, the spread of which can be reduced through condom use.[8] When and how birth control is practiced also varies. Women in developed countries tend to start using birth control in their late teens or early twenties to delay childbearing and, following the birth of a child, to achieve the desired spacing. In the developing world, contraception use frequently starts after the desired family size is achieved.

Third, abortion is one of the most common forms of modern birth control in the world and is assumed to be an important reason for low birth rates in much of the developed world.[9] Legal in much of the world, including Canada, the United States, most of Europe (except Ireland), China, India, and Russia, abortion rates are highest in China and Russia (approximately 55 and 31 per 100 in 1990, respectively),[10] and having an abortion is easier than accessing contraceptive devices in Russia.[11]

Finally, the inability to conceive is associated with voluntary or involuntary fecundity. Breast-feeding, for instance, reduces (but does not eliminate) the likelihood of pregnancy for as long as twenty-one months.[12] With modernization, breast-feeding has tended to decline, which may be of particular concern within the developing world where, in the absence of other birth control techniques, fertility may increase. Sterilization also provides a method for lowering fertility, although this is a more popular procedure in developed countries where it is generally used to prevent further pregnancies after the desired family size has been achieved.

Together, these four variables explain nearly all variations in fertility, with the importance of each determinant depending on the cultural, economic, health, and social factors within a population. In many African societies, babies are breast-fed until age two or three, and women may be expected to abstain from intercourse for up to two years after giving birth, both of which tendencies increase the spacing between births. Although Bongaarts provides insight into the key determinants of fertility, the question remains as to what determines the social forces that mould fertility choices. Why, for instance, would marriage be delayed? Why would contraceptive use increase? How do the cultural values attached to children change?

To answer these questions, we must turn to theories of fertility transition over time and space.[13] These may be roughly distinguished by microeconomic interpretations characterized by Richard Easterlin's "supply and demand" framework,[14] along with the "diffusion-innovation" perspective proposed by a number of authors.[15] Both frameworks find their roots within the demographic transition theory, which ascribed declines in fertility to societal changes related to industrialization and urbanization. In the face of declining mortality and improved economic opportunities, the demographic transition theory implies that people will eventually realize that more children will survive into their reproductive years than they can afford, resulting in a decline in fertility that preceded modern birth control methods. Urbanization and industrialization therefore set the stage for declines in fertility, such as in pre–twentieth century Europe and North America, creating a way of life that made it more expensive to raise children.[16] Rather than using children to augment household income, parents "invested" in them through such means as providing educational opportunities.

The linkages among **urbanization**, industrialization, and fertility within the demographic transition theory were, however, criticized, especially within the context of the developing world, where the correlation between development and fertility is weak. Several countries in Asia (e.g., Bangladesh) and Latin America (e.g., Haiti) remain poor and underdeveloped with low levels of urbanization but are also experiencing fertility declines. In other words, development and economic security are not sufficient conditions to cause fertility to decrease. The neoclassical theories of fertility decline build on the demographic transition theory. Easterlin's classic supply-demand framework defines fertility choice as the outcome of a rational calculation of the costs and benefits associated with fertility behavior, contextualized relative to cultural and household expectations. Families try to maintain a balance between the potential supply of children and the demand for surviving children. Where death rates are high, high fertility ensures the survival of children to an economically active age, and there is no incentive to control fertility. The response to high mortality reflects the valuing of children as a source of security and labor, a preference for sons, or the desire to "replenish" the population. In effect, children may be likened to pension plans, contributing to production and income within the household or the care of elders, making large families a necessity and an investment in future security.

If, on the other hand, supply exceeds demand, fertility regulation becomes important. The decision to control fertility is then based on the financial and social costs of raising a child as more children are being produced and surviving into their reproductive years. Casting fertility behavior as an economic choice means that children are, in many ways, seen as luxury items, subject to both time and investment. Investment is represented by the *direct costs* of education, clothing, food, and so forth, as well as *opportunity costs*, such as foregone investments and purchases of other consumer goods. Parents are then faced with a trade-off between quality and quantity. In the developed world, quality is emphasized, with resources concentrated on a relatively small number of children. Children in the developed world are not expected to contribute to the economic well-being of the household or to support parents in their old age. Instead, they represent large direct costs associated with education, clothing, and food, along with the indirect, or opportunity, costs of having children at a time when the same dollar value could be spent on other consumer goods and demands for leisure time.

Criticism of neoclassical determinants of fertility behavior has lead social scientists to link changes in fertility behavior to the diffusion of ideas across space.[17] As with any process, diffusion of social norms or new ideas varies spatially, with the timing of the fertility transition hinging on the diffusion of social norms and new ideas, including birth control techniques. In the past, the preference for small families diffused from urban areas and from high- to low-income groups. Although important, diffusion is not a spatially smooth process. For instance, poor or inadequate transportation or communication infrastructures, which are especially evident in **rural**, agricultural, and poor regions of the world, create barriers that alter the diffusion of new ideas or norms. Religious ideology remains a persuasive force limiting the success of family-planning programs and the promotion of birth control methods. Cultural practices may likewise preclude the use of contraceptive devices, such as the condom, which is viewed as interference during sexual intercourse.

The uptake of new ideas or norms also depends on the individual. If new ideas, such as birth control, are to be accepted, individuals must feel that they exert some power or control over life events. In societies where women lack control and power, fertility rates tend to remain high. The key, therefore, is to produce greater equity between males and females, which is accomplished by making improvements in educational attainment, occupational status, or income opportunities. Improved education status and paid employment have reduced fertility, with a near universal relationship between improved educational levels among women and decreased fertility. Women with higher levels of education also tend to have a higher uptake of family planning, to wait longer between pregnancies, and to stop bearing children at an earlier age than those who are less educated. There is an even stronger relationship between women's education and child health, with higher educational attainment linked to healthier and better-nourished children, which in itself promotes a reduction in fertility. Although the exact relationship is unclear, completion of education may delay entry into marriage and expands employment options, suggesting that women delay fertility in order to earn an income. Employment also exposes women to new ideas, behaviors, and influences outside of the family. However, gender equity in employment is vital: if employment does not translate into power and enable women to make decisions regarding health care, contraception, the timing of children, and so forth, then declines in fertility are unlikely to occur.[18]

THE ROLE OF THE STATE: FERTILITY REDUCTION

There has been growing recognition since the 1980s of the need to control population growth within developing countries. Despite its complexity, governments have not stopped attempting to influence fertility behavior. Although reductions in fertility have occurred, many governments, including those of Saudi Arabia, India, Sri Lanka, Pakistan, Niger, and Peru, still view their population growth rates as being too high. In response, they have enacted programs to reduce population growth rates by controlling fertility behavior and have met with varying levels of success. Two long-term and well-known examples are discussed below, both of which provide insights into the successes and shortcomings of fertility policy.

China

Identified as one of the most successful, albeit controversial, fertility-control programs, China's one-child policy has received considerable lay and academic attention.[19] Initially, China's government viewed family-planning and fertility-reduction programs as suspect, assuming instead that socialism would ensure the equitable distribution of resources across society. By the late 1960s, however, China's leadership recognized the limits to population growth and the need for population control. With a TFR in excess of 7.0, rapid growth was acknowledged to hinder attempts to improve the economy and raise the standard of living. Beginning in 1979, the Chinese government advocated its one-child program, with the goal of stabilizing the population at 1.2 billion, to be accomplished through a combination of social pressures, including propaganda, local political activism, and coercion, increased availability of contraception and family-planning resources, and a series of economic incentives and disincentives. Those committing to the program received cash bonuses, and one-child families were given preference in school admission, housing, and job applications, and employment in urban areas. In rural areas, the program was altered slightly so that families would receive the same food rations and the same-sized plot for private cultivation as a two-child family. Disincentives to large families were also employed, requiring families having more than one child to repay all benefits received.

By the late 1990s, China's TFR had dropped below replacement and is currently at 1.6. The apparent "success" of the program seemingly follows from the ability of the Chinese government to exert control over the population to limit births, a recognized feature of China's communist society. The program's success could also be attributed to the promotion of personal and national economic benefits and its link to broader health issues, which together engendered the desire for smaller families within the Chinese population. Yet, even as fertility rates declined and population growth slowed, the program was not without its critics. Internally, a significant proportion of the Chinese population resisted the one-child policy, reflecting deeper cultural issues or economic necessity and the importance placed on the birth of male children. Higher financial incentives were also attached to the birth of daughters among couples who endorsed the one-child policy, and the government allowed more than one child in some rural areas; still, the policy meant that approximately 50 percent of families would not have a son. Poverty further reinforced the importance and contribution of male children to family welfare. As a result, couples frequently opted to disregard the one-child policy in their efforts to have a son and also turned to prenatal scans and abortion to prevent the birth of unwanted daughters, leading to an imbalance in the number of boys relative to girls, or the "missing girls" phenomena.[20] Equally disturbing, reports of female infanticide and abuse of women who give birth to girls were not uncommon,[21] and it was suggested that the set of disincentives for higher-order births (i.e., second, third, or more) deterred women from seeking appropriate prenatal and pregnancy related care, increasing the risk of death for mother and child.[22]

The true success of the program has also been questioned since declines in fertility can be traced to the 1960s. Fertility decline was furthered in the 1970s by government policies of delayed marriage, longer spacing between births, and fewer children so that by the early 1980s, the TFR had already dropped below 3.0.[23] In other words, the decline in fertility levels would appear to have been well established by the mid-1970s. Far from inducing fertility decline, the one-child program may have simply enhanced the motivation for smaller families, codifying family size as a national goal through the provision of a set of incentives and disincentives.

Continued economic liberalization will likely promote small families in the coming years as the direct and opportunity costs of children are realized, particularly in urban areas. Conversely, economic liberalization may also promote fertility among the poor as a means of ensuring their economic success in an economy in which the gap between the rich and poor is widening increasingly, leading observers to question whether low fertility rates can be maintained over the longer term. Even now, with an estimated population of 1.3 billion in 2005, the original target population of 1.2 billion has been exceeded owing to demographic momentum and the youth of the population. The government has already loosened its restrictions on early marriages and has relaxed its one-child policy, permitting two children in certain circumstances, suggesting that a substantial demand for larger families may remain within the population, particularly in rural areas where economic liberalization has increased the pressure to have children as a means of family support and production. Chinese planners are also recognizing that the rapid reduction in fertility levels in just twenty-five years has resulted in a young population (aged fifteen and under) that is substantially smaller than previous generations, creating a heavy burden of old-age dependency. Like many countries in the developed world, the Chinese government is trying to cope with an **aging** population and a shrinking labor force to support the elderly.[24] Moreover, the erosion of traditional family structures means that children no longer care for their elderly parents, posing additional problems and making a further relaxation of the one-child policy to meet the problem of an aging population possible. At the same time, the Chinese government reaffirmed and codified the one-child policy in 2002, while also criminalizing coercive enforcement measures.[25]

India

In a country where the total population exceeded one billion in 2000, India's attempts at and success with fertility control contrast markedly with those of China and remain a key issue. Although the recognition of the need to control population growth emerged much earlier in India than in China, the government was primarily committed to rapid economic development as a means of fertility reduction. In other words, family planning was, at first, seen as a long-term objective: government policy emphasized economic development with the expectation that reductions in fertility would naturally follow as income prospects improved. With little progress in reducing fertility apparent and the population continuing to grow, its control was increasingly seen as crucial to India's economic success. That is, rather than fertility reductions stemming from economic improvement, fertility reduction was targeted as a means of improving economic performance, making the Indian government the first to initiate a national program to slow population growth in 1953.[26] Providing support mainly through family-planning clinics, progress was slow, and the impact on fertility was minimal, with the TFR remaining near 6.0 by the early 1960s. In response, the Indian government reorganized family-planning programs on multiple occasions throughout the decade, pursuing reductions in fertility along a number of fronts by investing in family-planning programs meant to educate the populace and provide the means for birth control, legalizing abortion, and providing financial incentives to make sterilization more acceptable to the poor. The government also initiated disincentives, including the denial of maternity benefits to women after the birth of their third child. However, the emphasis on family-planning programs tended to divert funds from needed general health programs, including maternity and child health services, both of which are crucial to the success of any program promoting fertility reduction. Therefore, the government's own policies worked counter to the intended results.

Not surprisingly, fertility failed to respond even as mortality rates continued to decline, meaning the population was growing at an ever-faster rate. With mounting frustration over the failure of family-planning programs and economic-development policies to bring about a decline in fertility, the Indian government instituted an enforced sterilization program in 1976. Officially, no one was coerced to participate in the program, but the requirement that government employees produce two candidates for sterilization, wide-scale bribery, and a series of disincentives, including the denial of licenses, essentially meant that sterilization was indeed forced on the population. Although some twenty-two million individuals were sterilized, most were older males who had already achieved their desired family size, meaning that the program was once again ineffective in reducing total fertility. The forced sterilization program also carried a heavy political price tag with the defeat of Prime Minister Indira Gandhi in the 1977 general election. Her defeat sent a clear message that population-control policies that fail to recognize the rights of the population and broader relationships can bring about the fall of the government. Subsequent governments continued to recognize the need for family-planning programs, although they pursued the policy much less aggressively, combining abstinence with monetary rewards and improvements in the scope of family-planning services. Interestingly, TFR had decreased to 4.75 by the early1980s, a decline that may better be attributed to increased literacy programs for women and an increase in the average age of marriage rather than to family-planning programs per se. Although still high, rates have continued to decline, even among the poor, as radio, television, and other forms of communication help popularize the idea that small families are better.

Although India has managed to reduce its fertility rate over the past decades, declines in the TFR have seemingly reached a plateau, and the current TFR of 3.0 is still well above the replacement fertility level.[27] With a population exceeding 1.1 billion, it is set to surpass China's as the world's largest by 2050, India initiated its most recent attempt to reduce fertility, the National Population Policy 2000, which aims to reduce the TFR to 2.1 by 2010 and to stabilize the population by 2045.[28] Emphasizing quality-of-life issues associated with smaller families, the program targets improvements in public health, immunization rates, women's education opportunities, and reproductive health. It remains to be seen, however, whether the policy can be implemented as it will require large-scale funding, and it is not clear whether this will be made available. Even if the money does become available, other administrative problems, including a slow-moving bureaucracy and corruption, may scuttle the program. Even as the central government has backed off of sterilization programs, individual states continue to promote it through a variety of methods, including coercion, using loans, housing, and land to entice people to be sterilized after having two or more children.[29]

The failure of family planning within India raises a number of issues. Critics have charged that Indian programs have been inconsistent and typically lacked direction, with demographic targets tied to oscillating rewards and disincentives. The program has also failed to offer more flexible birth control methods such as the pill or intrauterine device (IUD). Instead, it has focused on sterilization in a country with a history of low contraception use. Other contraceptive techniques still represent only a small proportion of contraceptive use within India. The causes of India's lack of success run deeper than inconsistent or narrow policy objectives that fail to account for the broader social context within which reproduction occurs, including the role of women, the interrelationship among classes, and the political consequences of fertility policies. Like China, there is an antigirl bias: sons are preferred over daughters as they provide economic security or additional labor, especially in rural areas, while women in Indian society are typically marginalized and their role limited to motherhood. As in China, couples are now terminating pregnancies if the baby is female, leading to a surplus of boys.[30]

Class within Indian society is particularly important as a determinant of fertility, with typically lower fertility rates in the better-educated, more literate south.[31] Unlike China, with its supposedly classless society, totalitarian government, and tight control of its population's actions, India, with its democratically elected government, has a fractious population divided along caste, religious, and ethnic lines. Vina Mazumdar notes, for instance, that the desire for small families came from India's middle class, where low fertility fit with their own beliefs and aspirations.[32] Elsewhere, high child mortality, illiteracy, the marginalized role of women, and traditional extended-family structures dominate fertility options, meaning that fertility is unlikely to decline quickly. In effect, a minimum of two economic and demographic realities can be observed, with the fertility policies representative of the middle class being imposed on the lower class without taking into account the household economies of this group.

The middle-class outlook was not completely accidental. In order to succeed, fertility policy would depend on improvements in employment, health, and gender equity among the lower class, but this would also threaten the current political and economic power structure. Internal political interests have also played an important role, with some Indian states failing to curb population growth, while others have succeeded. Fertility reduction has been greatest in the more literate and prosperous southern states, while future fertility reductions must come from the highly illiterate and large northern states. The democratic implication is that any reallocation of seats within the Indian government would lead to a loss of political power for those states where population controls were more successful and an increase in political power elsewhere—hardly an incentive to promote fertility reduction.[33] The reality of the demographic, political, and class relationships within India weakens any national attempts to reduce fertility.

India's population has not yet realized the benefits of smaller families, and family-planning programs have not been able to generate the social revolution needed to make small families the norm. The failure of family programs is hardly surprising given the complexity and multidimensionality of fertility behavior. Empirically, it may be difficult to distinguish the impact of family-planning programs from the effect of other societal changes, including improving economic conditions. More generally, India's failed attempts to encourage lower fertility are not representative of all fertility programs but do reflect the difficulty of implementing these sorts of policies. Indeed, family-planning programs have succeeded in altering fertility behavior when properly instituted, increasing the use of contraceptive methods and contributing to declines in fertility. Successful programs have explicitly recognized that a decline in fertility is as dependent on individual and societal motivations as it is on technology and the government. Government policies alone are insufficient to promote change, and the mere provision of a family-planning program is inadequate to reduce fertility in the absence of a social environment that encourages changes in fertility behavior. Most family-planning programs fall short of their goals because they fail to understand how to influence desired family size. As in the case of India, if birth control and smaller families contradict the interests of many, and individuals fail to see the benefit of smaller family sizes, declines in fertility are unlikely to occur. We are recognizing increasingly that for family-planning programs to succeed, they must work to change the context of the social and cultural environment to encourage smaller families. This means that population policy will need to extend beyond family planning to encompass a variety of segments within society, including the provision of health care, the removal of socioeconomic barriers to contraceptive use, the involvement of religious leaders, the involvement of males (as husbands and fathers), and a synergy between development initiatives, such as literacy and the communications infrastructure.[34]

THE ROLE OF THE STATE: FERTILITY PROMOTION

From the perspective of the developed world, one of the most important demographic events in recent history was the **baby boom**, which presented a departure from the long-term trend of declining fertility. Generally referring to those born between 1946 and 1964, it affected the United States, Canada, and other nations involved in World War II, although the demographic impacts tended to be greatest in North America. In the United States, the TFR peaked at 3.58 in 1957, up from 2.19 immediately after the war. In Canada, the TFR reached a slightly higher level (3.9) and peaked slightly later (1959). In both countries, the rise in fertility expressed the pent-up demand for children following the Depression, then the war, along with rising incomes and expectations. By the mid-1960s, fertility rates had once again dropped to levels similar to those observed prior to the baby boom. In Canada, the TFR had dropped below the replacement level of 2.1 by 1972. Surprisingly, Quebec led the decline, an issue discussed later in this section. Although the baby boom was demographically important, with boomers' numbers impacting the provision of education in the 1950s and 1960s, then careers and leisure pursuits, and now retirement, social welfare programs, and health care as the baby boom generation ages into retirement,[35] it was a short-term phenomenon. It represented only a temporary boost, rather than a sea change, in fertility behavior. Over the longer term, fertility rates continued a decline that had first been noticed decades earlier.

While many countries face overpopulation and rapid population growth, a handful of Western industrialized or former Soviet Bloc countries are confronting the opposite problem: too few births, an implication of the long-term trend toward lower fertility rates. Beginning in the 1970s, TFRs fell below replacement levels (2.1) in many industrialized countries, particularly in Europe. Already, thirteen European countries, including Austria, Ukraine, Russia, Germany, Hungary, and the Czech Republic, have negative population growth, meaning that deaths outnumber births. Other countries, including Japan and Canada, are also facing low fertility rates and slowing population growth. Even in China, where the government has long been concerned with rapid population growth, concerns have turned to an aging population and its support.

In most Western nations, the decline in birth rates to below replacement levels has been linked to deep societal and economic changes.[36] With the promotion of gender equity, women have become increasingly educated. Increased employment and career aspirations have provided greater financial autonomy, contributing to declines in fertility as women seek careers outside their homes. Rising consumer aspirations further reinforce the opportunity costs of children, even as fears of unemployment, downsizing, and the uncertain future of the welfare state temper optimism about economic prospects. Together, these effects have prompted many either to delay childbirth or to reduce the desired family size, challenging many long-held assumptions about the timing of marriage and children.

Seemingly paradoxically, low birth rates and a slowing or decreasing population growth rate have their own set of problems. Although the anticipated consequences of an aging society are still unclear, both the Population Reference Bureau and the Canadian *Review of Demography* have concluded that low fertility is a serious problem, having more disadvantages than advantages, making it a politically unsustainable position.[37] From a demographic perspective, low fertility results in an increasing proportion of elderly. In Canada, the elderly population (aged sixty-five plus) represented just 7.8 percent of the population in 1951, growing to 13 percent in 2005 (see figure 1.2a). Current projections place it at approximately 20 percent by 2026, altering the age distribution of the population from its typical pyramidal shape dominated by a young population to a rectangular one characterized by a proportionately larger elderly population (see figure 1.2b).[38] Although it has the highest TFR in the Western world, the United States has seen similar increases in its share of the elderly population, which represented just 4.1 percent of the population in 1900, 12 percent in 2005, and is projected to grow to nearly 20 percent by 2030.[39] In Europe, the elderly already represent more than 15 percent of the population in several countries, including Sweden (17 percent), the United Kingdom (16 percent), and Belgium (17 percent), with continued growth ensured.

Not surprisingly, economists have tended to assume that the marketplace will be able to react to population change. If children are scarce, they will become more valuable, and the system will correct itself, either by finding substitutes for children (unlikely!) or placing greater value on children, which will be achieved through various incentive programs. Yet, it is unclear what the economic effects of low or negative population growth will be. Ester Boserup, a Danish economist, promoted the idea that

Figure 1.2a. Population Pyramids: United States, Canada, and Mexico, 2005. *Source:*
U.S. Census Bureau, International Data Base, 2005.

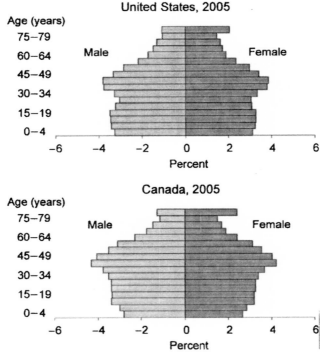

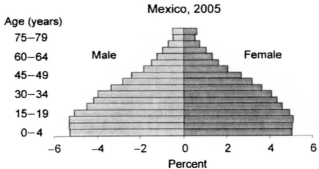

   The age profiles of countries with rapid population growth, such as Mexico, resemble a pyramid because each
age group (cohort) is larger than the one born before it (greater than replacement fertility). Populations growing
slowly, such as Canada and the United States in 2005, show less of a pyramidal structure in response to changes in
fertility and mortality. By 2025, the age pyramids of Canada and the United States are projected to be "rectangular,"
signifying the impact of an aging population and slower growth. The baby boom (ages thirty to forty-nine) is visible
in both Canada and the United States. The lower rates of mortality and longer life expectancies for females are also
observable within the pyramids.

Figure 1.2b. Population Pyramids: United States, Canada, and Mexico, 2025. *Source:* **U.S. Census Bureau, International Data Base, 2001.**

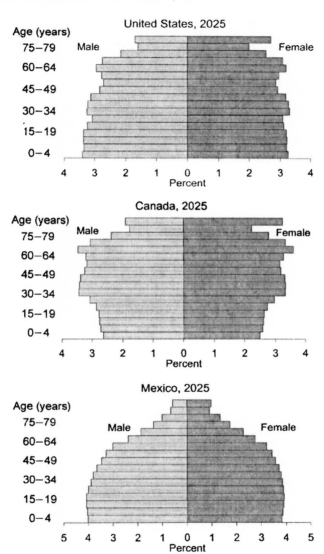

By 2025, the age pyramids of Canada and the United States are projected to be "rectangular," signifying the impact of an aging population and slower growth, while Mexico's age structure largely retains its pyramidal shape, although the effects of reduced fertility are apparent.

population growth triggered economic development:[40] over the long run, countries with growing populations would be more likely to post strong economic growth than stationary or declining populations. It has generally been assumed, for example, that population growth provides an economic stimulus, while declining population growth rates imply slower economic growth, a notion that most developed societies have adopted. Overall, however, the main economic impacts are expected to be minimal, with an aging population associated with higher savings rates, greater expertise, less unemployment, and higher innovation, although educational costs for retraining and continuing education of an older labor force are likely to increase. Likewise, low or negative population growth should not influence rates of technological change, consumption, or investment, although the distribution of these impacts across regions or age groups is unlikely to be equal, as is the case with the consumption of medical care.[41]

The negative economic impacts associated with low or negative population growth may be associated with greater inequalities within society. There is little doubt that countries with an aging population will face an increased burden of supporting the elderly, placing pressure on social welfare programs. Countries with low fertility rates will have smaller labor forces with which to support the elderly population and may face severe labor shortages that threaten their economic livelihood or stability.[42] The changing age structure of the population therefore raises questions regarding the provision of income security for the elderly, as well as housing, transportation, and other services, as has been highlighted by recent debates regarding the crisis (and reform) of Social Security in the United States. Health care provision is of particular concern since the elderly, particularly those older than seventy-five, consume a disproportionate share of medical services. Concurrently, the welfare of children may suffer as funds are diverted to meet the needs of the elderly population.

The largest negative consequences of low or negative population growth may, in fact, be political rather than economic.[43] Internally, countries may face a "graying of politics" as political and economic concerns increasingly represent those of older generations at the expense of the young. Internationally, a shrinking population has been associated with demographic marginalization. A "population implosion" may infringe on the very essence of nationality, with governments fearing that a declining population will threaten the ability of a country to defend itself. Even national identity is at stake, with national influence dependent on the vitality and size of a population.

Fearful of "demographic suicide" and the economic implications of an aging population, many countries have adopted pronatalist policies intended either to promote fertility directly or to ease the opportunity costs of children, with the expectation that fertility rates will increase. Faced with slowing or declining population growth rates since the 1970s, Eastern European countries have the longest history of pronatalist policies.[44] Policies have typically addressed the issue through a combination of financial incentives or restricted access to contraception and abortion services. Meant to ease the opportunity costs of children, financial benefits commonly include paid maternity and paternity leave, free or reduced-cost child care, and tax breaks for large families. Most of these programs are not advertised as fertility policies by explicitly targeting a desired number of children. Instead, policies are presented as antipoverty, prowoman, or profamily measures and are meant to influence socioeconomic conditions related to fertility decisions. Australia is slightly different: concerned with falling fertility (TFR reached a low of 1.73 in 2001), it has started to pay families who have children a $3,000 bonus. Since then, TFR has increased to 1.8, although critics suggest that this represents either a change in the timing of fertility (but no real increase in the number of desired children) or the "echo" of a large early-1970s **cohort** that is just now having children.[45]

Countries and national governments are not alone in their concern about declining fertility rates and slowing population growth. In Northern Ireland, the Protestant majority has expressed concerns that the Irish Catholic population, with its higher fertility rates, will eventually tip the demographic (therefore democratic) balance in its favor. Likewise, the Israeli government is fearful of the demographic implications of low fertility among the Jewish population and high rates among Palestinians. Despite high levels of education, Palestinian women in the Gaza Strip and West Bank have fertility rates of 6.6 and 5.0, respectively, rates that will allow the Palestinian population to double in twenty years under current fertility conditions.[46] Although Israel's population has benefited from immigration, the Jewish fertility rate is just 2.4 (higher among ultraorthodox Jews). Arabs and other non-Jews already make up approximately one-fifth of the population, an amount sufficient for Israelis to worry about the future viability of a Jewish democratic state.

Quebec, Canada's French-speaking province, provides yet a third example of regional concerns associated with fertility and population size. Historically, birth rates within the province were higher than the Canadian average as Quebecers resisted the adoption of contraception and fertility changes. Even in the late 1950s, at the peak of the baby boom, Quebec's TFR exceeded 4.0, giving the province one of the highest fertility rates in the industrialized world. The delayed uptake of newer fertility norms and contraceptive techniques reflected the control of the Roman Catholic Church and its traditional stance against contraception. In Quebec's case, the church also encouraged large families as a "demographic investment" that ensured the survival of French Canada within the Canadian confederation.[47]

Quebec lost its demographic advantage in the 1960s. The liberalization of the church and rapid emancipation of women contributed to declining fertility rates, enabling them to drop below the Canadian average. By the mid-1980s, Quebec had one of the lowest rates of fertility in the world at that time (1.37),[48] and its share of the Canadian population had dropped from 32.3 percent at the time of confederation in 1867 to 24 percent in 2001. Responding to this apparent crisis, Quebec's Commission de la Culture reported in 1985 that the province needed to take action to counter demographic trends that threatened the province's existence as a "distinct society," an issue that has dominated the province's politics since its foundation. The commission and other commentators pointed out that the demographic situation threatened the political strength of the province and its cultural sovereignty, in addition to posing the problem of providing for an aging population. Robert Bourassa, then premier of Quebec, echoed the concerns of the commission by declaring that increasing birth rates was the most important challenge for Quebec.[49] In response, Quebec initiated a series of profertility programs, including more generous tax deductions for children, higher family allowances, longer parental work leaves, and more day care opportunities. Beginning in 1988, the Quebec government also offered baby bonuses based on family size, with $500 (Canadian) for the first child, $1,000 for the second, and $6,000 for the third and all subsequent children. Revisions to this policy in subsequent years raised the bonuses slightly.[50]

Evidence from Eastern Europe and Quebec indicates that pronatalist policies are only moderately successful and their effects are short-lived. Over the short term, fertility rates frequently increase, but these increases do not hold up over the longer term. Statistics Canada, for example, identified a slight recovery in fertility rates in the years following the introduction of pronatalist policies, with the TFR reaching 1.6 in 1996, but dropping again to 1.5 in 1997 and remaining slightly below the Canadian average in 2000 with a TFR of 1.4.[51] If anything, most observers believe that incentives merely alter the timing of the first birth rather than changing the desired family size by increasing the number of "higher-order births" (i.e., second-, third-, or higher born children). Over the longer term, the relationship between financial incentives and other attitudinal factors related to fertility are difficult to measure and remain unknown. Certain demographic factors, such as there being fewer women in their childbearing years, mean that birth rates are likely to remain low. Restrictions on access to abortion services also have a short-term effect on fertility as couples quickly adjust their own practices or resort to illegal abortion.

Countries have also explored alternatives to fertility promotion by looking at other policies, such as delaying retirement to keep individuals in the labor force or delaying the start of welfare programs, as the United

States has done. Immigration offers an alternative to pronatalist policies, although it is a problematic one. Countries with traditionally high levels of immigration, such as Canada, Australia, New Zealand, and the United States, can still expect significant long-term population growth through immigration and a younger age structure, even though their fertility rates are at, or have dropped below, replacement level (U.S. = 2.0).[52] In Europe, governments may also choose to increase immigration, but do so with great risk. Europe has not, in the past, been a major destination for immigrants (excepting for short-term work programs), and current immigration numbers are insufficient to reverse population decline, while further increases in immigration levels may result in ethnic confrontation.[53] Most European countries have imposed strict immigration policies, and some have actively encouraged their foreign-born populations to leave.

THE ROLE OF THE INTERNATIONAL COMMUNITY: CONFLICTING MESSAGES

Although we like to think that reproductive choices are personal, the previous discussion indicates that states and their governments will often take either an active or an accidental role in promoting fertility. Growing concern within developed countries with rapid population growth in the post–World War II era prompted international institutions and governments to influence fertility policies.[54] At first, the developing world was slow to respond to programs promoting fertility reduction, arguing instead that economic development was the best contraceptive. Population policies were also viewed as an infringement on state sovereignty by former colonial or imperialist powers. With stagnating economies, high child mortality, and the increasing realization that women wanted to limit their own fertility, governments in the developing world increasingly warmed to the idea that population growth should be slowed. The United Nations became the driving force through its sponsorship of the first meeting on global population in 1954. Other UN organizations, including the World Health Organization (**WHO**) and United Nations Children's Fund (**UNICEF**), have incorporated reproductive health into their programs and under the auspices of the United Nations Population Fund (UNFPA).

The U.S. government has taken a more independent approach, preferring to direct its money through its own Agency for International Development (**USAID**), reflecting its own concerns and policy goals.[55] Largely driven by concerns that rapid population growth threatened U.S. security via trade, political conflict, immigration, or damage to the environment, USAID has been the largest single donor to family-planning programs. Initially, programs emphasized family-planning practices or specific demographic targets but grew to provide contraceptive information and related health services to support child and maternal health by the 1970s. Critics argued that the programs were too narrowly focused, failing to respect religious beliefs or making insufficient investments in social and economic opportunities. Most notably, abortion opponents criticized U.S. involvement in family-planning programs because of their belief that family-planning programs promoted abortion. In fact, U.S. law has prohibited the use of such funds to pay for abortion services since the 1970s.

The 1980s saw a significant shift in U.S. population policy during the Reagan administration. Supported by **economic optimists**, including Julian Simon, who argued that world population growth was "good," the administration declared at the 1984 International Conference on Population in Mexico City that population growth actually had a neutral effect on economic development. Reflecting its connections with the religious Right, the Reagan administration also opposed the use of funds for abortion services, withdrawing all financial support from any organization that provided such services, even when it used its own money to provide legal abortions. At the same time that the United States was reversing its position on population growth, developing countries had largely stepped back from their earlier opposition to family-planning programs. Instead, they promoted the benefits of small families and the need to slow population growth. Despite U.S. opposition, the 1984 conference ultimately supported family-planning initiatives and urged governments to make such services available.

After Bill Clinton took office in 1993, his administration waived funding restrictions set in place by the previous Republican administrations and increased funding to family-planning programs. Eight years later, within days of taking office, the Bush-Cheney administration reinstated restrictions to family-planning programs imposed at the time of the Mexico City conference.[56] The so-called global gag rule denies U.S. funding to private overseas organizations that use other (non-U.S.) monies to provide abortion services or lobby for changes to the abortion law in their own countries. Unfortunately, such restrictions actually undermine the success of family-planning programs. Broadly speaking, the number of family-planning providers will likely be reduced as funding disappears. Ultimately, the global gag rule will undermine family planning's objective of preventing unwanted pregnancies and improving maternal and child health. In fact, the ubiquity of abortion suggests that there is a large, unmet need for family-planning programs that can prevent the use of abortion services by providing counseling and discussing other options.[57] In cases where legal abortion is not an alternative, women may choose illegal abortions when faced with an unwanted pregnancy, increasing their risk of death or injury. Family-planning programs can also reduce fertility levels by helping with birth spacing, improving the odds of survival for both mother and child, preventing unsafe abortions, and reducing the incidence of sexually transmitted diseases, including HIV. Studies have clearly shown that as use of family-planning methods increases, abortion rates decrease, and that increased funding of family-planning programs reduces the incidence of abortion.[58]

Leading up to the fifth UN conference on population held in Cairo in 1994, discussions once again centered on the relationship between population growth and development. Despite the success of family-planning programs in the developing world, critics of these programs viewed them as infringing on personal liberties, specifically on the choice of individuals or couples to reach their preferred family size. Instead, they argued that family-planning programs should be better integrated into a broader view of health and that women's well-being should be of paramount importance. Responding to the critics, the conference redefined views of population growth and how to address it, linking population growth to **sustainable development**. Rather than focusing primarily on national interests, the conference promoted investment in human development, particularly the status of women. Family planning was to be integrated into a broader health agenda, including pre- and postnatal care, sexually transmitted diseases, and cancer screening. Infant, child, and maternal mortality and the alleviation of poverty were to be targeted, and universal access to family-planning services and a primary school education, as well as increased access for girls and women to higher education, were promoted. However, abortion was not promoted as a method of family planning, a clear recognition of the differing legal, moral, and religious viewpoints concerning abortion in different countries.

Although the success of the 1994 conference is still being evaluated, reviews give mixed results. Many countries have articulated and implemented new population policies, along with reproductive health programs; however, funding shortfalls by donor countries, including the United States and other developed nations, limit their reach and effectiveness. The success of the Cairo conference must also be evaluated within the context of broader health reforms and economic liberalization. Many developing countries had already started to change their policies and institutions, promoting a broader health agenda that incorporated reproductive health and gender equity. For example, the WHO's Health for All by 2000 (HFA 2000) program was an early promoter of societal health.[59] Initiated in 1977, HFA 2000 emphasized the promotion and protection of health, realized through the provision of primary health care, which stressed comprehensive basic services for all rather than sophisticated curative medical care for a few. Primary health care thus became WHO's basic strategy for health improvement, notably because of its concern with factors supporting health, including water supplies, sanitation, education, and the food supply, along with programs promoting child and maternal health and family planning. A particular emphasis has been placed on the health and education of children, adolescents, and women within the developing world. There is increasing recognition that childhood health is linked to health in later life; consequently, improved early childhood nutrition, greater access to immunizations, better hygiene, improved education opportunities, and safe water supplies have been promoted. Because societal or cultural norms often reinforce gender differences, programs have targeted equity issues, working to narrow gaps among women in literacy, education, and income opportunities.

WOMEN'S REPRODUCTIVE HEALTH

Underlying many fertility decisions and, ultimately, their outcome, is women's reproductive health, which includes safe motherhood, HIV/ AIDS,[60] adolescent reproductive health, and family planning. Clearly, these are not mutually exclusive concerns, although they are more often than not a concern of the developing world. Maternal mortality, for example, is greatest in sub-Saharan Africa (920 maternal deaths per 100,000 live births), with many countries experiencing rates in excess of 1,000. In comparison, maternal mortality is only 6 in Canada, 17 in the United States, and 12 in Western Europe.[61] Morbidity associated with poor reproductive outcomes is also significant.[62]

Not surprisingly, maternal mortality is associated with the absence of good medical care before, during, and after delivery. For instance, a majority of births in sub-Saharan Africa are not attended by skilled health personnel, and antenatal care is frequently lacking and sought out only when there is a complaint.[63] Equally problematical, there is frequently a lack of awareness about the importance of, and need for, medical care during pregnancy. Maternal mortality is compounded by the effects of gender roles and social and economic conditions within individual societies. For example, the cost and accessibility of reproductive health care providers may limit use, particularly in rural areas where trained providers are few, access to information is either limited or difficult, and the population simply lacks the funds for appropriate care.[64] Similarly, while women may prefer to seek female health care providers, few may be available, and husbands may be the ones who decide whether to seek care. As a consequence, males must also be included in reproductive health discussions. Complications from illegal and unsafe abortions are also a major cause of maternal death or morbidity, one that is common in areas where access to safe abortion is limited or illegal. In Nicaragua, complications from unsafe abortions have been identified as one of the leading causes of hospitalization among women, and upward of 8 percent of maternal deaths may be linked to complications associated with unsafe abortions.[65]

Adolescents are perhaps at greatest risk for negative reproductive-health outcomes, given their potential exposure to sexually transmitted diseases, unintended pregnancies, and complications from pregnancy and childbirth.[66] Worldwide, more adolescent girls die due to pregnancy-related complications than any other cause, and maternal mortality is four times as high for women younger than seventeen years. In part, their poor reproductive health reflects their societies' inability to address adolescent reproductive needs, early marriage, and lack of knowledge or experience in terms of family planning. Female genital cutting, or the removal of all or part of a young girl's external genitalia, remains a major reproductive health issue in some African and Middle Eastern countries and can lead to infertility and other health complications.

In large part, improvements in female reproductive health reflect increased access to trained health care providers and family planning, contributing to both maternal and infant health by reducing the number of unintended or unwanted pregnancies. As noted above in the discussion on the determinants of fertility, the use of contraceptive devices varies widely. There is, however, a relationship between family-planning programs and the practice of some form of family planning, be it contraception use or some other method to limit and space pregnancies. In Iran, which introduced family-planning programs in the 1980s, 74 percent of married women practice family planning. Correspondingly, rates tend to be lower in countries with newer or more limited family-planning programs. At the same time, the failure to use contraceptive devices, for reasons that include such diverse issues as fear of contraception's side effects, disapproval of husband or family, religious objections, and difficulties in obtaining contraceptives, limits the success of family-planning programs. Such unmet contraceptive needs are typically highest among poor and uneducated women.[67]

EMERGENT THEMES AND ISSUES

The low fertility rates that now characterize much of the developed world and their perceived social, economic, and political consequences will likely influence demographic decisions in the coming years, leading to programs and calls to increase TFR levels. Despite this rather paradoxical situation in light of concerns with high fertility elsewhere, the reduction of global fertility levels will likely be the dominant issue. Since the 1950s and the beginning of the population explosion in the developing world, demographers and governments alike have searched for indications that the characteristic high fertility levels found in the developing world would decrease. While fertility rates have declined as expected in most instances, they have stalled in others such that population growth will continue for the next few decades, fueled by population momentum associated with the young age structure, increased life expectancies, and above-replacement fertility rates. The multidimensional factors associated with fertility decline, which are further complicated by national and international policies, make it difficult to ascertain whether all countries will complete some form of fertility transition. Pressure within segments of China's population to have more than the allotted one child shows a continuing desire to have larger families, and the problems associated with a rapidly aging population may force the government to relax its fertility policy. However, it is also a misconception that China has its population under control. Large-scale population movements from rural to urban areas have lead to growing regional inequities, insufficient urban infrastructure, degradation of resources, and the potential for urban conflict. In India, despite a half-century of promoting fertility reductions, fertility rates remain relatively high, with a TFR of 3.0. Fertility rates continue to remain above replacement in many other regions. Despite early successes in reducing fertility in Bangladesh, which saw fertility rates drop from over 6.0 children per woman in the early 1970s to 3.0 in 2005, fertility rates have remained relatively unchanged through the 1990s. Similarly, Egypt's birth rate has remained greater than 3.0 since 1993, and it is uncertain whether it will be further reduced.[68]

After observing fertility transitions in Asia and Latin America, all eyes have focused on Africa, where fertility rates remain stubbornly high, and most African nations (notably in sub-Saharan Africa) have made little progress toward fertility transition.[69] In short, much of Africa is still waiting for the fertility transition. Africa arguably faces the most pressing fertility concerns: some fifty years after mortality levels were dramatically reduced in the developing world, Africa's TFR remains at 5.1, while sub-Saharan Africa still has a fertility rate of 5.6. Fertility rates this high, corresponding to an annual increase of 2.3 percent for Africa and 2.4 percent for sub-Saharan Africa, mean that the population will double in thirty years or less in both cases. While population growth is expected to slow, and there is emerging evidence that fertility rates will ultimately decline, the population of Africa will, under current conditions, double by 2050. In sub-Saharan Africa, only South Africa, Zimbabwe, Kenya, and Namibia would appear to have entered a period of transition in fertility behavior, which could be characterized by high contraceptive use, longer life expectancies, and a declining fertility rate, although HIV/AIDS threatens this success. Fertility reduction remains a distant goal among the majority of sub-Saharan countries.

Why has fertility remained so high in much of Africa? Given that fertility behavior is complex, it is not surprising that a combination of factors mediated through culture and society continue to promote high fertility on that continent. In general, poor economic development, subsistence agricultural practices, and low incomes maintain historically high fertility regimes, with many societies continuing to desire large families for the security that they provide. Strong lineage associations where children are expected to help the extended family mean that children provide both security and labor. In Africa, children are vital to the production of agricultural crops and are therefore a form of inexpensive labor.[70] Children may also provide additional income by working outside the home or migrating elsewhere and remitting income to the parents. The poor quality of transportation and communications systems; gender inequities in access to education, occupation opportunities, and power; and the continued absence of a strong family-planning program reinforce high fertility. In some instances, small families or attempts to limit family size are discouraged.

Although most observers expect fertility rates to decline in African states, the question remains as to when large-scale reductions will occur, how far rates will drop, and how long it will take to achieve significant reductions. Like explanations for fertility decline, the answers to these questions are also multidimensional. First, although contraceptive use is increasing, it is employed more to control the spacing of children or after the desired family size is achieved and less as a form of fertility control to limit family size. Less than 21 percent of married women use some form of modern birth control in many African nations, compared with 69 percent in North America. Second, mortality remains high in many African nations. As already noted, mortality rates have decreased within Africa, but perhaps not sufficiently to initiate fertility decline. The general rule is that life expectancy at birth must be greater than fifty years for fertility to decrease. This has only been achieved recently in some African states, while in others (particularly sub-Saharan states), life expectancy hovers near or remains below the fifty-year mark. Third, the HIV/AIDS crisis may reverse gains in life expectancy. Although there is no evidence that fertility choices will be affected, declines in life expectancy have already been noted. It has been estimated that life expectancies in Zimbabwe are now twenty-one years lower than they would have been without AIDS.[71] Fourth, gender equity is a distant goal in many societies. Women remain marginalized, literacy rates remain low, and rapid population growth and economic crises in the 1980s and 1990s prevented many countries from expanding educational opportunities to meet the growing population. Too frequently, the consequence is poor reproductive health. Health care systems are also casualties of high population growth rates and stagnant economies that have limited development, modernization, and investment in basic health care services.

Many systems are poorly funded or in ruin, preventing access to the most basic of health services at a time when both mother and child are in need.

In the past, policy options have offered little hope of reducing fertility levels in Africa,[72] as is evidenced by the experiences of the United Nations and other international groups that have worked since the 1950s to address population-growth issues. This is not to imply that progress in reducing fertility has not been (or is not) possible, but merely that the implementation of successful family-planning programs is challenging and that there is a particular need to target the underprivileged and those in rural areas through the provision of family planning and the encouragement of gender equality, education, and economic development. In general, countries that have invested in health and family planning have slower population growth and greater economic development than those countries that have not made such investments. African governments have recognized the intimate link between population and development and promoted programs to reduce fertility levels, but they have frequently lacked the financial ability to implement those programs fully. Alternatively, they have not sufficiently involved all stakeholders, including religious leaders and men who would work to ensure success by altering social, political, and economic forces influencing fertility choices that prove slow to change. Ensuring that fertility rates are reduced in Africa will provide an ongoing challenge.

NOTES

1. For example, the Population Reference Bureau projects that Latvia's current population of 2.3 million will decline to 1.8 million by 2050. Germany's population, currently 82.6 million, is projected to decline to 75.1 million by 2050. Two other European countries, the Czech Republic and Ukraine, had a TFR of just 1.2 in 2005.

2. Trudeau made this comment to the media during a December 22, 1967, interview, while he was the justice minister in Prime Minister Pearson's cabinet.

3. John C. Caldwell, "Toward a Restatement of Demographic Transition Theory," in *Perspectives on Population*, ed. Scott W. Menard and Elizabeth W. Moen, 42–69 (New York: Oxford University Press, 1987).

4. Sergei Maksudov, "Some Causes of Rising Mortality in the USSR," in *Perspectives on Population*, ed. Scott W. Menard and Elizabeth W. Moen, 156–74 (New York: Oxford University Press, 1987).

5. John R. Weeks, *Population: An Introduction to Concepts and Issues*, 7th ed. (Belmont, CA: Wadsworth, 1999).

6. John Bongaarts, "A Framework for Analyzing the Proximate Determinants of Fertility," *Economic Development and Cultural Change* 4 (1978): 211–35.

7. *World Population Data Sheet* (Washington, DC: Population Reference Bureau, 2005).

8. Peter Gould, *The Slow Plague: A Geography of the AIDS Pandemic* (Oxford, UK: Blackwell, 1993).

9. Weeks, *Population.*

10. Weeks, *Population.*

11. Stanley Henshaw, "Induced Abortions: A World Review, 1990," *Family Planning Perspectives* 22, no. 2 (1990): 76–89.

12. Weeks, *Population.*

13. Karen Oppenheim Mason, "Explaining Fertility Transitions," *Demography* 34, no. 4 (November 1997): 443–54.

14. Richard A. Easterlin, "An Economic Framework for Fertility Analysis," *Studies in Family Planning* 6 (1975): 54–63; Richard A. Easterlin and Eileen M. Crimmins, *The Fertility Revolution: A Supply-Demand Analysis* (Chicago: University of Chicago Press, 1985).

15. Weeks, *Population*, 1999.

16. As is discussed in chapter 6, fertility was already starting to decline (predominately among the upper classes) in Europe at the time of Malthus's writings. Had he foreseen that fertility decline would occur across all classes, his writings may not have been so dark.

17. John Cleland and Christopher Wilson, "Demand Theories of the Fertility Transition: An Iconoclastic View," *Population Studies* 41 (1987): 5–30.

18. Alene Gelbard, Carl Haub, and Mary M. Kent, "World Population beyond Six Billion," *Population Bulletin* 54, no. 1 (March 1999).

19. For additional information on China's one-child policy, see Jim P. Doherty, Edward C. Norton, and James E. Veney, "China's One-Child Policy: The Economic Choices and Consequences Faced by Pregnant Women," *Social Science and Medicine* 52 (2001): 745–61; Johns Hopkins University Population Information Program, "Population and Birth Planning in the People's Republic of China," *Population Reports* 1, no. 25 (1982); Jeffrey Wasserstrom, "Resistance to the One-Child Family," in *Perspectives on Population*, ed. Scott W. Menard and Elizabeth W. Moen, 269–76 (New York: Oxford University Press, 1987).

20. In some parts of China, approximately 135 boys are born for every 100 girls. The typical difference (the "sex ratio") is 105 boys for every 100 girls. See Ansley Coale and J. Bannister, "Five Decades of Missing Females in China," *Demography* 31 (1994): 459–80. The missing-girls trend has continued. See Jim Yardley, "Fearing Future, China Starts to Give Girls Their Due," *New York Times*, January 31, 2005, 2C. See also Eric Eckholm, "Desire for Sons Drives Use of Prenatal Scans in China," *New York Times*, June 21, 2002, 4A.

21. Wasserstrom, "Resistance to the One-Child Family," 269.

22. Doherty, Norton, and Veney, "China's One-child Policy," 745.

23. Weeks, *Population.*

24. Nancy E. Riley, "China's Population: New Trends and Challenges," *Population Bulletin* 59, no. 2 (June 2004).

25. Lori S. Ashford, Carl Haub, Mary M. Kent, and Nancy V. Yinger, "Transitions in World Population," *Population Bulletin* 59, no. 1 (March 2004).

26. Vina Mazumdar, "Fertility Policy in India," in *Perspectives on Population*, ed. Scott W. Menard and Elizabeth W. Moen, 259–68 (New York: Oxford University Press, 1987).

27. Carl Haub, "Decline in India's Birth Rate Slows," *Population Bulletin* 57, no. 2 (March 2002).

28. O. P. Sharma, "India Proposes Retooled Population Policy," *Population Today* 28, no. 3 (April 2000): 6.

29. Celia W. Dugger, "Relying on Hard and Soft Sells, India Pushes Sterilization," *New York Times*, June 22, 2001, 3A.

30. According to the 2001 Indian Census, there were an average of 927 girls for every 1,000 boys. In Delhi and Bombay, fewer than 900 girls were born, dropping to 845 girls per 1,000 boys in New Delhi's richest suburb (Shaikh Azizur Rahman, "Where the Girls Aren't," *The Globe and Mail*, October 16, 2004, F(2).

31. Haub, "Decline in India's Birth Rate Slows."

32. Mazumdar, "Fertility Policy in India," 259.

33. Sharma, "India Proposes," 6.

34. Iran has very successfully promoted family planning and contraceptive use, with the use of modern contraceptives rising from 24 percent in 1976 to 56 percent in 1997. See Farzeneh Roudi, "Iran's Revolutionary Approach to Family Planning," *Population Today* 27, no. 7 (July/August 1999): 4–5.

35. See, for example, David Foot, *Boom, Bust and Echo* (Toronto: McFarlane, Walters, and Ross, 1996); Doug Owram, *Born at the Right Time: A History of the Baby Boom Generation* (Toronto: University of Toronto Press, 1996).

36. Jean-Claude Chesnais, "The Demographic Sunset of the West," *Population Today* 25, no. 1 (January 1997): 4–5.

37. Review of Demography, *Charting Canada's Future* (Ottawa: Health and Welfare, 1989). Peter McDonald, "Low Fertility Not Politically Sustainable," *Population Today* (August/September 2001).

38. Eric G. Moore and Mark W. Rosenberg, *Growing Old in Canada* (Ottawa: Statistics Canada Cat. No. 96-321-MPE, 1997).

39. Judith Treas, "Older Americans in the 1990s and Beyond," *Population Bulletin* 50, no. 2 (May 1995).

40. Ester Boserup, *Population and Technological Change: A Study of Long-Term Trends* (Chicago: University of Chicago Press, 1981); Ester Boserup, *The Conditions of Agricultural Growth* (Chicago: Aldine, 1965).

41. Review of Demography, *Charting Canada's Future.*

42. See, for example, Moore and Rosenberg, *Growing Old*; Victor W. Marshall, *Aging in Canada*, 2nd ed. (Markham, Ontario: Fitzhenry and Whiteside, 1987); Judith Treas, "Older Americans."

43. Geoffrey McNicoll, "Economic Growth with Below-Replacement Fertility," *Population and Development Review* 12 (1986): 217–37; Kingsley Davis, "Low Fertility in Evolutionary Perspective," *Population and Development Review* 12 (1986): 397–417.

44. Henry P. David, "Eastern Europe: Pronatalist Policies and Private Behavior," in *Perspectives on Population*, ed. Scott W. Menard and Elizabeth W. Moen, 250–58 (New York: Oxford University Press, 1987).

45. Effective July 1, 2005, the bonus was increased to $4,000 per child. Robert Lalasz, "Baby Bonus Credited with Boosting Australia's Fertility Rate," Population Reference Bureau, 2005, at www.prb.org (accessed February 4, 2006).

46. Michael R. Fischbach, "The West Bank and Gaza—A Population Profile," Population Reference Bureau, 2005. See also Philippe Fargues, "Protracted National

Conflict and Fertility Change among Palestinians and Israelis," *Population and Development Review* 26, no. 3 (September 2000): 441–87.

47. Gary Caldwell and Daniel Fournier, "The Quebec Question: A Matter of Population," *Canadian Journal of Sociology* 12, nos. 1–2 (1987): 16–41; Roderic Beaujot, *Population Change in Canada* (Toronto: McClelland and Stewart, 1991).

48. Caldwell and Fournier, "The Quebec Question," 16.

49. Beaujot, *Population Change*.

50. Jean Dumas, *Report on the Demographic Situation in Canada 1990* (Ottawa: Statistics Canada Cat. No. 91-209, 1990).

51. Alain Belanger, *Report on the Demographic Situation in Canada 2002* (Ottawa: Statistics Canada, Cat. No. 919-209-XPE, 2002).

52. Mary Mederios Kent, "Shrinking Societies Favor Procreation," *Population Today* 27, no. 12 (December 1999): 4–5.

53. See the discussions by James F. Hollifield, Phillip L. Martin, Rogers Brubaker and Elmar Honekopp, and Marcelo M. Suarex-Orozco, in *Controlling Immigration: A Global Perspective*, ed. Wayne A. Cornelius, Philip L. Martin, and James F. Hollifield (Palo Alto, CA: Stanford University Press, 1992).

54. Gelbard, Haub, and Kent, "World Population."

55. Gelbard, Haub, and Kent, "World Population."

56. Peter H. Kostmayer, "Bush 'Gags' the World on Family Planning," *Chicago Tribune*, January 25, 2001, 2A. Note that Kostmayer was, at the time that he wrote the *Tribune* article, the president of Zero Population Growth (now Population Connections). Additional references can be found on the Population Connections website at www.populationconnection.org (accessed June 14, 2005). See also Liz Creel and Lori Ashford, "Bush Reinstates Policy Restricting Support for International Family Planning Programs," at www.prb.org (accessed February 2, 2006).

57. Timothy King, *Population Policies and Economic Development* (Baltimore: Johns Hopkins University Press, 1974).

58. Barbara Shane, "Family Planning Saves Lives, Prevents Abortion," *Population Today* 25, no. 3 (March 1997): 1.

59. Sarah Curtis and Ann Taket, *Health and Societies: Changing Perspectives* (London: Arnold, 1996).

60. Chapter 3 discusses the HIV/AIDS implications associated with women's reproductive health.

61. *Women of Our World Data Sheet* (Washington, DC: Population Reference Bureau, 2005). This discussion does not imply that women's reproductive health is not an issue in the developed world; instead, it tends to focus more on the pharmaceutical market, contraceptive choices, and infertility treatment, rather than on negative health outcomes for mother and child. Still, debates in countries such as Canada and the United States with respect to access to abortion services and attempts to limit access may push direct health outcomes to the surface once again.

62. A number of resources are also available online at the UNFPA website. See www.unfpa.org (accessed June 8, 2005).

63. Farzaneh Roudi-Fahimi, *Women's Reproductive Health in the Middle East and North Africa* (Washington, DC: Population Reference Bureau, 2003).

64. Ranjita Biswas, *Maternal Care in India Reveals Gaps between Urban and Rural, Rich and Poor* (Washington, DC: Population Reference Bureau, 2005).

65. Heather Luz McNaughton, Marta Maria Blandon, and Ligia Altamirano, "Should Therapeutic Abortion Be Legal in Nicaragua: The Response of Nicaraguan Obstetrician-Gynecologists," *Reproductive Health Matters* 2002 (10): 111–19.

66. Liz C. Creel and Rebecca J. Perry, *Improving the Quality of Reproductive Health Care for Young People* (Washington, DC: Population Reference Bureau, 2003).

67. Lori S. Ashford, *Good Health Still Eludes the Poorest Women and Children* (Washington, DC: Population Reference Bureau, 2005), and Lori S. Ashford, *Unmet Need for Family Planning: Recent Trends and Their Implications for Programs* (Washington, DC: Population Reference Bureau, 2003).

68. Carl Haub, "Flat Birth Rates in Bangladesh and Egypt Challenge Demographers' Projections," *Population Today* 28, no. 7 (October 2000): 4.

69. Thomas J. Goliber, "Population and Reproductive Health in Sub-Saharan Africa," *Population Bulletin* 52, no. 4 (December 1997).

70. Goliber, "Population."

71. Up-to-date statistics on the HIV/AIDS epidemic are available at www.unaids.org/wad2004/report.html (accessed June 14, 2005).

72. Goliber, "Population."

2

The (Un?)Certainty of Death and Disease

As the counterpoint to fertility rates, mortality rates declined from their historically high levels, initiating the demographic transition. In much of Europe and North America, improvements to human survival and longer **life spans** resulted in rapid population growth, aided by modernization and advances in sanitation and nutrition. Declines in mortality were apparent shortly after the onset of the industrial revolution, with Europe's population more than doubling between 1800 and 1900.[1] By the first half of the twentieth century, developed countries had completed their mortality transition, characterized by long life expectancies, low infant death rates, and slow population growth rates. In the developing world, the second half of the twentieth century brought rapid population growth, with the initiation of mortality declines in the postwar era. Here, the pace of mortality decline tended to be much quicker than that experienced in the developed world, assisted by the import of modern medicines, better health care, immunizations, and improved nutrition and sanitation.

The past one hundred years have seen remarkable improvements in life expectancy, yet, in the end, we all still die. Typically expressed as the number of deaths per one thousand people, death rates do not distribute equally. Instead, they vary by age, sex, socioeconomic status, race, ethnicity, and location, with the developed world characterized by lower death rates than elsewhere (see figure 2.1). Graphing the age-specific death rates of American and Mexican males and females (see figure 2.2), the "J" shaped function is a characteristic found in all countries and populations. The standard age pattern is characterized by differences between males and females and by death rates that are comparatively high in the first

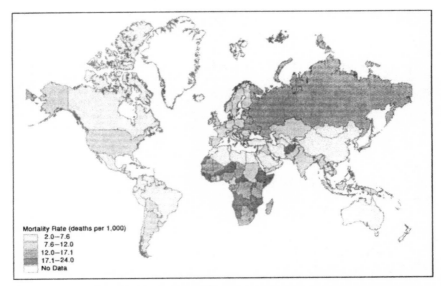

Figure 2.1.   World Variations in Mortality Rates, 2004. *Source:* **Population Reference Bureau, World Data Sheet, 2004.**

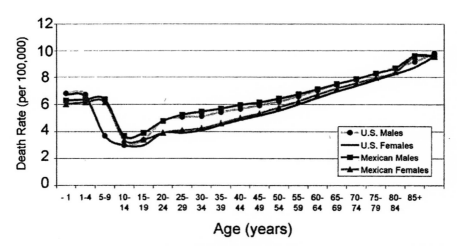

Figure 2.2.   U.S. and Mexican Age-Specific Death Rates by Sex, 2000. *Source:* **United Nations Demographic Yearbook, Historical Supplement, 2002.**

year of life, decline through childhood and adolescence, and then increase during old age. Women have lower death rates from birth onwards, with female life expectancies averaging eighty years in the developed world, an average of seven years longer than that for men. This sex differential is actually greatest for young adults, with the death rates of fifteen- to twenty-four-year-old males approximately three times that of females in the same age group, a difference that is largely attributed to the increased risk of HIV/AIDS, suicide, accidents, or homicides among young males. Moreover, despite overall gains in life expectancy over the past thirty years, fifteen- to twenty-four-year-old males have actually experienced increasing mortality,[2] even though most deaths in this group are preventable. Higher socioeconomic status, whether measured by education, income, or occupation, also confers greater life expectancy.

While death rates give a quick illustration of individuals' risk of dying, demographers typically prefer the complementary measures of life expectancy (the average duration of life beyond age x) or the infant mortality rate (the number of deaths of infants less than one year of age divided by the number of live births). Both measures provide descriptions of the mortality experiences of a population and a society's quality of life (see figures 2.3 and 2.4). As of 2005, global life expectancy at birth averaged sixty-seven years. With an average of seventy-six years, Western (developed)

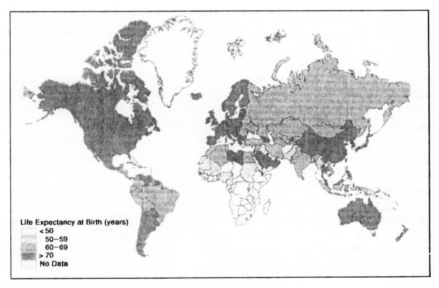

Life Expectancy at Birth (years)
< 50
50–59
60–69
> 70
No Data

Figure 2.3. World Variations in Life Expectancy at Birth, 2004. *Source:* **Population Reference Bureau, World Data Sheet, 2004.**

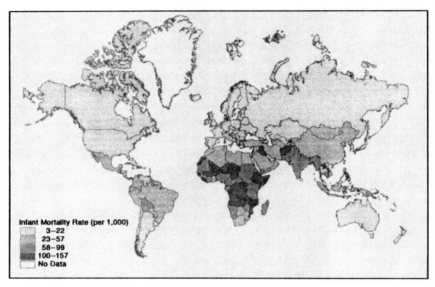

Figure 2.4.   World Variations in Infant Mortality Rates, 2004. *Source:* **Population Reference Bureau, World Data Sheet, 2004.**

countries enjoy some of the longest life spans and lowest infant mortality rates (six per thousand). Conversely, with an average life expectancy of just forty-eight years, countries in sub-Saharan Africa have among the shortest average life expectancies and the highest infant mortality rates (ninety-four per thousand). The two measures are obviously closely linked, with reductions in infant mortality rates historically extending life expectancy. More recently, Western nations have seen life expectancies increase through enhanced medical intervention and breakthroughs that can extend life among the elderly.

Of particular concern are threats to longevity and health from new diseases, along with inequalities in health within and among societies. Consequently, rather than focusing on the mortality process and its mechanics, as most population texts do, this chapter highlights two major themes. The first, the reemergence of infectious and parasitic diseases (IPDs), challenges population health in both the developed and developing worlds. With the advent and widespread use of powerful antibiotics in the mid-twentieth century, science thought that IPDs were controllable and ultimately could be eliminated as serious causes of death. The control of measles, mumps, polio, and other common childhood diseases, along with the complete eradication of smallpox further solidified the impression that modern medicine would overcome diseases that had been a scourge to humans for centuries. Yet, in the past two decades, IPDs have reemerged as threats to societal health. Drug-resistant strains of malaria and tuberculosis, increased societal resistance to immunization, and the emergence of new diseases such as HIV/AIDS and Ebola have further shaken science's complacency.

The second theme, inequities in the mortality experience, engages notions of equity, discrimination, and marginalization within modern society by contrasting the mortality experiences in the United States, Canada, and Russia. Race, in particular, has clear implications for mortality experiences, with African Americans or Canadian Aboriginal infant mortality rates and other health indicators approaching rates observed in the developing world. Minority groups such as African Americans or indigenous populations are doubly disadvantaged, having shorter life expectancies and higher infant mortality rates on average than their white counterparts. In contrast, Asian Americans reflect the other end of the health and socioeconomic spectrum, with a female life expectancy of eighty years.[3] Russia, on the other hand, which at one time proudly displayed its health system as a triumph of the state-controlled medical system, has experienced increases in mortality over the past three decades as economic conditions have deteriorated and its health care system suffered neglect.

THE (RE)EMERGENCE OF INFECTIOUS AND PARASITIC DISEASES

For much of human history, the average person could probably only expect to live between twenty and thirty years. Infant mortality rates were high, and approximately half of all deaths occurred before age five, usually associated with poor nutrition or infanticide. With advances in agriculture and the domestication of animals, humans were able to establish year-round settlements. Infectious diseases, such as bubonic plague, found a new home in human settlements and became the prevalent cause of death as denser populations and relatively poor sanitation allowed infectious diseases to thrive. Trade between settlements transported illness and disease across space.[4] The nineteenth and twentieth centuries saw improvements in housing, sanitation, and nutrition, allowing life expectancy in Europe and North America to increase to forty years. The poor health standards and living conditions observed in American, Canadian, and British cities during the industrial revolution gave rise to new public health initiatives. This intervention was spearheaded by the elite not out of goodness but from fear that their own health and, perhaps more importantly, their profits, hinged on the conditions of the working poor.[5] Although infectious diseases, including tuberculosis, bronchitis, pneumonia, influenza, and measles remained the main cause of death, their incidence declined with environmental improvements, occurring long before medical intervention was widely available.[6] Some diseases such as diphtheria, however, did not respond to societal improvements, declining only when large-scale immunization programs began. In fact, it wasn't until the 1950s that a decline in mortality, particularly among the older population, could be associated with the application of low cost public health programs. Since then, improvements to life expectancy within developed countries have generally been attributed to advances in medical and biological sciences, as opposed to general economic improvements or public health. The mortality transition also results in a shift in the ages when the majority of deaths occur. In countries at the beginning of the transition, younger age groups are at greater risk of dying since children are particularly susceptible to many infectious diseases. Even now, approximately 40 percent of deaths in the developing world occur among children less than five years old. In the developed world, most deaths occur among the elderly, with less than 2 percent of deaths occurring among those less than twenty years old.

Abdel Omran's **epidemiological transition** provides a useful framework for looking at these temporal trends in mortality, echoing the decline in mortality set out in the demographic transition theory.[7] However, Omran's theory asserts that modernization not only brings about reductions in overall mortality levels and the timing of death but also results in a shift in the major causes of death from infectious and contagious diseases to chronic, degenerative disorders. As recently as the mid-eighteenth century, tuberculosis, cholera, diarrhea, and pneumonia-influenza were the leading causes of death throughout the world. Through much of the later half of the twentieth century, resources were marshaled to control IPDs. By the late 1990s, only pneumonia and influenza remained among the top ten causes of premature death within the developed world. Instead, chronic noncommunicable and degenerative diseases such as cancer, diabetes, and liver, cardiovascular, or neurological diseases have replaced infectious diseases as the leading cause of death in the developed world. As the incidences of disease and premature death were reduced, individuals were able to enjoy longer life expectancies.

Countries occupy different stages in this transition and progress through it at different rates (see table 2.1). Unlike the developed world, where socioeconomic improvements resulted in declining mortality over a span of decades, most developing countries have moved quickly through the epidemiological transition, directly benefiting from the transfer of public health knowledge and medical technology from the developed world. This has meant that the developing world has experienced a much quicker decline in mortality levels than that experienced in the developed world. International campaigns have inoculated children against many common

Table 2.1. Leading Causes of Death in the United States and Mexico, 2002

	United States		Mexico	
Rank	Cause of Death[a]	Percentage	Cause of Death[b]	Percentage
—	All causes	100.0	All causes	100.0
1	Heart diseases	28.5	Heart diseases	16.2
2	Malignant neoplasms	22.8	Malignant neoplasms	12.7
3	Cerebrovascular diseases	6.7	Diabetes mellitus	11.9
4	Chronic lower-respiratory diseases	5.1	Accidents	7.8
5	Accidents (unintentional injuries)	4.4	Liver diseases	6.2
6	Diabetes mellitus	3.0	Cerebrovascular diseases	5.8
7	Influenza and pneumonia	2.7	Prenatal conditions	4.0
8	Alzheimer's disease	2.4	Chronic obstructive pulmonary diseases	2.6
9	Nephritis, nephritic syndrome, and nephrosis	1.7	Influenza and pneumonia	2.5
10	Septicemia	1.4	Homicide	2.2
11	Intentional self-harm (suicide)	1.3	Intestinal infectious diseases	N/A
12	Chronic liver disease and cirrhosis	1.1	Nephritis, nephritic syndrome, and nephrosis	N/A
13	Essential (primary) hypertension and hypertensive renal disease	0.8	Malnutrition and other nutritional deficiencies	N/A
14	Assault (homicide)	0.7		
15	Pneumonitis due to solids/liquids	0.7		
—	All other causes	16.7	All other causes	27.8

Source: United States, *National Vital Statistics Report* 48, No. 11 (2000). National Institutes of Statistics, Geography and Informatics, 2000. Mexico data found at www.inegi.gob.mx/est/contenidos/espanol/rutinas/ept.asp?t=mpob45&c=3222 (accessed June 25, 2005).
[a] Based on the ninth revision of *International Classification of Diseases.*
[b] Based on the tenth revision of *International Classification of Diseases.*

diseases, the most successful being that which eradicated smallpox in 1977. Still, many children remain at risk, and IPDs remain the leading cause of death in the developing world. Measles remains one of the five leading causes of death in children under five years.[8] Although the **prevalence** of measles has been reduced remarkably within the past five years, it continues to account for a large number of preventable deaths (an estimated 530,000 deaths, or about 4 percent) among children.[9] Worldwide, IPDs cause upwards of 54 percent of all deaths among children, while over

60 percent of deaths in Africa can be attributed to IPDs, especially among
the young and very old. One reason infectious diseases cause a larger
percentage of deaths in these areas is purely demographic. The proportion of the population surviving into older ages, where the risk of death
from chronic degenerative diseases is greater, is small in many parts of
the developing world. Instead, young populations, widespread poverty,
malnutrition, and inadequate public health care systems contribute to the
high death toll, even though a majority of existing IPDs can be prevented
through immunization, safe drinking water, proper food storage, safe-sex
practices, and personal hygiene.

In the postwar era, huge financial resources were committed to the eradication of infectious diseases. The successful defeat of smallpox in the
1970s seemed to confirm that infectious diseases could be greatly controlled
through large-scale public health initiatives. Another major program targeted malaria, an illness that has plagued humanity throughout history.
The drainage of swamps and the control of mosquitoes, the "vectors" that
carry malaria, through the application of the pesticide DDT resulted in
dramatic reductions in the number of new cases. But the gains were only
temporary. After 1963, commitment to the programs waned, and the disease returned, worse than before. Long-term use of DDT had given birth to
DDT-resistant mosquitoes, not to mention DDT's own deadly legacy linked
to cancer. Concurrently, inadequate treatment regimes, poor drug supplies,
and the misuse of drugs contributed to the rise of drug-resistant malaria.[10]
Despite worldwide attempts to control the disease, it is as prevalent today
as it was at the start of the campaign. The reemergence of malaria should
have served as a warning that complacency in the fight against infectious
diseases was not an option. The experience with malaria and other microbes indicated that diseases could emerge or reemerge as the causal mi-
crobe evolved into a more infectious form or as new pathways to infection
appeared. The rise of new IPDs, including the fearsome Ebola, a usually
deadly disease for which there is no known cure, as well as multi-drug-
resistant tuberculosis, malaria, and meningitis and new forms of cholera,
has further shaken our complacency in science's ability to control infectious
disease.

A variety of factors have been responsible for the reemergence of IPDs,
including change to the natural environment. Human-induced changes can
cause genetic changes in organisms or the vectors that transmit diseases
(e.g., as was the case with DDT resistant mosquitoes). Further, the misuse of antibiotics contributes to the rise of drug-resistant forms of malaria
and tuberculosis, and HIV/AIDS has resulted in an increase in tuberculosis and pneumonia. Agricultural practices affect the environment within
which microbes live and spread, and social, economic, and political conditions have facilitated their return and spread. Population movement has

long been an important avenue for the spread of disease. Historically, the bubonic plague came to Europe from Asia, and European explorers brought smallpox to North America and Oceania, decimating the indigenous populations who had no resistance to the disease. Settlement and urbanization have concentrated populations and enabled the sustained presence of diseases that were formally epidemic in small areas or for short periods. Cholera, nearly nonexistent in rural areas, quickly rose to epidemic proportions with urbanization as people were brought together, and the risk of contagion escalated in crowded and unsanitary conditions. Today, rapid urbanization in the developing world repeats this process as migrants settle in crowded and inadequate conditions. More recently, the surge in IPDs has been due to a breakdown in the provision of public health, with civil strife being a prime cause as it disrupts the distribution of needed drugs and food, and refugees fleeing conflict frequently find themselves living in poor and unsanitary conditions that promote the spread of disease. In 1994, more than half a million refugees fled fighting in the Congo and settled in refugee camps in neighboring countries. Within thirty days, some fifty thousand people died as cholera moved through the camps.[11] Similar numbers of dead were reported among Rwandans fleeing the genocide in Rwanda. Ongoing conflict and social disruptions in Afghanistan sustain the threat of cholera there.

The twenty-first century brings with it new challenges in the control of IPDs. Rapid population growth and urbanization has meant that governments have not been able to provide adequate or basic health care or infrastructure such as clean water. Perhaps more worrisome is the speed and ease of the transference of disease. The rapidity of movement across countries through jet travel poses additional challenges. Airplanes offer a highly effective means of transportation for disease, with the potential to spread disease across the world in a matter of hours. The arrival of a Congolese woman in Hamilton, Ontario, with symptoms similar to Ebola, when she had just left the Congo hours earlier, prompted North America's first Ebola scare in February 2001.[12] Although Ebola was ultimately ruled out, it is only a matter of time before a real case arrives in North America. Yet, it may not be the arrival of such fearsome diseases that threaten population health. Severe Acute Respiratory Syndrome (SARS) leapfrogged from China to Hong Kong to Toronto, Canada, in a matter of weeks in spring 2003 through air travel. Now, the World Health Organization (WHO) is closely watching the development of avian flu, with fears that it may be the next pandemic.

Additionally, there is an increasing number of cases of societal rejections of immunization. In North America and elsewhere in the developed world, rejection may be based on religious grounds or (unfounded) fears that immunization is linked to increased incidence of childhood autism, or both.[13] Elsewhere, the failure to immunize and thus protect children from preventable IPDs is also based on religious grounds. In Nigeria in 2004, for example, the government in the northern state of Kano stopped immunizing children against polio, a disease that is spread through feces, and can result in paralysis in one in two hundred people, amid fears and claims by religious leaders that the vaccine made girls infertile.[14] The WHO had hoped to eradicate polio; instead, it was fighting to contain the virus, which had spread quickly to countries including Sudan, Benin, Botswana, Chad, Ghana, Togo, Ivory Coast, Cameroon, and the Central African Republic. In these cases, the spread of the virus was likely due to the relatively porous borders in the region, while air travel has likely resulted in its spread to countries including Afghanistan, Indonesia, Egypt, Niger, Nigeria, and Pakistan.

WORLDS APART: VARIATIONS ON MORBIDITY, MORTALITY, AND LIFE EXPECTANCY

Since the 1950s, most countries have seen an increase in life expectancy and a reduction in infant mortality. Reductions were particularly dramatic in developing countries with the ability to treat or eradicate infectious diseases such as malaria, smallpox, and yellow fever and where improvements in basic health status had immediate effects. Despite improvements in indicators such as life expectancy or infant mortality within the past fifty years, widespread variations remain, even in the developed world. As of 2005, life expectancy in the developed world averaged seventy-six years, being slightly longer for women (eighty) than men (seventy-three). In the developing world (excluding China), life expectancies are lower, averaging sixty-four and sixty-one years from birth among women and men, respectively.[15] Improvements have been slower in sub-Saharan Africa than any other region,[16] with life expectancies there being just forty-eight years, compared to seventy-eight years in North America, seventy-two years in Latin America, and sixty-eight years in Asia. In fact, life expectancies have dropped since 2001 by two years in sub-Saharan Africa, a direct impact of the HIV/AIDS epidemic. At ninety-four deaths per one thousand births, infant mortality rates are also higher in sub-Saharan Africa. In comparison, infant mortality rates are only seven per thousand in North America, seven in Europe, and fifty-one in Asia.

In summarizing worldwide variations in life expectancy and infant mortality, it is apparent that we tend to make two assumptions. First, we assume that health indicators will consistently improve. We have come to expect improvements in life expectancy as medical science continues to make discoveries and as the population is increasingly taught to make positive lifestyle choices (i.e., not smoking or maintaining physical fitness) that will extend or protect life. Second, we generally assume that poor indicators of health are found only in the developing world. In other words, we assume that the Western, developed world has the advantage of an accessible and developed health care system that ensures population health. Yet, neither of these assumptions is correct as recent declines in life expectancy and increases in infant mortality in Russia show. Even within the developed world, with access to cutting-edge medical systems, we do not have everything right. Health and mortality differentials in the developed world are particularly problematic, not because they represent populations that require large-scale intervention and have little access to health care but for the exact opposite reasons. That is, in the presence of a large health care infrastructure, poor mortality experiences within segments of the population seem to be a paradox, yet they are common throughout much of the developed world. Rather than focusing on the triumphs of the medical system, the following sections look at its failures and shortcomings.[17]

Russians

As recently as 1900, Russian life expectancy was only slightly greater than thirty years, reduced by infant mortality rates that most likely reached three hundred per thousand and a child mortality rate of up to 50 percent.[18] Within a relatively short time, the former Soviet Union had successfully reduced mortality and increased life expectancy within its population, with rates in the early 1960s comparable to those found in the United States and elsewhere in the developed world. Despite these dramatic improvements in health in the postrevolutionary period, the Soviet Union could not keep pace with the West with respect to basic health outcomes from the 1960s onward. As life expectancy and infant mortality continued to improve in the West, they deteriorated in the former Soviet Union. By the 1990s, observers of Russia's demographic system noted that male life expectancy had dropped from sixty-five years in 1987 to fifty-seven years in 1994. Similarly, female life expectancy dropped by more than three years to an average of seventy-one years.[19] Although there is some disagreement as its cause, most placed this decline within the context of the breakup of the Soviet Union in 1989 and its corresponding economic and social turmoil, along with inadequate health services, lack of prescription medicine, alcohol abuse, and smoking behavior.

Russia's mortality experiences run counter to typical expectations, demonstrating that mortality and the epidemiological transition are not unidirectional. While debate as to the exact causes of the deterioration of health outcomes continues, these causes reflect a much longer process dating back more than thirty years to the Soviet era. Infant mortality in the Soviet Union was always relatively high, but research in the 1970s by Christopher Davis and Murray Feshbach notes that infant mortality rates started to diverge from those in the West.[20] Whereas infant mortality rates continued to decline in the West, in the former Soviet Union they stabilized at approximately twenty-five and then increased to over thirty by the mid-1970s. At about the same time, the Soviet Union stopped publishing detailed mortality statistics, a point that speaks for itself.[21] Davis and Feshbach attribute the increase in the infant mortality rate to social, economic, and medical causes, including increased smoking and drinking among mothers, poor maternal nutrition and health, inadequate health care during pregnancy, and unsanitary conditions in hospitals. They also noticed strong regional differences in mortality, with the rise in infant mortality highest in the Central Asian republics, including Uzbekistan and Kazakhstan, along with the Caucasian Republics of Georgia and Armenia.

The declining life expectancy among Russian men in the 1990s was not new either; instead, it reflected longer-term trends, with Soviet indices worsening relative to the West as early as the 1970s. After a temporary improvement in life expectancies in the 1980s, which was attributed to an aggressive antialcohol campaign under President Mikhail Gorbachev, the gap between the Soviet Union and the West continued to grow through the 1990s. As with infant mortality, the gap widened in part due to increasing life expectancy in the West, but it also reflected deeper institutional problems within the Soviet Union itself, including inadequate health services and general neglect of the Soviet and Russian health care system. Alcohol abuse and high rates of cardiovascular disease and injury also contributed to declining life expectancy.

Although male life expectancy had rebounded to sixty-six years by 2001, it dipped again to just fifty-nine years in 2005. Russia's infant mortality rate has continued to drop, moving from sixteen in 2001 to twelve in 2005. Still, it remains to be seen whether these measures will improve in the near future. The democratically nascent Russia continues to grapple with economic and social reform, and its health care system remains in a state of crisis. Russia must first catch up to the levels of infant mortality and life expectancy observed in the 1960s before they can approach Western levels. In the meantime, political uncertainty and stalled economic reforms mean that Russia's health institutions remain underfunded, and social and economic conditions remain poor—neither situation is conducive to improvements in life expectancy.

African Americans

Russia's poor health outcomes and the neglect of its health care system contrast markedly with American trends and health experiences. Americans have access to some of the best health care in the world, and their health care system consumes a significantly higher proportion of the gross domestic product than those in other developed countries.[22] A casual observer might, therefore, expect the United States to have the lowest infant mortality rate or the highest life expectancy. In fact, with an infant mortality rate of 6.6 and a life expectancy of seventy-eight years from birth, health indicators within the United States are rather poor by Western standards. Instead, the honors of lowest infant mortality rate and longest life expectancy go to Singapore (1.9) and Japan (eighty-two years), respectively. In fact, one hardly needs to travel far within the United States to observe health indicators that are more akin to those found in the developing world, placing American indicators closer to the bottom of the developed world's list than the top.

In large part, the poor performance of American mortality indicators reflects the poor health status and mortality conditions of its minority populations.[23] Health disparities are particularly noticeable among African Americans. Despite dramatic improvements in life expectancies since 1900 (from approximately 33 years to 72.3 years in 2002), they remain shorter than those of white Americans, who average 77.7 years of life.[24] African American mortality rates are nearly double those observed within the white population at every age except the very oldest as they have higher rates of death than whites for almost every major cause, especially heart disease, cancer, HIV/AIDS, and homicide. The increased risk of death is magnified among young African American males, where homicide is the leading cause of death, while white men are more likely to die in accidents (see table 2.2).[25] Blacks are also several times more likely to die from AIDS than whites. Smaller geographic scales show these same disparities. Across the United States, infant mortality rates are highly variable, with many of the Southern states having above average rates, including Mississippi (10.5), Louisiana (9.8), and South Carolina (8.9). The District of Columbia had a 2004 infant mortality rate (IMR) of 10.6, second only to Delaware (10.7).[26] Within the state of Illinois, which is one of the richest states in the United States, the 2004 IMR (7.7) was worse than the national average (6.8). This value, however, comprises a white 2000 IMR of just 6.5 and an IMR of 16.3 among African Americans,[27] rates that are comparable to Sri Lanka (16.8) and Russia (16.5)! At an even smaller scale, the 2000 IMR within the city of Chicago was 15.9 among African Americans, but just 7.1 among whites.

While the disparities in the mortality experiences of black and white Americans are startling, they are hardly surprising as they reflect the continued marginalization of blacks within American society, measured by inequalities in education, economic status, and occupation, despite improvements in their overall economic and social status since the 1930s.

Table 2.2.   Leading Causes of Death: Black and White Males Aged 25–34 in the United States, 2002

	Black Males			White Males		
Rank	Cause of Death[a]	Number	Rate	Cause of Death	Number	Rate
—	All causes	6,848	264.5	All causes	20,798	128.3
1	Assault (homicide)	2,129	60.1	Accidents (unintentional injuries)	7,986	49.3
2	Accidents (unintentional injuries)	1,309	50.6	Intentional self-harm (suicide)	3,495	21.6
3	HIV disease	634	24.5	Malignant neoplasms	1,472	9.1
4	Diseases of the heart	619	23.9	Assault (homicide)	1,435	8.9
5	Intentional self-harm (suicide)	447	17.3	Diseases of the heart	1,420	8.8
6	Malignant neoplasms	290	11.2	HIV disease	532	3.3
7	Diabetes mellitus	113	4.4	Diabetes mellitus	266	1.6
8	Cerebrovascular diseases	74	2.9	Congenital malformations, deformations, and chromosomal abnormalities	231	1.4
9	Anemias	73	2.8	Cerebrovascular diseases	195	1.2
10	Chronic lower-respiratory diseases	58	2.2	Chronic liver disease and cirrhosis	193	1.2
—	All other causes	1,102	42.6	All other causes	3,573	22.0

Source: United States, *National Vital Statistics Report* 53, no. 17 (2005).
[a] Based on the tenth revision of *International Classification of Diseases.*

Although legislation has reduced the social and economic gulf between the two groups, it remains substantial. For instance, median income in 2003 was $23,520; yet for blacks, the median income was only $19,794. Similarly, blacks experience lower educational attainment, with only 14.4 percent completing four or more years of college, compared to 23.8 percent in the total population. Also, minority children in poverty are less likely to be covered by health insurance.[28] Minority children suffer disproportionately from economic deprivation, and the proportion of children in poverty among blacks was approximately 2.5 times that of white children in 2003.[29] The prevalence of poor mortality outcomes is also an indicator of social problems within the African American community, including socioenvironmental and personal risks and inadequate service provision.

Poor health outcomes among African Americans are also linked to broader health concerns, including housing conditions, access to public health, and poor infrastructure. Latent racism and ongoing economic inequalities will perpetuate these differences for the foreseeable future. The marginalization of African Americans also extends to a health care system that provides fewer services and clinics in poor areas and in which blacks are less likely to be insured, thus less likely to use health care facilities, than their white counterparts.[30] Moreover, differences in mortality by race remain even after a comparison of individuals with similar levels of income and education.

The fact that the United States trails other developed countries on key population indicators reflects its patchwork health care system, which is dominated by user-pay or private health insurance as opposed to the state-funded, universal health care programs seen in countries such as the United Kingdom or Canada. African Americans' lower socioeconomic position within American society makes it unlikely that they will be able to afford private medical plans, meaning that those who are in greatest need of care can least afford it. In 2003, for instance, 14.5 percent of black children had no health care insurance. By comparison, just 7.4 percent of white, non-Hispanic children lacked some form of health insurance.[31] While public health programs such as Medicare or Medicaid are available for the poor or elderly, these programs are limited and means tested. For those who do not qualify, private health insurance has become too expensive, and an estimated forty-four million Americans have no insurance,[32] meaning that they forego medical treatment, rely on social service agencies for assistance, or use emergency room services, for which the cost of medical attention is significantly greater. The structure of the American health care system also extends to the location of service providers. Physicians, clinics, and institutions locate in areas with higher financial returns, and inner-city areas have fewer services. The number of public hospitals providing care for the poor declined from 1,778 in 1980 to 1,197 in 1999, having fallen victim to hospital closures, acquisitions, or mergers.[33] Inner-city areas have difficulty recruiting doctors and frequently depend on federal programs such as the National Health Services Corp, created in 1970 to provide basic care to inner-city neighborhoods. These structural barriers to care mean that poor, inner-city areas are frequently underserviced, a situation that has worsened under the Bush administration, which has cut a variety of health programs for people without health insurance.[34]

Canadian Aboriginals

The United States does not have a monopoly on poor health among its sub-populations. Making up approximately 4 percent of the Canadian population, Aboriginal peoples (the indigenous Canadian population including

Inuit, Metis, and North American Indians, or First Nations) bear a disproportionate burden of illness regardless of the indicator used,[35] despite the existence of generous government health programs.[36] For example, the 2000 life expectancy of First Nation males was only 68.9 years, compared to approximately 76 years for Canadian males at the time. For females, life expectancy is approximately 76.6 years, 5 years less than the Canadian average of 81 years. High infant mortality rates (16.3 among Inuit, 13.8 among Native American Indians) exceed the Canadian average of 5.2, with disparities heightened in more remote locations or on reservations.[37]

Responsibility for Aboriginal health care lies with the federal government and is administered through provincial or territorial plans. Status Indians (individuals registered under the Indian Act of 1876, which formally recognized their Aboriginal heritage and brought them under the control of the federal government) and the Inuit also receive nonmedical services such as drug, eye, and dental care through the Medical Services Branch of Health Canada. Like the United States, the poor health outcomes of Canadian Aboriginals are linked to their economic and social conditions, as well as to their history of oppression and marginalization, reinforced by racism and discrimination. The impacts of colonialism, both pre- and post-1876, have had widespread and long-term impacts on the health of the population. Early on, epidemics of smallpox, measles, and tuberculosis destroyed large parts of it. Under federal control, Aboriginal children were often removed from their parents and forced into residential schools that replaced their traditional culture and way of life with a European one. The stress associated with cultural dispossession and **assimilation** into Western society has weakened traditional cultural structures and values by removing traditional sources of support and identification. Such factors likely influence Aboriginal health negatively by promoting the disintegration of the community, hindrance of good health care practices, and participation in risky health behavior.

Marginalization and discrimination cannot account for all health disparities. Environmental conditions such as lack of running water or unsafe water, poverty, poor housing conditions, and low self-esteem reinforce high rates of alcohol and substance abuse, which are themselves partly responsible for the observed disparities in health. Geographic remoteness and physical access to health care play a role in the health status of the Aboriginal population. While residents of urban areas may have access to a greater variety of services, they also may not use them to their full benefit. In remote, rural areas, on-reservation service provision may only take the form of a resident community health representative and a doctor who fills in on a semiregular basis.

EMERGENT THEMES AND ISSUES

Changes in the mortality experiences of populations were among the most significant advances of the twentieth century. Unlike the twentieth, the twenty-first century will likely see less-dramatic changes to life expectancy within the developed world. Similarly, the developing world will likely see some change, although the degree of change and its direction are unclear. It is, in fact, likely that life expectancy will decrease in parts of the developing world as infectious diseases, including HIV/AIDS, continue to take their toll. As we look ahead to the coming decades, we can raise four nonexclusive issues relating to the mortality and morbidity experiences of populations, including the implications of aging societies, the threats to mortality gains posed by urbanization, the renewed threat of IPDs, and the provision of health services and other programs to improve population health.

First, the twentieth century witnessed remarkable improvements in life expectancy, with a concurrent increase in life expectancy after age sixty-five. Advances in medical technology have meant that an increasing number of people are surviving into old age, but it is among the "old elderly," variously referred to as those older than seventy-five, eighty, or even eighty-five, that the largest increases in morbidity (sickness) are observed. Therefore, are improvements to life expectancy a double-edged sword? For example, what are the implications of aging Western societies in terms of increased morbidity, service provision, and support of a growing elderly population? Has this increase come at the expense of an increasing number of years of morbidity?

Answering these questions is not simple as they imply a debate over quality versus quantity. The extension of the quantity of life may come at the expense of quality in terms of deteriorating and chronic health conditions, increased reliance on others, such as family or service providers, for support, and expensive medical intervention. The increasing disability among the elderly further raises value-laden questions regarding the need for medical intervention to save or prolong a life at all costs and may require a shift in thinking and resources to improve the quality of life or "years of health." The incidence of death from heart disease in America has, for example, declined in the past three decades. This has also meant, however, that people tend to live longer with heart disease. In large part, this is due to better medical treatment and the advent of new drugs that have increased survival rates.[38] However, since illnesses like heart disease cause only half of the reported disability and loss of functioning, improvements in health do not necessarily lead to increases in life expectancy. Most individuals will now experience some period of disease and disability before death, with health status among the elderly increasingly associated with nonfatal conditions, including arthritis, vision loss, and Alzheimer's. These conditions and others will become increasingly important causes of disability and loss of function in old age.

A larger elderly population and the growing numbers of disabled elderly imply a greater need for support. We generally expect that as life expectancy increases, the number of disabled people, particularly among the old elderly, will increase as well, placing ever-greater strains on the health care system. Institutional support, in the form of nursing homes or chronic care facilities for an increasingly old and disabled elderly population, will require policy attention. As noted by Eric Moore and Mark Rosenberg,[39] keeping up with the demand for space in institutions will be a crucial issue. Market-driven systems will create service-rich and service-poor areas if the use and provision of services reflects an ability to pay. While this may be acceptable in the U.S. health care environment, countries with socialized medicine programs, including Canada and England, may face a service-provision crisis or large variations in the type, quality, and quantity of resources available for the elderly.

Second, although this chapter has not specifically addressed urbanization, this phenomenon poses additional, specific challenges to mortality and morbidity experiences. Currently, 41 percent of the developing world's population resides in urban areas, and we project that a majority of the developing world's population will live in urban areas by 2020. Historically, urban areas have experienced fertility decline, creating a reason for optimism if these urbanization patterns continue. In the nineteenth century, urban residents in Europe and North America were among the first to practice family-planning techniques widely, helping to spread the idea of smaller families to rural areas. Fertility is also lower in cities in the developing world where the costs of childbearing are higher and family-planning services are more available. Historically, mortality and disease rates have also been lower in urban areas relative to rural areas.[40]

While urban areas may confer health benefits, significant emerging health concerns may place urban residents at a disadvantage with respect to mortality experiences in the near future. Urban health advantages hide the huge disparity between the urban poor and their wealthy counterparts, particularly in the developing world, where mortality experiences are frequently far worse in poor urban than rural areas.[41] One study in Bangladesh, for example, found that infant death rates varied from 95 to 152 per 1,000 people in urban areas, higher than rates in both middle-class urban areas (32) and rural Bangladesh.[42] Continued in-migration from rural areas and increasing population density may push mortality and morbidity higher in urban areas. Many cities in the developing world have grown faster than their infrastructures, leaving large proportions of their populations without adequate and safe water or proper sanitation, allowing diseases associated with poverty to increase in urban areas. It is important to realize, however, that while the poor may bear a greater burden of disease, they alone do not experience increased mortality and health deprivation in urban areas. Cities in the developing world have high levels of air and water pollution, with air pollution in parts of Asia having a marked impact on health. Children are at the greatest risk. Infectious diseases, including HIV/AIDS, also pose a larger risk in urban areas. Poor living conditions are a key factor in the transmission of disease, while more permissive sexual norms than those in rural settings, as well as the presence of male migrant workers who frequent prostitutes, promote HIV infection.[43] One UN estimate found that HIV infection rates were up to four times higher in urban areas. These trends will likely diminish the traditional health advantages provided by urban areas in the future.

Third, IPDs remain a threat to health. In the developed world, there is a need for action to avoid epidemics associated with the importation of disease. Despite safety nets designed to prevent the entry of diseases, such as the health screening of immigrants, the system is not foolproof. Systems and procedures must be in place if epidemics are to be avoided. The developing world faces its own set of problems. Among these, the poor living conditions associated with rapid urbanization and poverty in many cities of the developing world create an ideal breeding ground for disease. Clearly, steps must be taken to rectify these problems, whether by controlling internal migration or by providing appropriate infrastructure. Controlling internal migration is difficult and only possible in authoritarian regimes like China. Even there, where internal migration is supposedly controlled, the illegal migration of Chinese peasants to cities in search of new opportunities remains a problem for authorities. Provision of appropriate nutrition and sanitation or infrastructure is no less problematic given the huge fiscal and political implications of a world in which economic and food assistance is frequently tied to the political agendas of the developed world. Yet, less than half of the population has access to clean water in some developing countries, and more than one-third of the world's population under the age of five is underweight and undernourished, which compromises the current and future ability of these children to survive.

Finally, improvements in life expectancy and infant mortality can hardly be removed from the provision of health care and related services. While some authors have called for a medically driven response to the problems of IPDs and other health threats via the development of new vaccines, antibiotics, and improved laboratories, these methods carry a high price tag and may involve years of research and development.[44] Frequently, their applicability in the developing world is limited as is demonstrated by the reluctance of drug companies to provide drugs to combat HIV/AIDS in these locations. As discussed in chapter 3, the HIV/AIDS epidemic poses a particular challenge in parts of Africa, Asia, and the Caribbean. In sub-Saharan Africa, life expectancy has retreated to below fifty years as a consequence of HIV/AIDS and currently averages just thirty-seven years in Zambia, forty-five years in Malawi, and forty-four years in Rwanda.[45] The economic and social impact of HIV/AIDS and its demographic implications—orphans and a shrinking labor force—are staggering, creating the potential for civil unrest and war. The monies and resources to deal with HIV/AIDS are limited, and Western drug companies may be disinterested in finding an inexpensive cure—their fortunes await them in the developed world.

If expensive medical programs and intervention cannot provide the assurance of basic population health, other directions must be pursued instead. As a starting point, improvements to life expectancy must be achieved through a renewed commitment to public health programs and basic health care, providing a frontline defense against IPDs, improving maternal health, and dealing with other health concerns. The idea of providing basic health care is, of course, not new since the WHO and other groups have been promoting it for some time. Unfortunately, the provision of basic health care has fallen off the radar screens of many countries and agencies as they wrongly believe that this goal has been met. With less than half of the population in the developing world having access to health care, the numbers tell the true story. In China, huge numbers of rural residents are without primary health care, as the system of rural-based health care (China's highly regarded "barefoot doctors") and free rural clinics has disintegrated over the past decade. In its place, market-driven health care, with its higher costs and profit orientation, has taken hold. Poor rural residents are unable to afford even basic medical care in local, private clinics, and the cost of basic medicines is beyond the means of most people. Recent Chinese health statistics also tell of the decline of health care, with a quadrupling of tuberculosis cases in the past fifteen years, declining immunization rates, increasing maternal mortality, and increasing infant mortality in rural areas.[46] Unfortunately, China's declining basic health care system is more the rule in the developing world than the exception. Elsewhere, public health care has diminished in the face of civil strife, ethnic rivalries, and overburdened governments that lack the financial ability to implement health programs.

The provision of basic health care to meet the needs of the population is only one piece of the health puzzle, being insufficient on its own to ameliorate or remove inequalities in morbidity or mortality. Instead, we are increasingly realizing that the broader determinants of health, including education, sanitation, nutrition, lifestyle options (i.e., smoking, drinking, and drug use behavior), housing conditions, and personal power, impact health and mortality experiences directly.[47] Despite the importance of these factors and their contribution to health, governments have been relatively slow to address disparities. The Canadian government, for example, has attempted to address health disparities within the Aboriginal population, although past attempts to improve their health status have tended to focus on a rather narrow, biomedical definition of health that can be addressed simply by the importation of Western medicine and its biomedical model. Consequently, health policy has typically reacted to departures from health, neglecting the broader determinants of health, which comprise a synthesis of public health and social science literature and include issues such as lifestyle options, nutrition, housing, work, education, and income, as well as mechanisms related to societal power, social identity, social status and control over life circumstances.[48] More generally, governments have focused their resources on the delivery of health care to their domestic populations. Addressing the broader determinants of health also means that governments and other institutions must focus on reducing economic and social disparities at both the national and international levels, with the goal of equalizing health indicators between advantaged and disadvantaged groups like African Americans or Aboriginals. In large part, the gap in mortality and morbidity rates between Aboriginals and the Canadian population could be closed through a combination of improved living standards, lifestyles, social control, access to health care resources, and equity between groups.[49]

Clearly, however, investments in public infrastructure to provide clean drinking water, sanitation, appropriate housing, and public education or other programs, let alone the provision of basic health care services, are limited within the developing world. While needed, such a broad response to health conditions and mortality experiences will likely be constrained by budgets and inadequate resources, as noted in chapter 1. Attempts to provide such things as clean drinking water and infrastructure on such a large scale are frequently slowed by population growth, which in turn slows the attainment of these goals in low-income countries and creating a young population that places large demands on costly educational, social, and health services. Solutions will not come easily or inexpensively.

NOTES

1. Alene Gelbard, Carl Haub, and Mary M. Kent, "World Population beyond Six Billion," *Population Bulletin* 54, no. 1 (March 1999).

2. Joseph A. McFalls Jr., "Population: A Lively Introduction," *Population Bulletin* 58, no. 4 (December 2003).

3. John R. Weeks, *Population: An Introduction to Concepts and Issues*, 7th ed. (Belmont, CA: Wadsworth, 1999).

4. For a discussion of the geographical diffusion of illness, see Andrew Cliff and Peter Haggett, "Spatial Aspects of Epidemic Control," *Progress in Human Geography*, 13 (1989): 315–47; Andrew Cliff and Peter Haggett, *Atlas of Disease Distributions: Analytical Approaches to Disease Data* (Oxford: Blackwell, 1988); Peter Gould, *The Slow Plague: A Geography of the AIDS Pandemic* (Oxford: Blackwell, 1993).

5. Michael Bliss, *A Living Profit* (Toronto: McCelland and Stewart, 1974); Terry Copp, *The Anatomy of Poverty* (Toronto: McCelland and Stewart, 1974).

6. Thomas McKeown, *The Role of Medicine: Dream, Mirage, or Nemesis* (Princeton, NJ: Princeton University Press, 1979).

7. Abdel Omran, "The Epidemiological Transition: A Theory of the Epidemiology of Population Change," *Milbank Memorial Fund Quarterly* 49 (1971): 509–38.

8. Acute respiratory infections and malaria are also major killers among children less than five years old, accounting for 19 percent and 8 percent, respectively, of all deaths to children. See Jennifer Bryce, Cynthia Boschi-Pinto, Kenji Shibuya, Robert E. Black, et al., "WHO Estimates of the Causes of Death in Children," *The Lancet* 365, no. 9465 (March 2005): 1147–53.

9. See www.unicef.org (accessed June 27, 2005).

10. S. Jay Olsahansky, Bruce Carnes, Richard G. Rogers, and Len Smith, "Infectious Diseases—New and Ancient Threats to World Health," *Population Bulletin* 52, no. 2 (July 1997).

11. Olsahansky, Carnes, Rogers, and Smith, "Infectious Diseases."

12. Joanna Frketich, "Anatomy of Ebola Scare in Hamilton," *Hamilton Spectator*, February 17, 2001, 1A.

13. Kreeston M. Madson, Anders Hviid, Mogens Vestergaard, Diana Schendel, Jan Wohlfahrt, Paul Thorsen, Jorn Olsen, and Mads Melbye. "A Population-Based Study of Measles, Mumps, and Rubella Vaccination and Autism," *New England Journal of Medicine* 347, no. 19 (2002): 1477–82.

14. World Health Organization at www.who.org (accessed June 28, 2005).

15. *World Population Data Sheet* (Washington, DC: Population Reference Bureau, 2005).

16. Thomas J. Goliber, "Population and Reproductive Health in Sub-Saharan Africa," *Population Bulletin* 52, no. 4 (December 1997).

17. From a theoretical standpoint, the biomedical model and the body as machine, two dominant themes in Western medicine, have been criticized. For reviews of this literature, see Sarah Curtis and Ann Taket, *Health and Societies* (London: Arnold, 1996); Kelvyn Jones and Graham Moon, *Health, Disease and Society* (London: Routledge, 1992).

18. Sergei Maksudov, "Some Causes of Rising Mortality in the USSR," in *Perspectives on Population*, ed. Scott W. Menard and Elizabeth W. Moen, 156–74 (New York: Oxford University Press, 1987).

19. John Haaga, "High Death Rate among Russian Men Predates Soviet Union's Demise," *Population Today* 28, no. 3 (April 2000): 1.

20. Christopher Davis and Murray Feshbach, *Rising Infant Mortality in the USSR in the 1970s* (Washington, DC: U.S. Bureau of the Census, Series P-95, no. 74, September 1980).

21. Maksudov, "Some Causes," 156.

22. In 2002, for example, the United States spent 14.6 percent of its GDP on health care. In Canada, it was 9.6 percent. See www.who.int/countries/en/#C (accessed June 28, 2005).

23. Readers can refer to Linda Pickles, Michael Mungiole, Gretchen K. Jones, and Andrew R. White, *Atlas of United States Mortality* (Hyattsville, MD: U.S. Department of Health and Human Services, 1996).

24. "Deaths: Final Data for 2002," *National Vital Statistics Report* 53, no. 5 (2004). Available online at www.cdc.gov/nchs/data/nvsr/nvsr53/nvsr53_05acc.pdf (accessed June 28, 2005).

25. McFalls, "Population."

26. *Kids Count Data Sheet* (Washington, DC: Population Reference Bureau, 2004).

27. See Illinois Department of Public Health at www.idph.state.il.us/health/statshome.htm#Leading%20Causes (accessed June 28, 2005).

28. See U.S, Bureau of the Census at www.census.gov/population/www/socdemo/educ-attn.html (accessed June 28, 2005).

29. Carmen DeNavas-Walt, Bernadette D. Proctor, and Robert J. Mills, *Income, Poverty, and Health Insurance Coverage in the United States: 2003* (Washington, DC: United States Bureau of the Census, August 2004).

30. Norman J. Waitzman and Ken R. Smith, "Separate but Lethal: The Effects of Economic Segregation on Mortality in Metropolitan America," *The Milbank Quarterly* 76, no 3 (1998): 341–73.

31. DeNavas-Walt, Proctor, and Mills, "Income, Poverty, and Health Insurance Coverage." There has been a continuing decline, however, in the percentage of children without health insurance. See the National Center for Health Statistics at www.cdc.gov/nchs/products/pubs/pubd/hestats/healthinsur.htm#table%201 (accessed June 28, 2005).

32. *Health, United States 2004* (Hyattsville, MD: National Center for Health Statistics, 2004).

33. Sheryl Gay Stolberg, "After Two Centuries, Washington Is Losing Its Only Public Hospital," *New York Times*, May 7, 2001, 1A.

34. Robert Pear, "Bush Budget on Health Care Would Cut Aid to Uninsured," *New York Times*, April 4, 2001, 3B.

35. The indigenous populations in the United States, Australia, and New Zealand show similar discrepancies in morbidity and mortality statistics, representing a common history of oppression, racism, and discrimination that has created a population that remains marginalized.

36. Numerous authors have written on the health of the Aboriginal population. See T. Kue Young, *Health Care and Cultural Change: The Indian Experience in the Central Artic* (Toronto: University of Toronto Press, 1988); Peter H. Stephensen and Susan J. Elliott, *A Persistent Spirit: Towards an Understanding of Aboriginal Health in British Columbia* (Vancouver: University of British Columbia Press, 1995); Health and Welfare Canada, *Aboriginal Health Care in Canada* (Ottawa: Ministry of Supply and Services, 1992).

37. Health Canada. *A Statistical Profile on the Health of First Nations in Canada* (Ottawa: Health Canada, 2004).

38. Judith Treas, "Older Americans in the 1990s and Beyond," *Population Bulletin* 50, no. 2 (May 1995).

39. Eric G. Moore and Mark W. Rosenberg, *Growing Old in Canada* (Ottawa: Statistics Canada Cat. No. 96-321-MPE, 1997).

40. See the broader discussion of urban issues, including the perspectives from the developing and developed worlds, in Martin P. Brockerhoff, "An Urbanizing World," *Population Bulletin* 55, no. 3 (September 2000).

41. Trudy Harpham and Carolyn Stephens, "Urbanization and Health in Developing Countries," *World Health Statistics Quarterly* 44, no. 2 (1991): 62–69.

42. Referenced from Brockerhoff, "An Urbanizing World," 23.

43. United Nations, *AIDS and the Demography of Africa* (New York: United Nations, 1994).

44. Olsahansky, Carnes, Rogers, and Smith, "Infectious Diseases."

45. Up-to-date statistics on the HIV/AIDS epidemic are available at www .unaids.org (accessed June 28, 2005).

46. Elisabeth Rosenthal, "Without 'Barefoot Doctors,' China's Rural Families Suffer," *New York Times*, March 14, 2001, 2A.

47. Robert G. Evans and Gregory L. Stoddart, "Producing Health, Consuming Health Care," *Social Science and Medicine* 31, no. 12 (1990): 1247–1363.

48. Evans and Stoddart, "Producing Health."

49. See K. Bruce Newbold, "Problems in Search of Solutions: Health and Canadian Aboriginals," *Journal of Community Health* 23, no. 1 (1998): 59–73.

3

The Impact of HIV and AIDS

While the previous chapter introduced mortality experiences and briefly discussed the HIV/AIDS epidemic, this chapter takes a more detailed look at the disease, along with its web of interrelated demographic, social, and economic effects. After all, the human immunodeficiency virus, or HIV, the virus that causes acquired immune deficiency syndrome, or AIDS, has caused an epidemic far more extensive than that forecasted. In 2005 alone, 3.1 million people worldwide died of AIDS, including 570,000 children. Worse, the toll is expected to grow significantly within the next decade. Another 40.3 million people were living with HIV/AIDS in 2005, a number that we can assume will only increase and represents only a portion of the true number of infected, given the difficulties of reporting or screening in many countries. Most HIV cases (95 percent) are found in the developing world, where the scale of the epidemic has profound economic, social, demographic, and political implications.

HIV most likely entered North America sometime in the 1970s; the world was introduced to HIV and AIDS in 1981 when it was identified among gay men in the United States. Globally, it was likely around long before that. Reexamination of a blood sample taken in 1959 confirmed the presence of HIV/AIDS at that time.[1] Commonly thought to have emerged somewhere in Central Africa and present day Congo, the scientific community is still at a loss to explain exactly where it came from, although the most plausible theory is that the virus somehow moved from monkeys across the species barrier into humans, perhaps through hunting, religious, or cultural ceremonies; evidence all but cements this theory.[2] With little interaction and population mobility, it potentially survived for decades within the human population, albeit at very low levels and within a spatially confined area. Civil war in the Congo in the early 1960s likely facilitated its movement into the larger population, carried by soldiers and aided by refugee movements and famine. It would emerge as a major public health concern and a leading cause of death throughout the world within a generation.

Technically, AIDS is not a single disease but a complex of diseases and symptoms that lead to a degenerative death. Nearly 100 percent fatal, HIV kills by destroying the body's immune system, increasing its susceptibility to infections and other malignancies. Frequently, opportunistic infections such as tuberculosis or once rare forms of pneumonia or cancers (i.e., Kaposi's sarcoma) are the direct causes of death, but their development is facilitated by the initial HIV infection. The disease follows a slow progression for the first five to ten years after infection with few outward signs of its presence. Yet, this slow progression makes it even deadlier, giving infected people years to spread it unknowingly. Eventually, HIV infection leads to full blown AIDS, a transition that occurs when an HIV-infected person has at least one of the following: opportunistic infection, malignancy, dementia, loss of 15 percent of body weight, or a T-helper (a type of blood cell) count below two hundred.[3]

Carried by blood or other body fluids, the virus is transmitted through a number of pathways. In the North American and European context, homosexual activity carries the greatest risk of infection, with men having sex with men (MSM) accounting for 63 percent of new infections in the United States in 2003, although the patterns of HIV transmission are changing with an increasing proportion of people being infected through heterosexual intercourse.[4] Risk of infection is increased by unsafe sexual practices and grows with the number of sexual partners. Injecting drug use and the sharing of contaminated needles is also a major pathway, accounting for approximately 20 percent of all infections in the United States. Only 12 percent of all infections are attributable to heterosexual contact, although this proportion is slowly but steadily increasing, with unsafe heterosexual intercourse accounting for 73 percent of all new cases in the United States among women in 2003. Mother-to-child transmission is also an important pathway, with pregnant infected women having a 25 to 50 percent chance of passing the infection to the child (either during pregnancy, childbirth, or breast feeding), although numerous options exist to control transmission of infection from mother to the child, including **antiretroviral drugs**. While MSM still accounts for the majority of HIV cases reported in North America, infection through injected-drug use is rising in both Canada and the United States.[5] Injected drug use also accounts for 70 percent or more of infections in China, the Russian Federation, Ukraine, and Vietnam. HIV has also "leaked out" of these high-risk groups into the heterosexual community, aided by prostitution or homosexual contact. The movement of the

HIV epidemic into the heterosexual population poses far greater challenges to its control.

In North America and Europe, the openness with which the disease is discussed has helped slow its spread, as is reflected by the low adult prevalence rates of 0.7 percent in North America and 0.3 percent in Western Europe (see table 3.1).[6] Public education campaigns publicizing the dangers of risky behavioral choices have largely been successful. Elsewhere, the disease is much more prevalent and threatening. In sub-Saharan Africa, a continent where the epidemic has hit particularly hard, the adult prevalence rate is 7.2 percent, with one-quarter to one-third of adults infected in some countries. Here, transmission of the virus is predominately through heterosexual contact, placing a much larger proportion of the population at risk and creating a greater potential for the disease to spread rapidly than is the case when it is contained within a given subpopulation. The differences between Africa and elsewhere in the primary transmission route of HIV/AIDS are highlighted by the far higher prevalence rates among women. In sub-Saharan Africa, women make up 57 percent of the infected population, and rates of infection among women equal or surpass male infection rates. Outside of Africa, females typically have lower infection rates, with women representing 25 percent of the HIV-infected population in North America and Western Europe.

Prevalence among men is linked to notions of masculinity and risk taking, making them candidates for infection.[7] However, their behavior also directly contributes to HIV prevalence among women, who often have less power within sexual relationships, are less able to engage in safe sex, or are unable to decide with whom intercourse occurs. Notions of masculinity and sexual power are not the only factors that facilitate the spread of HIV. Instead, a number of nonexclusive social, behavioral, and biological factors are thought to assist the establishment of the HIV epidemic or drive it to higher levels within the general population, although it is not known exactly how each of these factors contributes to the spread of HIV.[8] Social and behavior factors include:

- *Condom use.* Condoms effectively protect against the transmission of sexually transmitted diseases (**STDs**), including HIV. Increases in the availability and use of condoms are still insufficient to slow the spread of epidemics. Oftentimes, their use may be discouraged by political, cultural, or religious beliefs or stigmatized due to association with commercial sex workers (prostitutes). In other cases, condom use could jeopardize relationships, implying potential contact with HIV or engagement in risky behavior. Moreover, condoms do not help in a stable relationship in which pregnancy is desired.

Table 3.1. Regional HIV/AIDS Statistics and Features, 2005

Region	Epidemic Started	Adults and Children Living with HIV/AIDS	Adults and Children Newly Infected with HIV	Adult Prevalence Rate[a] (%)	HIV-Positive Adults Who Are Women (%)	Main Models of Transmission[b]
Sub-Saharan Africa	Late 1970s Early 1980s	25.8 million	3.2 million	7.2	57	Hetero
North Africa and Middle East	Late 1980s	510,000	67,000	0.2	47	Hetero IDU
South and Southeast Asia	Late 1980s	7.4 million	990,000	0.7	28	Hetero IDU
East Asia	Late 1980s	870,000	140,000	0.1	18	IDU Hetero MSM
Latin America	Late 1970s Early 1980s	1.8 million	200,000	0.6	32	MSM IDU Hetero
Caribbean	Late 1970s Early 1980s	300,000	30,000	1.6	50	Hetero MSM
Eastern Europe and Central Asia	Early 1990s	1.6 million	270,000	0.9	28	IDU
Western and Central Europe	Late 1970s Early 1980s	720,000	22,000	0.3	27	MSM IDU
North America	Late 1970s Early 1980s	1.2 million	43,000	0.7	25	MSM IDU Hetero
Oceania	Late 1970s Early 1980s	74,000	8,200	0.5	55	MSM
Total		40.3 million	4.9 million	1.1	46	

Source: Reproduced by kind permission of the Joint United Nations Program on HIV/AIDS (UNAIDS).
[a] The proportion of adults (15–49 years of age) living with HIV/AIDS in 2005 population numbers.
[b] Hetero (heterosexual transmission), IDU (transmission through injecting drug use), and MSM (sexual transmission among men who have sex with men).

- *Multiple sex partners.* The high incidence of multiple sex partners, including pre- and extramarital intercourse, increases the likelihood of infection, particularly when partners are concurrent (i.e., many within a short period of time) rather than serial, as is typical in monogamous relationships.
- *Age mixing.* Sexual intercourse between older men and younger women or girls has occurred as older and richer men seek out supposedly uninfected populations, coercing or enticing young girls into sexual relationships. Unfortunately, many of the men are already infected and thus introduce HIV to a new generation. Magnifying the problem, girls are less likely to be informed about HIV and how to prevent transmission, even if engaging in consensual sex.
- *Use of prostitutes.* The frequent use of commercial sex workers, with most clients engaging in unprotected sex, promotes the spread of HIV into the heterosexual population. Prostitution has thrived because of tourism, urbanization, and poverty. In portions of Africa, prostitutes are associated with long-haul trucking, facilitating its spread over long distances and into the family on the truckers' return home.
- *Rapid rates of urbanization.* As males migrate to urban areas in search of employment, they frequently leave behind wives and families but become involved in new sexual relationships in the city. STD rates are also higher in cities because of the larger population size and the breakdown of traditional social norms that limit sexual contacts. The presence of STDs increases the likelihood of infection, with the individual ultimately returning home to rural areas or smaller villages and exposing the family to HIV.
- *Status of women.* In many developing societies, women are frequently economically or politically disadvantaged. Their lack of power and economic dependence forces them to rely on marriage or prostitution, undermining their control over the circumstances in which sex occurs or the use of safe-sex practices. Women may search for alternative ways, including prostitution, to support their children and augment their incomes.

Biological factors include:

- *High rates of STDs.* STDs, particularly those that cause skin lesions, facilitate the transmission of HIV during unprotected intercourse.
- *High viral load.* HIV levels are typically highest when a person is first infected and again in the late stages of the disease, with higher viral loads increasing the likelihood of transmission.
- *Rates of male circumcision.* Although the epidemiological effect is still debated, countries with high levels of circumcision before puberty

have limited epidemics. In some countries with higher prevalence rates, circumcised men have lower rates of infection than uncircumcised ones, even after controlling for other covariates, including education, income, and age effects.[9]

Given variations in the prevalence of HIV/AIDS, this chapter follows two avenues of discussion. First, it focuses on the African crisis, illustrating the potential demographic and related social and economic effects, including decreased economic productivity, lowered incomes, and the social costs of a growing population of AIDS orphans. Second, the chapter references the debate over the provision of anti-AIDS drugs in the developing world. Until recently, in the absence of a cure, the outlook has been bleak for most Africans infected with HIV. New drug therapies, while not providing a cure, have promised to improve health in the developed world. These same drugs remained beyond the reach of most patients in Africa, with drug companies clinging to their need to charge high prices owing to the high cost of drug development and research. Ultimately, however, the drug companies backed down, agreeing to sell the drugs at significantly reduced rates, an outcome that promises to reshape the epidemic. The final section of this chapter discusses emerging trends and issues within the HIV/AIDS dialog, including the ongoing need for public education, the continued threat of HIV/AIDS in the developed world, and the emergent crises within parts of Asia or the Caribbean.

THE AFRICAN CRISIS

The challenges posed by HIV/AIDS vary from place to place but are perhaps felt most acutely within sub-Saharan Africa, where AIDS has become the leading cause of death. The first case of AIDS was reported in the Congo in the early 1980s, beginning among individuals engaged in high-risk sexual behavior, including prostitutes and their clients. The virus quickly spread into the general population where it is much more difficult to control, infecting more women than men and spreading outward from the major centers of population hierarchically, eventually spreading through rural populations.[10] With an adult (aged fifteen to forty-nine) infection rate of 7.2 percent, the total number of people with HIV/AIDS in sub-Saharan Africa in 2005 was 25.8 million. Sub-Saharan Africa represents over 60 percent of the world's cases, and 80 percent of the children living with HIV are found in the African continent.[11]

Although infection rates are high in the region, the prevalence of HIV/AIDS is unequal, meaning it is inaccurate to speak of a single, African epidemic. Although initially centered in the countries of central and eastern

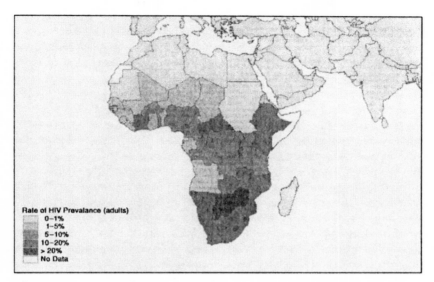

Figure 3.1. HIV Prevalence Rates in Africa, 2004. *Source:* United Nations, 2004.

Africa, the epidemic has exploded in Africa's southern countries, while prevalence rates remain steady at 5 percent or less in many West African states, and East Africa has seen some modest declines in HIV prevalence among pregnant women in urban areas (see figure 3.1).[12] The epidemic peaks in southern Africa, where 38 percent of all adults (aged fifteen to forty-nine) in Botswana and 38.2 percent in Swaziland are infected. Growing from just 1 percent in the early 1990s, the prevalence rate in South Africa is now 20.9 percent among adults. Swaziland, Zimbabwe, and Namibia all have adult infection rates greater than 19 percent (38.2, 24.9, and 21.3 percent, respectively). In other words, between one in four and one in five adults in southern African countries carry the virus. Albeit somewhat lower, prevalence rates among the young tend to track adult infection rates in these countries, ominously pointing to a continuation of the disease in younger generations, with high prevalence rates among pregnant women as high as 39 percent in Swaziland and 27.9 percent in South Africa.

Spatial variations in HIV/AIDS prevalence are likely rooted in a complex web of behavioral, social, and biological factors that interact with the continent's varied economic, social, and political systems.[13] The exact reasons for the spatial variation remain unclear, however, and a number of theories have been advanced to explain it.[14] One possibility is that patterns of sexual activity or networking within sub-Saharan Africa promote heterosexual infection. Premarital and extramarital intercourse, age at first intercourse, number of partners, polygamy, the low status of women, wife inheritance,

and the use of and frequency of contact with prostitutes have been im-
plicated as practices that increase the risk of infection. While there are elements of truth to the networking theory, it is important to place it within the
proper social, cultural, and political context of sub-Saharan Africa, rather
than creating an ethnocentric version that portrays African societies as sexually promiscuous.[15] A second theory relates to the increased prevalence
of other STDs in sub-Saharan Africa, with STDs resulting in lesions to the
skin, facilitating infection. A third theory suggests that the presence of
other infections, such as malaria or tuberculosis, can increase the amount
of HIV in the blood, thereby increasing a carrier's ability to infect a partner.

While there are now successful models for controlling HIV/AIDS on the
continent, many sub-Saharan countries were slow to adopt HIV/AIDS-
awareness programs or simply to recognize the existence of the virus. The
discussion of sex or sexuality was taboo in many societies, and HIV/AIDS
carried a stigma that governments and individuals alike tried to avoid,
denying that it was a problem and failing to invest in public education.
Countries lost time in introducing measures to contain HIV because they
did not fully understand the disease and its significance or because governments denied that it was occurring. The Kenyan government denied that
AIDS existed in the early and mid-1980s and, along with other governments
in the region, rejected condom use. As recently as 1999, the South African
president Thabo Mbeki questioned whether HIV causes AIDS.[16] Since
then, he has recanted, and the country has moved to the forefront of AIDS
awareness and the provision of low-cost AIDS drugs to its population.
Economic disparities and poor health systems further hamper HIV/AIDS
control. In many countries, access to condoms, anti-AIDS drugs, and health
care facilities were limited for economic, political, or cultural reasons, and
countries lacked sufficient screening facilities. Many unknowingly carry
the virus and infect others, with one estimate suggesting that upward of
90 percent of the infected population are unknowing carriers.[17]

Demographic, Economic, and Social Implications of the AIDS Crisis in Africa

Sub-Saharan Africa is a region coping with the cumulative impact of
HIV/AIDS. The disease has probably lasted longer there than elsewhere
in the developing world since it is thought to have originated there. There,
HIV threatens to destroy decades of progress measured by health and economic indicators, as well as to generate personal suffering and hardship.
In 2005, it was estimated that 3.2 million sub-Saharans were newly infected
with HIV,[18] representing a modest drop from 3.8 million new infections in
2000.

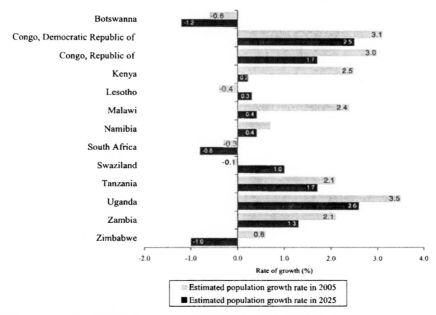

Figure 3.2.   Estimated Population Growth Rates in Selected African Countries, 2005 and 2025. *Source:* **U.S. Census Bureau, International Data Base, 2005.**

The most obvious effect of the HIV/AIDS epidemic is the increase in mortality rates.[19] Already high relative to the developed world, mortality rates are expected to be higher in countries affected by AIDS than they would be otherwise. Even now, AIDS causes approximately one in five deaths in sub-Saharan Africa, and mortality rates are expected to climb from fifteen per one thousand to twenty-five per one thousand within the next twenty-five years (see figure 3.2). The increase in death rates is even greater in Botswana, a country with an adult prevalence rate of 38 percent, where mortality rates are projected to grow from a current twenty-eight per one thousand to thirty-two per one thousand by 2025.[20] Despite higher mortality rates, AIDS was not expected to alter population growth rates, which were expected to remain positive given high levels of fertility and the effect of population momentum; the U.S. Census Bureau originally projected that AIDS deaths would not slow the overall rate of population growth. This is still true globally but not for individual countries. U.S. Census Bureau projections from 2000 have altered this view, with estimates that Botswana, South Africa, and Zimbabwe will experience negative population growth by 2025. Several other sub-Saharan countries will see their

growth rates approach zero within the next twenty-five years, declines that
are far faster than would be expected without AIDS.

AIDS deaths are premature deaths and, consequently, alter the age structure of the population, as well as infant mortality and life expectancy, the
two traditional markers of development discussed in the previous chapter. AIDS mortality is increasing child mortality in sub-Saharan Africa,
reversing improvements in health indicators that had been occurring since
the 1970s and 1980s. In Zimbabwe, there has been little decline in child
mortality when declines should be expected, and it is projected that the
infant mortality rate will be more than twice as high as it would have been
without the prevalence of AIDS by 2010.

AIDS is also associated with declines in life expectancy (see figure 3.3)
and an increase in death rates (see figure 3.4). In Zimbabwe, AIDS is expected to reduce life expectancy (from birth) from its 1997 level of fifty-
one years to thirty-nine years in 2010, with further reductions expected
by 2025. As of 2005, life expectancy at birth had already fallen to forty-
one years.[21] Without HIV/AIDS, it is estimated that life expectancy would
have increased to 69.5 years within the next 10 years. For children born in
some countries, including Botswana, Lesotho, and Zambia, life expectancies have already dropped below forty years. Life expectancies are similarly

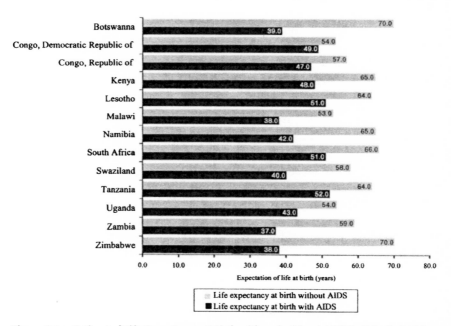

**Figure 3.3.   Estimated Life Expectancy at Birth with and without AIDS in Selected African
Countries, 2000–2005. *Source:* United Nations, 2005.**

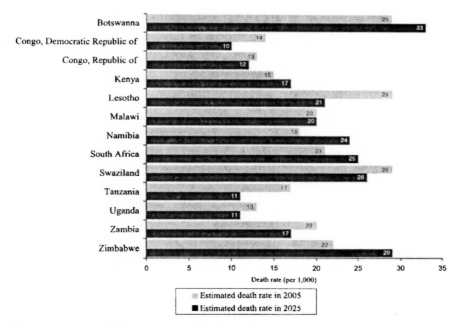

Figure 3.4. Estimated Death Rates in Selected African Countries, 2005 and 2025. *Source:* U.S. Census Bureau, International Data Base, 2005.

expected to drop in other sub-Saharan countries, with declines projected to be greater than twenty years in Zimbabwe (25.5 years), Namibia (20.2 years), and Lesotho (23.5 years). In South Africa, fifteen-year-olds have a greater than 50 percent chance of dying from HIV-related causes.[22] Consequently, the traditional population pyramid, which has a wide base representing the young and tapers to represent increasing ages, is being restructured and characterized as a population "chimney" in countries that have high HIV prevalence rates (see figure 3.5) because AIDS "hollows out" the young adult population, generating a base that is narrower as there are fewer young children. With fewer women reaching and surviving their childbearing years and, thus, having fewer children, the most dramatic changes occur when young adults who were infected in their adolescence die, particularly those in their twenties and thirties, substantially shrinking the adult population.

But the effect of HIV/AIDS is far more insidious, reaching into almost every corner of daily life and affecting both individuals and societies. In the countries worst affected by the epidemic, HIV occurs against a backdrop of deteriorating public services, poor employment, and poverty, all of which work concurrently to reduce the ability of communities and individuals to cope. Existing evidence suggests that households bear a large

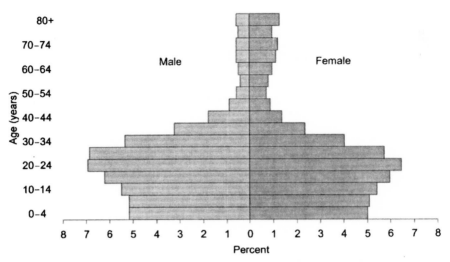

Figure 3.5. Projected Population Structure with AIDS, Botswana 2025: The AIDS "Chimney." *Source:* **U.S. Census Bureau, International Data Base, 2005.**

part of the burden, with differences in the ability to cope based on wealth and income.[23] In poor households, the death of an adult member reduces money for food, and poor households receive little financial help from family and friends. Many other households are unable to cope with the death of a family member, or the burden of care associated with either sickness or death. Socially, fear and shame are still associated with the disease, hindering prevention and care while potentially exposing others to the virus. The death of just one parent also disrupts life and economic abilities, a situation which may be amplified if the father dies: because women lack property and inheritance rights in many African countries, the epidemic compounds the burden placed on AIDS widows who face the loss of their economic livelihoods. Often times, children are left with a future that only reflects what the streets can offer.

Although AIDS tends to kill proportionately more young or middle-aged people who were infected in adolescence, its effect on the very young is startling, and it has created a **cohort** of AIDS orphans. Worldwide, it is estimated that fifteen million children are AIDS orphans; twelve million of them are found in sub-Saharan Africa.[24] Worldwide, the number of orphans is expected to balloon to forty million by 2010, with eighteen million in sub-Saharan Africa.[25] Orphaned children face a variety of social and economic challenges. Economically, the large number of orphans increases the burden on communities and governments to provide food, shelter, health care, and schooling. Young orphans are rarely able to cope with agricultural tasks, leading to crop failure and the death of livestock. Socially, AIDS orphans may be burdened by the psychological damage of seeing a parent die. Immediately relevant is the question of who raises the orphaned child. Grandparents or extended family members are frequently called on to raise them, but this occurs at the same time that they had expected to have a reduced role in the family. Instead, they are forced into the parenting role once again, which includes the need to provide economic security. However, the increased number of orphans has altered the ability and willingness of families and communities to help, and the task threatens to outstrip the capacity of the extended family system. For those lacking an extended family, street gangs provide an alternate "family," but one that exposes them to violence and antisocial behavior, as well as STDs or HIV as they exchange sex for food and money. Although the number of orphans is large, it represents only a portion of the children who are affected by HIV. Millions more are living with parents who are ill, becoming primary care givers for their parents or siblings.[26] Like orphans, they are more likely to drop out of school and to suffer from malnutrition, and they may be compelled to work.

HIV/AIDS also threatens the economic stability of countries by straining already fragile health care systems, decreasing the quality and quantity of labor, reducing economic output, and decreasing the amount of disposable income. The epidemic has increased the demand for health care, as well as the costs of providing care and drugs and of maintaining and improving infrastructure. In order to deal with the epidemic, countries have generally placed a larger share of domestic spending on HIV/AIDS, which tends to draw expenditures away from other needs. Staffing health centers and training that staff pose additional hardships, particularly due to AIDS-related illnesses or the death of health care workers from AIDS. Concurrently, non-AIDS patients are frequently crowded out of health care facilities, and tuberculosis is emerging as the leading cause of death among those infected with HIV.[27]

HIV/AIDS knows no boundaries and spares no occupational or social group. From an educational standpoint, the epidemic threatens the coverage and quality of education. As teachers die of AIDS, African countries will be faced with a teacher shortage, and class sizes are likely to increase, while governments face the costs of training replacement teachers over the longer term. Failure to do so or to meet the demand for teachers will result in a population that lacks the skills needed to participate fully within the economy. Moreover, education may not be reaching those who need it the most. This includes orphaned children who may be forced to drop out of school because they must earn a wage or work on the family farm or because they can no longer afford school fees. In turn, there is an increased likelihood of infection, with the Joint United Nations Program on

HIV/AIDS (UNAIDS) studies demonstrating that those with lower levels of education are more likely to engage in casual, unprotected sex.[28] On a larger scale, HIV/AIDS is stripping sub-Saharan countries' ability to build for the future, robbing them of the ability to generate and supply what Thomas Homer-Dixon calls "ingenuity," threatening their very survival.[29]

The impact of AIDS is also felt within the labor force, where it reduces the number of workers and degrades the quality or productivity of work at the same time that it undermines education and the ability of the system to provide needed skills. Responsible for a large burden of sickness, HIV/AIDS leads to increased absenteeism from work, greater medical costs, and higher costs for training new workers. Faced with high prevalence rates and lower productivity, companies may outsource their labor requirements. Alternatively, companies may reduce their investments in areas with high HIV prevalence. Either way, the cost of caring for sick workers shifts from the company to households or governments and undermines the economic security of workers.

While it is difficult to measure the economic impact of HIV/AIDS, growing evidence suggests that as HIV prevalence increases, the growth of national income, measured by **gross domestic product** (GDP), falls.[30] Among countries with prevalence rates greater than 20 percent, GDP growth may be reduced by as much as 2 percent per year. In South Africa, UNAIDS estimates that the overall economic growth in the coming decade may be between 0.3 and 0.4 percent per year lower than it would be without AIDS, which translates into a 17 percent reduction in GDP (relative to the estimated GDP without AIDS) by 2010. This means that household income will be reduced at the same time that countries are spending more on the care of AIDS patients or orphans. AIDS will alter the distribution of income, with the number of households in poverty increasing and poor households seeing a drop in income. In South Africa and Zambia, it is estimated that income in AIDS-affected households, most of which are already poor households, will be reduced by 60 to 80 percent due to coping with AIDS-related illnesses.[31] While the large pool of unemployed may replace unskilled workers, the impact of HIV/AIDS on the education of future workers will likely cause a shortage of skilled workers. Investment, which promotes long-term economic growth, will suffer as money is diverted to health care expenditures.

ANTI-AIDS DRUGS: THE PROMISE AND BATTLE

For the first two decades of the epidemic, medicine offered relatively little hope for those diagnosed with HIV/AIDS, making it a terminal disease.

Scientists searched frantically for a vaccine, but the virus's ability to mutate and the number of HIV strains has made vaccine development exceedingly difficult.[32] To date, the greatest advances have been associated with protease inhibitors, a class of drugs introduced in 1995–1996. While not a cure, the drugs reduce the viral load within an infected person, inhibiting the progression of HIV into AIDS. Those with the ability to pay for these medicines (mainly in the developed world) are able to prolong their lives and maintain a relatively good state of health.

At the same time, the developing world has been largely overlooked or bypassed in the rush to find a cure or treatment, even though it endures a disproportionate share of the disease. Any involvement by the drug companies in the developing world has tended to be short term, and there have been allegations that they tested new drugs and therapies on unsuspecting populations. Then, once the trials were completed, the infected populations were left with no drugs and little long-term hope. Arguing that they need to cover the high cost of research and development and hiding behind patent laws, drug manufacturers such as Merck, Squibb, and Bristol-Myers insisted on charging developed-world prices in the developing world. But the estimated cost of US$10,000 to US$15,000 per year for drugs has placed them beyond the reach of most of the HIV-infected population. In countries where per capita health care expenditure can be measured in the tens of dollars and household income is less than $1,000 per year, individuals and governments had little hope of extending drug coverage without dramatically increasing their health budgets. If they did, it was typically at the expense of some other needed program, meaning that the majority of sub-Saharans had little hope of securing treatment. Poorer countries could, at most, prevent new infection through public-education programs and perhaps treat a limited number of patients.

Moving to stem rising international criticism of their pricing policies while protecting their intellectual property rights, drug companies encouraged private deals with individual countries. However, while drug costs would be substantially reduced (up to 90 percent), the deals would restrict the number of people able to receive the drugs, giving the programs limited reach.[33] More problematically, such stopgap solutions raised a host of ethical issues and slowed the development of longer-term programs. For instance, such programs clearly could not be equitable: who would receive the medicines (children versus adults, wealthy versus poor, newly versus long-term infected), and who would decide? Furthermore, is it appropriate to limit the supply of needed drugs when 20 percent or more of a country's population is infected? Finally, what is the potential for blackmail and extortion in the distribution of drugs, particularly in countries where corruption is commonplace? Would those with the greatest need (i.e., the poor) be bypassed as those with more resources or political connections receive the drugs?

In the face of the growing crisis, governments and nongovernmental organizations (NGOs) struggled to enact a coherent AIDS drug plan that would provide drugs to those who needed them. They were faced with a difficult, if not impossible, task. Recognizing their inability to secure drugs through normal market mechanisms and led by countries like Brazil and India, governments sought ways to skirt patent laws and provide their population with low-cost drugs.[34] While member countries of the World Trade Organization (WTO) must grant twenty-year patent protection to drugs, they can circumvent the rules. One option, called "parallel importing," allows the importation of a patented drug without the owner's consent. In addition, "compulsory licensing" allows a country to use a patent without consent if the owner does not provide the product at a reasonable market price. By declaring a national emergency, countries can invoke these safeguards, but the process is slow and can take years as it winds its way through hearings and the WTO bureaucracy and approval process.[35]

In 1997, Brazil began producing a generic version of several antiretroviral drugs.[36] Although they cost the government approximately US$3,000 per year per victim, they were offered for free to those infected with HIV. To date, the results have been impressive. Success in Brazil and other countries, such as Haiti, has muted fears that such programs would fail due to an inadequate health care infrastructure that would not only limit the ability of programs to reach patients but was ill prepared to distribute drugs and monitor compliance with a strict drug regimen.[37] Critics noted that even simple, short-term drug programs, such as tuberculosis treatment regimens, had limited and sporadic compliance in many cases as a result of overburdened and underfunded health care systems. Instead, Brazil successfully built AIDS clinics despite the relatively poor existing health system and demonstrated that the poor could take their medication on time, with compliance rates equal to those found in North America. Critics also assailed the program's expense. While expensive, it has stabilized the epidemic, paying for itself in reduced death rates from AIDS, reduced hospital stays and costs, reduced sick days, and increased productivity among the infected. In Brazil, the government estimates that it has saved US$2.2 billion in hospital costs that it would have paid out otherwise.[38] However, similar successes have been observed in Haiti and Mozambique, countries with arguably fewer resources given years of unrest and civil war. In Mozambique, the health system lacked the staff and resources to provide AIDS medications, but the government stepped in and trained the unemployed in AIDS management.

In the face of the mounting AIDS crisis and increasing criticism that its policies were preventing millions from receiving needed care, drug companies were forced to reduce the cost of their anti-AIDS medicines. The United States and other developed countries also pressured drug companies to alter their policies. A decision by the Clinton administration, for example, sided against the U.S. drug companies when it stated that the U.S. government would not discourage other countries from producing or acquiring generic drugs. But even with announced price reductions by the major drug manufacturers for patients in the developing world beginning in 2001, the cost remained at approximately $600 per year per victim, although UNAIDS estimated that the cost to provide antiretrovirals had dropped to US$300 per person per year in 2003.[39] In addition, countries such as Brazil, India, and South Africa were determined to resist drug companies' pressures and patent laws that they viewed as only benefiting the drug companies. These countries asserted their right to import or produce generic drugs that still promised to be cheaper than the prices offered by the drug companies. Not surprisingly, the major drug companies opposed initiatives within the developing world, arguing that they violated patent laws and intellectual property rights and that Brazil and other generic-drug producers were essentially stealing their intellectual property. The debate over drug pricing appeared elsewhere as well. In South Africa, the government moved in 1997 to allow the importation of generic drugs through parallel importation, a move challenged in the courts by the major drug manufacturers who cited the need to protect intellectual property rights, trade, and patent laws (see figure 3.6). The legal challenge was heard before a South African court in spring 2001 and was seen as a test of drug companies' ability to protect their patents against governments looking for a way to fight the AIDS epidemic. Finally, the drug companies backed down, setting a precedent and allowing the South African government to import and produce cheap anti-AIDS drugs, potentially changing the face of the epidemic in South Africa and elsewhere.[40]

Most countries with national AIDS plans now have established programs that provide access to antiretroviral drugs through either reduced-cost or free programs. Brazil, Chile, Barbados, Argentina, and Costa Rica, among other countries, provide universal coverage for AIDS drugs. In other cases, drugs are provided at a hugely discounted rate, and countries have set targets for the proportion of the population able to access appropriate treatment. UNAIDS has also campaigned to provide antiretrovirals to three million people in the developing world by 2005 through its so-called "3-by-5" initiative. Although the number of people taking antiretroviral treatments had tripled in sub-Saharan Africa and Asia to 500,000 and

Figure 3.6.   The Drug Companies' Response to AIDS in Africa. *Source:* **Kirk Anderson, reproduced with permission.**

In 2001, the major drug companies took the government of South Africa to court over that country's importation or production of generic anti-AIDS drugs, a violation of existing patent laws. The drug companies ultimately backed down in the face of national and international pressure.

155,000, respectively, this represented a fraction of the need, given the large number of cases. UNAIDS admitted in July 2005 that it would not meet its target.[41]

EMERGENT THEMES AND ISSUES

Due to education and prevention, HIV/AIDS has seemingly been controlled in North America and Europe, confining the epidemic largely to specific (and typically high-risk) populations. By 1999, HIV infection was no longer among the fifteen leading causes of death in the United States for the first time since 1987, when it was first ranked.[42] Infection rates and, ultimately, death rates dropped as educational programs meant to modify behavior were implemented in the 1980s and 1990s. Antiretroviral drugs have increased survival rates and reduced the number of deaths from AIDS. Mother-to-child transmission of HIV has also been reduced following the introduction of drugs to prevent perinatal transmission.

Not all of the news emerging from the developed world is good, however. Despite the gains made over the past two decades in educating the public and reducing the number of new infections, complacency is not an option. Prevention methods may be stalled, with no further reductions in the number of AIDS cases and deaths in many countries. Alarmingly, the number of new infections has risen slightly, particularly among women, and there is a growing resurgence among gay men. An increasing proportion of infections through heterosexual contact is especially troubling, indicating that the disease is spreading into the larger population. There is, therefore, a potential for the prevalence of HIV/AIDS to increase in developed countries, attributable to three effects. First, individuals may be more likely to engage in risky behavior than they were just ten years ago, reversing a trend that had been observed since the emergence of the epidemic—this is an issue of "prevention fatigue." Unlike the 1980s and early 1990s, when HIV/AIDS was largely felt within the gay community, few young homosexual men have seen their friends die from AIDS or other opportunistic infections and, thus, they are increasingly engaging in high-risk sexual behavior, such as unprotected sex and sex associated with drug use, which decreases inhibitions. The U.S. Centers for Disease Control and Prevention have noted declines in safe sex and a resurgence of HIV among gay men.[43] Similarly, the proportion of injected-drug users who report sharing a needle has increased. Although there is no evidence to indicate that infection rates are currently increasing within this population, the potential exists.

Second, the emergence of antiretroviral drugs, while providing hope and extending life for those with HIV, has led to the mistaken assumption among some that these new drugs cure AIDS. At a minimum, AIDS is now seen as a survivable, but "chronic," condition, similar to other common afflictions, although there is emerging evidence that the virus is increasingly drug resistant. More fearsome, New York City health officials identified in early 2005 a particularly aggressive strain of the virus that was resistant to nearly all drugs.[44] The hope for longer-term discoveries, such as a cure or vaccine that will eliminate or reduce the threat of HIV/AIDS, remains but will not likely be fulfilled in the near future. Furthermore, given the complications posed by the range of virus subtypes and the ability of the virus to mutate, they may never be available. In the absence of a suitable vaccine, prevention is the key.

Third, HIV/AIDS disproportionately impacts racial and ethnic minority groups, and not all groups have benefited equally from the new treatments. No longer confined to homosexuals and injected-drug users, HIV/AIDS is increasingly defined as an epidemic of the poor and minorities. In the United States in 2005, for example, African Americans accounted for 48 percent of all new HIV cases, although they represented just 12 percent of the population. HIV/AIDS is found disproportionately among the young, who are more likely to be promiscuous or to use injected drugs, making HIV the sixth leading cause of death among the young aged twenty-five to thirty-four (all races, both sexes), the fifth leading cause of death among those aged thirty-five to forty-four, and the second leading cause of death among black males aged thirty-five to forty-four.[45] The disproportionate impact on racial and ethnic minorities has been increasing, and disparities likely reflect inequalities in the insurance and medical systems in the United States. Infections are also rising among black heterosexual women, who account for over 70 percent of all new HIV cases among women in the United States. Clearly, race is not a risk factor per se, but poverty, joblessness, substance abuse, poor health care, low levels of education, and high rates of STDs increase the risk of infection.[46] Consequently, while the developed world tends to think of HIV prevalence rates as being much lower than those found in other countries, certain populations have tremendous potential for an explosion of incidence of the disease similar to what is observed in other parts of the world.

Controlling or stopping the spread of HIV within the developed world therefore continues to require both immediate action and long-term reforms that target factors that promote its transmission. While recognition of the importance of prevention and educational campaigns in slowing the spread of HIV/AIDS is hardly new, we sometimes forget that such campaigns have been the cornerstone of HIV-prevention policies over the past two decades. Over the longer-term, reforms to improve public health care are needed. Over the short term, there is an ongoing need to convince people to change their sexual behavior by reducing the number of partners, using condoms, delaying sexual activity, and seeking treatment for STDs. Standard prevention messages will not be effective for everyone, however. For example, the young will differ from their older counterparts in terms of how they perceive risk and how to change their attitudes, creating a need for research that clearly identifies the role of behavior and how it can be modified. Similarly, it is easy to promote the use of condoms among male homosexuals or of clean needles within the injected-drug user population. In fact, efforts to contain the spread of HIV/AIDS by restricting it to these at-risk populations would be successful simply because they are identifiable and themselves contained. Once HIV is established within the heterosexual population, prevention campaigns and care of those infected become more expensive, but preventing HIV/AIDS from leaking out of high-risk populations is difficult. For example, drug users and prostitutes frequently face criminal charges, making it difficult to work with these populations or to provide education and preventing them from seeking assistance for fear of identification or arrest. Moreover, education and intervention programs must be packaged in a culturally appropriate manner so that they offer a number of alternatives rather than promote just one or two.

While the outlook might be guardedly positive within the developed world, it is much less so within the developing world, where unprotected sex and injected-drug use continue to feed a heterosexual epidemic, despite prevention campaigns. While Africa is feeling the brunt of the epidemic, no country or region is immune to its effects. In fact, the world may have only seen the beginning of the epidemic. By 2005, the Caribbean had the second highest prevalence rate (1.6 percent) outside of sub-Saharan Africa. Approximately two-thirds of the cases occurred in the heterosexual population, reflecting the main mode of transmission through multiple sex partners and unprotected sex.[47] The current rate in Haiti, which has a similar sexual-networking pattern to that observed in sub-Saharan Africa, is greater than 3.0, but may run much higher, making it the only country outside of Africa to have such a high rate. Furthermore, Haiti's life expectancy dropped from fifty-seven to fifty-one years in 2004, and it is projected to fall even lower, although there are signs that in Haiti the number of new infections is decreasing. In Eastern Europe, prevalence rates remain below 1 percent, but a rising number of infections is worrisome. The Russian Federation now reports the largest number of cases in the region, with a steady increase in prevalence rates and many of the infections (80 percent) attributed to injected-drug use. Although prevalence rates remain low among other populations, including homosexuals and pregnant women, more women are being infected through heterosexual intercourse, meaning that the epidemic is spreading. Moreover, the estimated number of infections most likely underestimates the true number since the national registration system captures only a portion of all infections.[48] At the same time, increasing numbers of reported STDs may facilitate the transmission of HIV into the heterosexual population in the near future; signs are already emerging that infection is increasing in the general population. Elsewhere in Eastern Europe, the numbers are increasing as well, with most new cases attributed to injected-drug use, a problem augmented by the fall of communism, opened borders, economic troubles and unemployment, and decreases in police controls that traditionally curbed drug use and prostitution.[49] The Ukraine, for instance, went from just 183 cases in 1992 to over 68,000 official cases in 2002 and remains the worst affected country in Europe with a prevalence rate of 1.4 percent and the epidemic spreading into the broader population.[50]

The situation is similar in Southeast Asia and the Pacific, where there is a large potential for growth in the number of infections aided by an active and overlapping sex trade, use of injected drugs, and human migration. Thailand, where the prevalence rate dropped from 2.15 percent in the late 1990s to 1.7 in 2005, demonstrates that the AIDS epidemic can be controlled through education and safe-sex practices, particularly in its sex trade, which reaches throughout Asia and into Europe. Condom use rates have improved with awareness campaigns that have targeted both clients and prostitutes, a population where, historically, use of condoms has been low, with workers lacking the power to insist that their clients use protection. Still, there is the potential for growth of infections within the heterosexual population, particularly among heterosexual couples in which the husband or partner uses prostitutes. Cambodia, which had the highest prevalence rate in the region in the 1990s, has also seen similar declines in HIV/AIDS infections. Evidence from Vietnam and Indonesia suggest that the epidemic is just starting to expand rapidly in both of these countries, with transmission primarily through heterosexual sex and injected-drug use. Like the situation in sub-Saharan Africa, measures of life expectancy and infant mortality have been rolled back, reflecting the impact of HIV/AIDS, with life expectancy in Thailand and Cambodia already reduced by approximately three years. Although longer-term projections made by the U.S. Census Bureau show an increase in life expectancy within these countries, they assume that the virus will not make further inroads into the population. Infant and child mortality has been affected most in countries that had already reduced mortality due to other causes. Finally, China has only recently acknowledged HIV/AIDS as a problem, despite evidence of rapid growth in the rate of infection there.[51]

Fortunately, there is some room for optimism in the fight against HIV/AIDS, although any report of success is subject to important caveats and exceptions. First, the move by drug companies in 2001 to reduce the price of anti-AIDS drugs and to allow countries to import or produce generic versions of the drugs is significant, although patent laws and protection continue to constrain access to generic versions, with the United States closely watching Brazil and other countries who plan to break patent laws on AIDS drugs. Ultimately, this may ensure that the drugs are available for all who need them, but even now, only a small portion of those in developing countries who needed AIDS drugs were receiving them.[52] It is important to recognize, however, that the success of programs to provide anti-AIDS drugs can only be measured in the coming decades. This assumes, of course, that governments and other groups can overcome problems in the distribution, financing,[53] and compliance issues associated with these new programs and that the emergence of drug-resistant strains does not thwart attempts to control the virus. Funding for drug-distribution programs has increased, but it is generally acknowledged that more is needed. While Brazil, Haiti, and portions of Africa, such as Kenya and Uganda, have shown that programs providing free or low-cost AIDS drugs can work, replicating these successes may be difficult in places with lower incomes, poorer health care systems, or greater numbers of infected people. Even in

South Africa, where average incomes are higher than in most other African nations, the prospect of establishing and maintaining a long-term drug program is nothing short of daunting. Moreover, there is concern as to whether generic drug makers, particularly small or unknown companies that might spring up to fill the need for drugs, can provide reliable versions of the antiretroviral drugs. Products that are not full-strength or are absorbed by the body differently could promote the growth of drug-resistant viruses or fail the patient, and contaminated or substandard drugs could kill.

Similar difficulties arise in the prevention of mother–to-child transmission. Although the risk of infection can be reduced dramatically through drug intervention, using AZT and other antiretrovirals that have proven effective, these regimens require strict compliance and are expensive, limiting their use to a small number.[54] However, research has shown that the antiretroviral drug nevirapine can be administered to the mother during labor and to the infant after birth at one-tenth the cost of AZT (about US$4) with the same effectiveness as AZT. Geography, however, means that distributing and promoting awareness of the drug remain problematic. Other interventions, including the use of infant formula rather than breast milk (which can pass HIV) and caesarean delivery of children, have proven effective in reducing HIV transmission in developed countries but are not always available or are costly in the developing world. Moreover, breast-feeding is a near universal practice in Africa. Short of these interventions, improved antenatal care, confidential counseling and testing of women (many women are reluctant to be tested for HIV), short-course drug therapy, and strengthened family-planning programs would be beneficial in slowing the spread of the disease.

Also, there are some indications that the rate of new infections may be leveling off in sub-Saharan Africa, with Uganda frequently set forth as the poster child for decreased HIV prevalence.[55] Since 1992, HIV infection levels have steadily declined from 13 percent in the early 1990s to 4.1 percent in 2003. Declines have been especially notable among pregnant and young women, and similar declines in infection rates have been observed in countries across East Africa, including Zambia, Kenya, and Burundi. A number of reasons account for this change, including education promoting delayed sexual activity, use of condoms, and limiting the number of sexual partners. In addition, the leveling off in the number of new infections may reflect the disease's duration, after which it leaves behind a relatively small pool of uninfected people. Unfortunately, Uganda's experience is not the rule. With only a few areas showing stabilization in the prevalence of HIV/AIDS, the epidemic has not yet peaked in Africa and may quickly expand if countries in western Africa, including Nigeria, which currently has a prevalence rate of 5.5 percent, see a rapid increase in the number of HIV/AIDS cases.

Clearly, the fight against HIV/AIDS in the developing world cannot be relaxed. Instead, governments and NGOs still face the challenges of providing health care to a growing population, reducing the number of new infections, and coping with the cumulative impact of HIV/AIDS. Many countries have intervention programs that include a comprehensive AIDS program promoting condom use, sexual abstinence, delayed intercourse, social openness and the ability to discuss HIV/AIDS, and mutual fidelity between partners, but they vary in their effectiveness and in the populations that they reach. Promoting the status and equality of women through improved education, employment, income, and political opportunities is crucial.[56] In addition to giving them fertility control, status and equity have a direct bearing on whether women protect themselves from HIV infection and on the resources available to them. While chapter 1 referenced the linkage between fertility, health, and the provision of basic health care services, a similar linkage can and should be made with HIV and STDs, with clinics offering education and screening services. Improved primary or basic health care is also essential. If a primary health care system is to be promoted, access to HIV/AIDS education and drugs can easily be made available to a much wider public. Unfortunately, access to AIDS drugs may yet reflect geography and class, with people near hospitals and with jobs that provide drug coverage having the best chance of receiving them, while the poor and those in rural areas will have far fewer opportunities. Most likely, the success of education and drug programs will require the assistance of the developed world to cover cost shortfalls and help establish the health care network.

The battle against the epidemic must also be contextualized in terms of socioeconomic and political instability. As it grows, the epidemic may also encourage economic and political instability, creating a self-reinforcing loop. Such instability may increasingly characterize countries that have been hard hit by HIV/AIDS, devastating their economies. Not only does AIDS impact the age structure of the population, but it also jeopardizes future economic growth by removing economically active adults from the work force and reducing economic output. Just as it removes the young and educated from the labor force, HIV/AIDS threatens professionals such as doctors, nurses, and teachers, along with the leadership structure of countries. Declining incomes and decreased economic opportunities have the potential to create an environment that fosters political instability as populations search for answers, assistance, and guidance.

Finally, the HIV/AIDS epidemic is becoming increasingly associated with women and the young, two groups that are at increasingly greater risk of infection, in both the developed and developing worlds. As of 2005, women accounted for approximately 46 percent of all cases worldwide, and they bear the brunt of the epidemic in terms of the provision of care to sick relatives, lost jobs and incomes, and discrimination. Likewise, the young aged fifteen to twenty-four represent more than half of all new HIV cases, a troubling statistic since this is the group that needs schooling and education if the epidemic is to be controlled in the future.[57]

NOTES

1. Peter Gould, *The Slow Plague: A Geography of the AIDS Pandemic* (Oxford: Blackwell, 1993).

2. Gina Kolata, "The Genesis of an Epidemic: Humans, Chimps, and a Virus," *New York Times*, September 4, 2001, 3C.

3. John R. Weeks, *Population: An Introduction to Concepts and Issues*, 7th ed. (Belmont, CA: Wadsworth, 1999).

4. Statistics are for all races and both sexes. See the National Center for Health Statistics at www.cdc.gov/nchs (accessed June 29, 2005). The specific statistics can be found at www.cdc.gov/nchs/fastats/aids-hiv.htm (accessed June 29, 2005).

5. UNAIDS, *AIDS Epidemic Update, 2005*, at www.unaids.org (accessed February 4, 2006).

6. UNAIDS defines the adult population as those aged fifteen to forty-nine since this group is the most sexually active and, therefore, subject to the greatest risk of infection. Although the risk of infection continues beyond age fifty, it is thought that most members of this group who engage in high-risk behavior are already infected. All HIV prevalence rates within this chapter are drawn from UNAIDS at www.unaids.org (accessed February 4, 2006).

7. Gould, *The Slow Plague*.

8. Thomas J. Goliber, "Population and Reproductive Health in Sub-Saharan Africa," *Population Bulletin* 52, no. 4 (December 1997).

9. UNAIDS, *AIDS Epidemic Update, 2005*.

10. Gould, *The Slow Plague*.

11. UNAIDS, *AIDS Epidemic Update, 2005*.

12. In Somalia, the adult prevalence rate is just 1.0 percent; this low infection rate is associated with the country's isolation due to civil war and devout Muslim population. While 1 percent is low, UNAIDS views it as a critical takeoff point, from which infections could quickly rise if controls are not put in place. However, within the country, HIV/AIDS is not seen as a problem, echoing the denials in the 1990s of other countries, and observers question whether the low incidence rate is truly representative.

13. See the edited volume of *African Rural and Urban Studies* (vol. 3, no. 2 [1996]) for a discussion of AIDS in sub-Saharan Africa. See also www.unaids.org (accessed June 29, 2005).

14. Lawrence K. Altman, "The AIDS Questions That Linger," *New York Times*, January 30, 2001, 1D. For an academic analysis of the spread of HIV/AIDS in Africa, see Bakama B. BakamaNume, "The Spatial Patterns of HIV/AIDS Infection in Uganda: 1987–1994," *African Rural and Urban Studies* 3, no. 2 (1996): 141–62; Gould, *The Slow Plague*; Veronica Ouma, "A Spatial-Temporal Analysis of HIV/AIDS

Diffusion in Kenya: 1986–1993," *African Rural and Urban Studies* 3, no. 2 (1996): 113–40.

15. Ezekiel Kalipeni and Joseph Oppong, "Rethinking and Reappraising AIDS, Health Care Systems, and Culture in Sub-Saharan Africa—Introduction," *African Rural and Urban Studies* 3, no. 2 (1996): 7–11.

16. See, for example, Helen Schneider and Joanne Stein, "Implementing AIDS Policy in Post-Apartheid South Africa," *Social Science and Medicine* 52 (2001): 723–31.

17. Gould, *The Slow Plague.*

18. In 2004 alone, it is estimated that 4.9 million people worldwide were infected with HIV.

19. Goliber, "Population."

20. Projected life expectancies, mortality rates, and infant mortality rates included in this chapter are drawn from the U.S. Census Bureau's IDB (follow the "HIV/AIDS" link at the bottom of the page), at www.census.gov/ipc/www/idbsum.html (accessed June 29, 2005).

21. *World Population Data Sheet* (Washington, DC: Population Reference Bureau, 2005).

22. UNAIDS, *AIDS Epidemic Update, 2005.*

23. UNAIDS, *AIDS Epidemic Update, 2005.*

24. UNAIDS, *AIDS Epidemic Update, 2005.*

25. UNAIDS, *AIDS Epidemic Update, 2005.*

26. See *USAID Efforts to Address the Needs of Children Affected with HIV/AIDS* (Washington, DC: USAID, 2000), at www.usaid.gov/pubs/hiv_aids (accessed June 29, 2005).

27. For a more general discussion of the impacts, see UNAIDS, *2005 Report on the Global AIDS Epidemic.*

28. UNAIDS, *AIDS Epidemic Update, 2005.*

29. Thomas Homer-Dixon, *Environment, Scarcity, and Violence* (Princeton, NJ: Princeton University Press, 1999); UNAIDS, *AIDS Epidemic Update, 2005.*

30. UNAIDS, *AIDS Epidemic Update, 2005.*

31. UNAIDS, *2004 Report on the Global AIDS Epidemic.*

32. Two types of HIV are currently recognized, HIV-1 and HIV-2. Both are transmitted identically and cause clinical AIDS. HIV-2 is less easily transmitted and has a longer incubation period. HIV-1 is the predominant virus worldwide, having several subtypes (A–J, O, and N) that vary by geographic area. Subtypes A and D, for example, are found in sub-Saharan Africa, while B is found in North America, Japan, Australia, and Europe. They differ primarily in their genetic makeup and may vary in their transmission routes. Subtype B is most prevalent among homosexuals and injected-drug users, and subtypes E and C are associated with heterosexual transmission. See www.unaids.org/en/Resources/FAQ.asp (accessed June 29, 2005).

33. Although most deals were not made public, it was reported that the Ugandan government negotiated a cost of approximately $500 a month per patient. In Senegal, the price was reduced to a yearly cost of approximately $1,000, but the program was apparently limited to a few hundred individuals. See Tina Rosenberg, "Look at Brazil," *New York Times Magazine*, January 28, 2001, 3–7.

34. Surprisingly, although India produces generic AIDS drugs for export, only a small proportion of Indians who need such treatment receive access to free or reduced-cost treatment (which currently costs approximately $25 per month, although this is a large amount for many Indians). See Somini Sengupta, "Spread of AIDS in India Outpaces Scant Treatment Effort," *New York Times*, May 27, 2004, 3A. See also Gumisai Mutume, "Pressure Mounts for Cheaper Anti-AIDS Treatment," at www.prb.org (accessed June 29, 2005).

35. Drug companies have argued that if countries turn to compulsory licensing, the development of new AIDS drugs will be reduced. Drug companies have also wanted to prevent this to protect their profits and intellectual property rights in the developed world, fearing the illegal importation of cheaper drugs.

36. Rosenberg, "Look at Brazil."

37. To be successful, the drug cocktail, which includes AZT, ddI, and protease inhibitors, must be taken according to a strict regimen for the remainder of the victim's life, given current scientific thinking. Current drugs do not remove the virus from the body but simply reduce it to low numbers and slow its ability to reproduce. Patients may stop taking the drugs, given the adverse side effects associated with many, when their health improves. Failure to comply will result in the virus's returning at full strength and the decreased effectiveness of the drugs.

38. UNAIDS, *AIDS Epidemic Update, 2005*.

39. Price reductions were offered in response to the cost of generic drugs entering the market. Rachel L. Swarns, "AIDS Drug Battle Deepens in Africa," *New York Times*, March 8, 2001, 1C; Rachel L. Swarns, "AIDS Obstacles Overwhelm a Small South African Town," *New York Times*, March 29, 2001, 3C.

40. Andrew Pollack, "News Analysis: Defensive Drug Industry Fuels Fight over Patents," *New York Times*, April 19, 2001, 1A.

41. Stephanie Nolen, "UN Says It Will Miss AIDS Target," *The Globe and Mail*, June 30, 2005, 16A.

42. In 2002, it was ranked twenty-two.

43. Lawrence K. Altman, "Swift Rise Seen in HIV Cases for Gay Blacks," *New York Times*, June 1, 2001, 1A; Sheryl Gay Stolberg, "In AIDS War, New Weapons and New Victims," *New York Times*, June 3, 2001, 1A.

44. Marc Santora, "Rare AIDS Strain Is Very Aggressive, Study Says," New York Times, March 18, 2005, 3B.

45. National Vital Statistics Reports, *Deaths: Leading Causes for 2002* 53, no. 17 (2003). The U.S. National Center for Health Statistics publishes yearly statistics on causes of death, with the most recent year being 2002. See www.cdc.gov/nchs.

46. Kevin Sack, "AIDS Epidemic Takes Toll on Black Women," *New York Times*, July 3, 2001, 1A, and UNAIDS, *AIDS Epidemic Update, 2005*.

47. Tony Fraser, "Caribbean Faces AIDS Epidemic, *Population Today* 28, no. 7 (2005): 10.

48. UNAIDS, *AIDS Epidemic Update, 2005*.

49. UNAIDS, *AIDS Epidemic Update, 2005*.

50. UNAIDS, *AIDS Epidemic Update, 2005*.

51. Bates Gill and Sarah Palmer, "The Coming AIDS Crisis in China," *New York Times*, July 16, 2001, 19A.

52. UNAIDS, *AIDS Epidemic Update, 2005.*

53. Even at sharply reduced prices, AIDS drugs remain out of reach for much of the population. Governments or other groups will likely be required to bridge the gap.

54. See USAID, *USAID Efforts to Prevent Mother-to-Child Transmission of HIV/AIDS* (Washington, D.C.: USAID, 2000), at www.usaid.gov/pubs/hiv_aids (accessed June 29, 2005).

55. Yvette Collymore, "Uganda Beats Back HIV/AIDS," *Population Today* 27, no. 11 (November 1999): 5.

56. See Lori S. Ashford, "New Population Policies: Advancing Women's Health and Rights," *Population Bulletin* 56, no. 1 (March 2001).

57. UNAIDS, *AIDS Epidemic Update, 2005.*

4

≈

Immigration: Closing or Opening the Door?

Between birth and death, the human population is relatively free to move. Population movement is harder to measure than birth or death events, dependent as it is on time and space constraints, yet it has a large potential to alter the population distribution.[1] Migration has become an increasingly important vehicle of population change, with three dominant themes, namely, migration from rural to urban areas, international labor migration (legal and illegal), and refugee flows. Of all population movements, international migration perhaps generates the greatest political, economic, and demographic interest owing to the large numbers of individuals crossing international borders. Fundamentally an economic process, international migration is motivated by a combination of "push" factors in the place of origin, including poor employment prospects, large populations, and low wages, with the major sending regions being Asia, North Africa, and Latin America. Principal receiving countries include the United States, Canada, Australia, Western Europe, Scandinavia, and Russia,[2] where higher wages and increased opportunity serve as immigrant "pulls."

As articulated by Douglas Massey and his colleagues, immigration is a complex demographic process.[3] Diverse explanations of immigration include neoclassical theory (supply and demand of labor), dual labor markets within developed countries where immigrants fill undesirable and low-paid positions, "chain immigration" and networks that reflect the persistence of immigrant flows, institutional theories postulating the existence of institutions that promote or organize flows, and cumulative causation theories. Notwithstanding the diversity of these explanations, no single theoretical viewpoint captures all of immigration's nuances, in part because national policies have also created and influenced immigration flows, either intentionally or unintentionally. In the past, immigration was an important component of nation building in Canada, the United States, Australia, and New Zealand; indeed, it remains a "myth" in many of these countries. The enduring and near legendary status of places like Ellis Island in New York and Canada's Pier 21 in Halifax, as well as of Australia's settlement by ex-convicts, is an important component of each nation's development and psyche. Countries have also encouraged labor recruitment through programs such as the **Bracero Program** that recruited Mexican laborers for work in the United States or Germany's guest-worker program. Consequently, immigration decisions must be considered within the broader context of national policies that promote or impede it.

Notwithstanding the historical significance of immigration flows, the developed world debated the costs and benefits of immigration throughout much of the twentieth century, and governments have moved to limit the number of entrants allowed. Despite the increased emphasis placed on immigration control, there is growing concern that receiving states have effectively lost control over their borders. This **immigration gap**, the difference between immigration policy and outcome articulated by Wayne Cornelius, Philip Martin, and James Hollifield,"[4] arises from a variety of national and international factors. Globalization, economic restructuring, liberal politics, and state policies that have encouraged immigration have worked to undermine state attempts to control it, provoking public opposition and calls for even tighter immigration policies.

In Europe, national identity and concerns with cultural and linguistic protection, as well as differences between foreigners and the native born, have driven a backlash against immigrants. In Germany, cultural and religious differences, along with economic concerns, fuel anti-immigrant sentiment. This backlash has increasingly given rise to European political forums such as Germany's "skinheads," France's Front National, and Austria's Freedom Party, all of which espouse antiforeigner sentiments.[5] More recently, France rejected the European Union constitution in spring 2005, in part based on fears that the country would be flooded with either poor Eastern European or non-European immigrants. Anti-immigrant groups are finding increasing political strength elsewhere in Europe, including Spain and Italy, where anti-immigrant violence has erupted, even though they, like other European countries, need foreign workers due to declining birth rates and an increasingly elderly population. Like other European countries, Spain and Italy have never defined themselves as immigrant importers and have only imported labor recently. Historically, they have been exporters of labor, and the shift from exporter to importer status is a difficult one for the average person to accept and is made even more difficult by large numbers of illegal immigrants.

The fact that Canada, the United States, and Australia define themselves as "nations of immigrants" may only delay large-scale anti-immigrant backlashes. In North America, concerns center on the economic and fiscal effects of immigration, including whether immigrants negatively influence wages and employment among the native born. Immigrants' ability to assimilate into North American society has also dominated policy and lay discussions. In the United States, these concerns have intensified, owing to illegal immigration and threats of terrorism. In fact, anti-immigrant sentiments are already present within the United States in response to the perceived negative consequences associated with immigration, including changes to the larger society and its institutions, as well as economic effects. Academically, the "Balkanization" debate has captured many of these concerns, suggesting that significant, negative spatial segmentation by race and ethnicity is associated with labor force competition between the native- and foreign-born populations.[6] Invoking Mark Ellis and Richard Wright's arguments, Balkanization takes a negative view of immigration, ethnic antagonism, spatial disintegration, and groups' ability to coexist peacefully. From a legislative perspective, California's **Proposition 187**, welfare reform, and a refocusing of resources on the U.S.-Mexican border to staunch illegal immigration provide sufficient evidence of mounting American concern with immigration. Canada, on the other hand, has largely avoided protracted immigration debates. Immigration there is viewed as an asset; its immigration policy is clear and has largely succeeded, although illegal immigration and refugee flows do represent areas of concern.

Spotlighting the policy and political implications associated with immigration, this chapter considers legal and illegal immigration from the European and North American viewpoints. Most developed countries have instituted restrictions and barriers to immigration and recast it as a national-security issue. But, if a country tries to close its doors to further immigration, will it succeed? The experiences of Europe and the United States, including the 1986 Immigration Reform and Control Act (**IRCA**) and recent clampdowns on illegal border crossings, suggest not. In fact, restricting legal immigration may only serve to increase illegal immigration or other "backdoor" immigration through family-reunification programs or seasonal-worker admission. Both Europe and the United States face a large gap between the realities of controlling immigration and politics, caught between employers, who desire cheap labor, and U.S.-born workers whose power and livelihood are threatened.[7] In Europe, anti-immigrant sentiment is more pronounced. While immigration is often portrayed as an economic issue within the receiving country, it also engages the rather thorny question of who (or what) constitutes a "nation." Such issues lie at the root of anti-immigrant violence in Europe and right-wing political parties that have risen in response to perceived threats to national identity.

POLICY AND REALITY: THE IMMIGRATION GAP

Over the past hundred years, most governments have attempted to control the movement of populations into and out of their countries, and state governments wrote and rewrote immigration law throughout the latter half of the 1900s to reflect emerging economic and demographic needs, as well as the reality of the civil rights movement. While many policies appeared to succeed at first, states have found it increasingly difficult to control immigration since the 1980s. Despite their best attempts to impose tighter entry restrictions and other controls, labor-importing states face an immigration-control crisis, defined by Wayne Cornelius and his colleagues as the "gap" between immigration-control policies and their outcomes.[8] While governments desire to control immigration, the reality is that they have less confidence in their ability to do so now than they did fifteen to twenty years ago. The gap between immigration policy and reality is aided and abetted by three concurrent factors.[9]

First, various domestic factors have limited the state's ability to control its borders. For example, programs like Germany's guest-worker program or the United States' Bracero Program were meant to be short term, with workers cycling in and out of the country as needed. The very existence of such programs, however, legitimized and concretized the movement of workers across international borders, connected regions, and created pathways for future immigrants by spreading information about jobs and receiving areas. Existing immigrant communities within the receiving regions have served as anchors for new arrivals, cushioning the stress of relocation. When states have attempted to restrict immigration, these networks maintain flows through illegal immigration and family reunification. Likewise, policies meant to close the border have created permanent residents out of temporary workers. Concerned with labor shortages, employers maintained their existing pool of immigrant workers. Workers, on the other hand, feared that they would not be able to return should they leave their host countries and instead remained. Both France and Germany have, at different times, declared their borders closed to further immigration, only to see the number of foreign-born inhabitants increase through family-reunification clauses or other "backdoor" immigration routes, including illegal immigration. Similarly, U.S. domestic policies have failed to deter illegal immigration. Nowhere is policy's inability to deter illegal immigration better illustrated than by the IRCA, which sought to allow

California's agricultural growers to continue to use undocumented workers at the same time that other employers were required to verify the employment eligibility of workers.

Second, a number of factors from outside the state have contributed to the gap between policy and reality, including globalization and economic restructuring. Globalization opens economies to greater trade and capital flows and increases demand for cheap labor within industrialized countries. Stopping or controlling immigration becomes increasingly difficult because of the underlying demand for inexpensive labor. With globalization, employers have shown an increasing insensitivity toward economic fluctuations. That is, employer demand for cheap labor remains strong even in conditions of relatively high unemployment, and employers have been successful in recruiting workers and co-opting state policies for their benefit. Concurrently, population growth and economic restructuring within the labor-exporting countries promote economic and social disparities and create a ready pool of labor that encourages emigration. A second exogenous factor is that advances in communications and transportation technology are increasingly accessible to immigrants, aiding the expansion of international migration networks and sustained immigration flows.

Third, the rise of liberalism and the extension of human rights to foreigners within developed countries have further legitimized their position within host countries, hampering state efforts to control immigration. Policies aimed at protecting rights (e.g., asylum) have helped immigrants enter and remain in host countries. Canada, for instance, has had problems in the administration of its refugee policy,[10] and Germany's generous asylum policies were seen as a quick and easy way to gain entry. Although some of the rights the foreign born acquired in the 1960s and 1970s have been lost through new legislation, they remain a barrier to immigration control.

THE NORTH AMERICAN EXPERIENCE: THE DOORS REMAIN OPEN

Both the United States and Canada have long prided themselves as being nations of immigrants, with immigrants arriving in search of economic opportunity and political or religious freedom, or to reunite with their families. Despite the long history of immigration to both countries, public attention has increasingly focused on the size, origin, and implications of large-scale immigration.[11] Over the past fifty years, polling has charted increasing opposition to immigrants within the United States. Ongoing and emerging debates reflect associated concerns: How will immigrants assimilate into or incorporate themselves within the host society? How will the larger society be changed? Will society become "Balkanized" along ethnic or racial lines?

Discussions of the costs and benefits of immigration reflect a long-running debate within most countries that receive a large number of immigrants. Answers to these questions cut across economic, social, fiscal, and demographic perspectives.[12] Undoubtedly, public awareness is higher in those locations that are primary magnets for immigrants, including California, New York, Illinois, Florida, and New Jersey in the United States and Ontario, Quebec, and British Columbia in Canada, but concerns with the number and impact of immigrants are not limited to these areas. Recent reports, including U.S. Census 2000 data, indicate that the foreign born are increasingly found in areas that have not been traditional destinations for immigrants.[13] States like Iowa, which can hardly be described as immigrant "magnets," are now counting larger foreign-born populations. New arrivals frequently fill low-paying or unskilled positions, and their presence forces communities to deal with issues of immigration and assimilation previously unknown to small-town America.

Economically, the bulk of evidence from Canada, the United States, and elsewhere indicates that immigration has a rather minimal, but positive, impact on economic well-being.[14] Immigration most directly benefits the immigrants themselves: they are financially better off in their host countries than they were in their countries of origin, even though they tend to earn less, on average, than the native born and predominately occupy low-paying, low-skilled positions in the workforce. Domestically, immigrants increase the supply of labor, boost production and demand for goods, and serve as a potent short-term policy tool to alleviate skill shortages quickly. Although the economy as a whole may gain, immigration also creates losers, including the less-skilled native born who compete directly with immigrants in the job market and who may see their wages fall. Again, however, the available evidence suggests that immigration has only a small negative impact on the wage and labor opportunities of the native born. In the formal sector, minimum-wage laws, unions, and low unemployment rates have ensured "wage stickiness," although workers in the informal economy or in regions that receive large numbers of immigrants may be somewhat more disadvantaged.

The debate over whether immigrants pay more in taxes than they receive in benefits is contentious. In an analysis of the impacts of immigration on U.S. society, the National Research Council (NRC) found that immigrant-headed households make small positive contributions to federal tax revenues.[15] At the state and local levels, the picture is less clear, with net fiscal burdens reported in immigrant-receiving states, such as New Jersey and California. In other words, the NRC calculated that immigrants receive more in services than they pay in taxes in these two states. However, the increased burden is explained by the fact that both states are important immigrant destinations with large numbers of immigrants. In turn, immigrant households tend to have a greater number of school-age children and therefore receive more transfers. Likewise, immigrant households tend to have lower incomes and less property, so they consequently pay lower taxes. Fiscal burdens may be particularly acute at the local level. In Phoenix, Arizona, the burgeoning Hispanic population, much of which is believed to be there illegally, has exerted pressures on institutions such as local school boards, hospitals, and libraries, even as their presence has been acknowledged to sustain the state economy by providing low-wage labor.[16] If the state or federal government does not reimburse local costs, the burden will fall to local taxpayers, a situation that it is easy to imagine will generate increased calls for immigration control.

Long-term projections of the fiscal costs and benefits of immigration indicate that they balance out over the lifetime of an immigrant's residency. Immigrants, like the native born, pose greater burdens during childhood and old age, owing to the costs of education and health care. During their labor force years, they tend to make a net fiscal contribution. Fiscal burden also varies by origin and education, with European and North American immigrants making a net fiscal contribution, while immigrants from Central and South America create a fiscal burden owing to their lower incomes, lower levels of education, and greater number of school-aged children. It is important to realize, however, that education and service provision to poorly educated or low-income native born pose similar fiscal burdens. In other words, the question of fiscal burden is not just an immigrant issue.

Demographically, immigration has frequently been touted as a solution to the problems of an aging population. As noted in chapter 1, most developed countries have entered a period characterized by below-replacement fertility levels. Economic development associated with urbanization, industrialization, economic uncertainty, and the welfare state has translated into a reduced need or desire for children. The result is an increasing proportion of elderly and a decreasing share of the population aged fifteen and younger. In effect, we are seeing a fundamental change in the age distribution of the population away from the traditional "pyramidal" structure, in which a large share of the population is concentrated in the younger age groups, toward a "rectangular" structure with a more even distribution of the population across all ages. In response, immigration could be used to offset the demographic implications of an aging population if young immigrants were targeted as the most desirable entrants. Indeed, the relatively high fertility levels in the United States (relative to Canada and other developed nations) reflect higher fertility among minority groups, particularly Hispanics.[17] Most studies, including those of the NRC, have found that immigration merely postpones or alleviates the onset of an aging population, although it is likely that immigration has allowed the United States to maintain relatively high fertility levels. In part, family reunification offsets the desired demographic effects as young adults sponsor their parents. Moreover, the dynamics of demographic change now under way within the developed world imply that the population will continue to age statistically in the coming decades.

Instead, the most visible impact of immigration will be changes to the cultural, racial, or ethnic composition of receiving countries as immigrants account for an increasing share of the population, issues that most developed countries are already grappling with. Socially, opposition to immigration has frequently focused on the perceived cultural and racial differences between immigrants and the native born, but this raises debates over whether the receiving country has one culture or many. In Europe or Canada, the answers to this question are simple but reflect polar ends of the spectrum. Most European states see their borders as encompassing a single nationality, hence their concern with increasing numbers of foreigners and the "dilution" of national identity. In Canada, on the other hand, the federal government has fostered and actively promoted the nation's identity as a multicultural society for the past thirty years. In the United States, the answer is less clear but no less important. The unifying vision of the "melting pot" contrasts with the reality of immigration. Immigration to the United States may have altered impressions of culture, but it does not necessarily suppress the cultural identity of immigrants, making the United States a de facto multicultural society as well (see figure 4.1). Even among groups that have been long-term residents of the United States, such as Germans or Scandinavians, their cultural heritage is embraced by the larger population, and their identities have left lingering impressions on the cultural and economic landscape.[18]

United States

For much of the first century of the United States' existence, immigration was largely unrestricted; the Supreme Court only ruled that the federal government had authority over immigration in 1875.[19] The years between 1875 and 1920 witnessed increasing regulation of entry into the United States, aimed at excluding those with criminal records, diseases, and unacceptable moral standards, as well as anarchists and members of particular groups. The 1882 Chinese Exclusion Act represented the first of several acts that restricted Asian immigration, with the Japanese excluded in 1907, and all Asians excluded in 1917. During the 1920s, national quotas were established that favored northern and western Europeans in an effort to maintain the racial and ethnic mixture in the United States. The 1921 Immigration Act

Figure 4.1.   The United Immigrants of America. *Source:* **Kirk Anderson, reproduced with permission.**

THE UNITED IMMIGRANTS OF AMERICA

With an increasingly diverse immigrant population, the United States must acknowledge that it is truly a nation of immigrants, with a multicultural, not melting pot, society.

was the first to place quantitative restrictions on immigration, with annual immigration from a given country limited to 3 percent of the number of foreign born from that country residing in the United States in 1910, when northern and western Europeans dominated the country. In effect, the law shifted immigrant origins away from unfavored regions, including southern and eastern Europe, emphasizing instead an Anglo-Saxon immigration agenda. Interestingly, the quotas did not place restrictions on immigrants from the Western Hemisphere. Canadians were seen as no different from the existing American population stock, and immigration from Central and South America was not deemed a problem. In subsequent years, quotas were made increasingly tight, altering either the percentage or pushing back the base year, further reducing the number of immigrants allowed entry. However, imposing restrictions on immigration simply gave rise to illegal immigration. In response, Congress established the U.S. Border Patrol in 1924, charged initially with apprehending illegal entrants.

The blatantly racist restrictions within American immigration policy were not removed until 1952 with the passage of the Immigration and Nationality Act. This act introduced a preference system for those with needed skills. For the first time, limits were placed on immigrants from the Western Hemisphere, and a preference system was set in place, with priority given to family members of American citizens and permanent residents, as well as those with needed job skills. The **quota system** was finally lifted in the 1965 revisions to the Immigration and Nationality Act, replacing it with a new system of hemispheric limits, which had a significant impact on the nature of American society. Although it was unintended, the family preference category dramatically shifted immigration away from traditional origins such as Europe and toward new origins in Central and South America and Asia. Prior to 1965, Europeans represented the majority of immigrants arriving in the United States, but they represented just 13.5 percent in 2004. Instead, approximately 36 percent of all immigrants were from the Americas by 2004, with Mexico representing the single largest country of origin (18.5 percent).[20] With 34.9 percent of immigrants, Asians were the second largest group. Minor adjustments were made to the immigration act through the 1970s and 1980s, a period marked by an increasing awareness of the scope of illegal immigration, and the Immigration Act of 1990 was the last major revision. Although family reunification remained a significant reason for immigration, the act increased the number of immigrants admitted on a yearly basis and expanded the number of visas given on economic grounds to 140,000 per fiscal year (see tables 4.1 and 4.2).[21]

In framing immigration policy, U.S. legislators have attempted to balance competing economic, social, and humanitarian goals. For example, some argue that a large illegal immigrant workforce is not beneficial to the United States. Competing interests have, however, lead to policy gridlock, a fragmented policy agenda, and other unanticipated consequences, resulting in a gap between the goals of national immigration policy and the results of those policies.[22] In her analysis of U.S. immigration, Kitty Calavita argues that historical and current policies are best summarized as a triad of oppositions between employers and workers, between an economy that needs unskilled workers and a political class unwilling to confront the conflicts this creates, and between human rights and border control.[23]

The contradictions inherent in U.S. policy are demonstrated by the Bracero Program (1942–1964) of contract-labor importation, which legitimized migrations between Mexico and the United States. In legitimizing immigration, it created long-term connections between the two countries and essentially condoned illegal immigration. The 1986 IRCA further exemplified these contradictions. Meant to solve the problem of illegal immigration, sanctions were put in place for employers who hired undocumented workers. At the same time, IRCA immediately provided exemptions for California's agricultural growers to continue to use undocumented workers under the Special Agricultural Workers Program. Immigration control was further undermined when IRCA failed to require

Table 4.1. Class of Admission of Legal Immigrants to the United States, Fiscal Years 2002–2004

	2002		2003		2004	
	Number	*%*	*Number*	*%*	*Number*	*%*
Total, all immigrants	**1,063,732**	**100.0**	**705,827**	**100.0**	**946,142**	**100.0**
New arrivals	384,427	36.1	358,411	50.8	362,221	38.3
Adjustments	679,305	63.9	347,416	49.2	583,921	61.7
Preference immigrants	**362,037**	**34.0**	**241,031**	**34.1**	**369,685**	**39.1**
Family-sponsored immigrants	**187,069**	**51.7**	**158,894**	**65.9**	**214,355**	**58.0**
Unmarried sons/daughters of US citizens	23,567	12.6	21,503	13.5	26,382	12.3
Spouses of alien residents	84,860	45.4	53,299	33.5	93,609	43.7
Married sons/daughters of US citizens	21,072	11.3	27,303	17.2	28,695	13.4
Siblings of US citizens	57,570	30.8	56,895	35.8	65,671	30.6
Employment-based immigrants	**174,968**	**48.3**	**82,137**	**34.1**	**155,330**	**42.0**
Priority workers	34,452	19.7	14,544	17.7	31,291	20.1
Professionals with advanced degrees	44,468	25.4	15,459	18.8	32,534	20.9
Skilled workers, professionals, other workers	88,555	50.6	46,613	56.8	85,969	55.3
Special immigrants	7,344	4.2	5,456	6.6	5,407	3.5
Employment creation	149	0.1	65	0.1	129	0.1
Immediate relatives of US citizens	**485,960**	**45.7**	**332,657**	**47.0**	**406,074**	**42.9**
Spouses	294,798	60.7	184,741	55.5	252,193	62.1
Children	97,099	20.0	78,024	23.5	76,347	18.8
Orphans	21,100	4.3	21,320	6.4	11,170	2.8
Parents	94,063	19.8	69,892	21.0	77,534	19.1
Refugees and asylees	**126,084**	**11.9**	**44,927**	**6.4**	**71,230**	**7.5**
Refugee adjustments	115,832	91.9	34,496	76.8	61,013	85.7
Asylee adjustments	10,252	8.1	10,431	23.2	10,217	14.3
Other immigrants	**89,596**	**8.4**	**87,173**	**12.4**	**99,025**	**10.5**

Source: 2004 Yearbook of Immigration Statistics.

Table 4.2. Immigrants Admitted to the United States by Selected Country of Birth, Top Ten Origins, Fiscal Years 2002–2004

Rank	2004 Country	Number	Percentage	2003 Country	Number	Percentage	2002 Country	Number	Percentage
—	All countries	946,142	100.0	All countries	705,827	100.0	All countries	1,063,732	100.0
1	Mexico	175,364	18.5	Mexico	115,864	16.4	Mexico	219,380	20.6
2	India	70,116	7.4	India	50,372	7.1	India	71,105	6.7
3	Philippines	57,827	6.1	Philippines	45,397	6.4	China	61,282	5.8
4	China	51,156	5.4	China	40,659	5.8	Philippines	51,308	4.8
5	Vietnam	31,514	3.3	El Salvador	28,296	4.0	Vietnam	33,627	3.2
6	Dominican Republic	31,492	3.2	Dominican Republic	26,205	3.7	El Salvador	31,168	2.9
7	El Salvador	29,795	3.1	Vietnam	22,133	3.1	Cuba	28,272	2.7
8	Cuba	20,488	2.2	Colombia	14,777	2.1	Dominican Republic	22,604	2.1
9	Korea	19,766	2.1	Guatemala	14,415	2.0	Ukraine	21,217	2.0
10	Colombia	18,678	2.0	Russia	13,951	2.0	Korea	21,021	2.0

Source: 2004 Yearbook of Immigration Statistics.

employers to check the veracity of legal documents. IRCA also provided amnesty for illegal **aliens**, allowing them to apply for legal status if they had resided in the United States prior to January 1, 1982. While nearly three million immigrants were legalized, the amnesty program did not meet its goal of reducing illegal immigration over the long run. Instead, apprehensions of illegals entering the country skyrocketed within three years, and it was clear that others were rushing to fill the need for illegal labor. Subsequent studies demonstrated that the law did not provide a substantial deterrent to illegal immigration.[24]

Almost two decades after IRCA, different policies to deal with illegal immigration continue to give mixed signals.[25] President Bush's Fair and Secure Immigration Reform proposal, tabled in January 2004, proposed turning illegal workers into guest workers, with incentives to return home at the end of the employment certificate. A Democratic bill would allow illegal workers to become legal immigrants, while the Agricultural Job Opportunity, Benefits, and Security Act bill debated in Congress in spring 2005 would apply only to agricultural workers, allowing workers meeting specific criteria to apply for temporary legal status. Like IRCA, these three programs are meant to eliminate illegal workers. Yet, if Mexico and other Latin American nations do not experience sustained economic growth, the result of each of these programs could be the creation of additional networks that link immigrants within the U.S. and Mexican labor markets and additional illegal entry.

Beyond policy, enforcement also bears on the presence and number of illegals within the country: the stronger the enforcement, the greater the number of apprehensions. The Pew Hispanic Center, for example, estimated that 10.3 million illegal immigrants resided in the United States in 2004, with as many as 800,000 people entering the country illegally each year, despite the increased attention to border security.[26] Given the tight economic conditions and low unemployment rates of the late 1990s, reports suggested that the then Immigration and Naturalization Service (INS) was no longer pursuing illegal aliens once they were inside the United States. More recently, concerns about terrorism have largely diverted the focus from illegal immigrants already within the United States to restricting entry. In most cases, this quiet agenda caters to employer demands for inexpensive labor and is reminiscent of the Bracero Program where apprehended illegal Mexicans were returned to the Mexican side of the border, only to be issued papers immediately for legal employment in the Bracero Program. Such mixed signals further encourage migration from labor-exporting countries.

Ultimately, the imbalance between policy goals and realities may engender greater hostility toward immigrants, placing increased pressure on the government to restrict immigration. In 1986, for example, 1,615,854 illegal

Figure 4.2.   Caution. *Source:* Author's photo.

A roadside sign in San Diego warning motorists on busy Interstate 5 of the potential for people, including women and children, to be on the highway, posted in response to illegal immigrants' entering the United States in this area and escaping custody.

aliens were apprehended along the U.S.-Mexican border, and aliens were brazenly entering the country by running directly past immigration agents at border crossings (see figure 4.2). Such images provoked fears that the United States had lost control of its borders, and calls for tighter restrictions intensified. Searching for ways to control immigration and responding to public concerns, legislators moved to restrict immigrant access to welfare and social benefits, as illustrated by California's Proposition 187, Arizona's Proposition 200, and welfare reform in 1996, and to make entry more difficult, as exemplified by increased border-patrol measures.

California's Proposition 187,[27] designed to remove public funding from all illegal immigrants, polarized immigration viewpoints within that state and pushed local immigration concerns into the national and international spotlight.[28] Propelled by the real and perceived costs posed by illegal immigrants, including welfare (ab)use, criminal activity, and employment costs, California lawmakers attempted to curb the tide of illegal immigration into the state and to encourage some who were already resident to leave. The proposition was designed to exclude illegal immigrants from schools and colleges, deny nonemergency health care to illegal aliens, require the police to verify the legal immigrant status of all people arrested, and require teachers and health care workers to report illegal aliens to the INS. While its provisions did not affect legal immigrants within the state, it none-the-less created an atmosphere in which all people of color, both legal and illegal, became suspect. Internationally, both Mexico and El Salvador expressed concern with Proposition 187, citing human rights violations. More realistically, both were likely concerned with the potential negative economic effects associated with a large number of returning workers.

Passed by public vote in November 1994 with 59 percent of the vote, Proposition 187 received broad-based support throughout the state and revealed the depth of frustration among California's voters with illegal immigration. Shortly afterward, a federal court found Proposition 187 unconstitutional, ruling that immigration was a federal, not a state, matter, and that federal law requires free public education to all children. The widespread support for Proposition 187 had considerable ethnic and spatial variation in voting behavior, stressing the complexity of the immigration debate and providing insight into public reaction to immigration and anti-immigrant sentiments.[29] Ethnic divisions in voting patterns followed expected patterns, with 63 percent of white non-Hispanics voting in support of the proposition. Greater support was found among middle- or upper-income white and Republican voters, expressing a simple anti-immigrant sentiment. African Americans and Asians were moderately likely to support the measure, voting 56 and 57 percent in favor, respectively, while only 31 percent of Hispanics supported Proposition 187. Analysis of the vote at the local scale shows additional variations, with greater support in Hispanic neighborhoods with higher socioeconomic status, suggesting a desire to control illegal immigration and mirroring white, non-Hispanic sentiments. Even in inner-city Hispanic communities, there was a surprising degree of support for the measure.

William Clark, a professor of geography at the University of California, Los Angeles, suggested that voter response to Proposition 187 could not be characterized simply as a nativist or racist reaction but, instead, reflected local responses to immigration. Recalling the findings of the NRC, Californians were forced to deal with the real and perceived consequences of immigration locally, where potentially significant (and costly) fiscal effects were more likely to occur.[30] Thus, Proposition 187 may simply have been a reaction to high immigration levels in the late 1980s, local fiscal implications, and the recession of 1990–1991, which seemingly increased the cost of service provision by the state and local governments. Clark also suggested that the voting behavior placed California at odds with the nation's role as a receiver of immigrants and with business's desire for low-cost labor.[31] George Sanchez raised a darker implication, arguing that Proposition 187 scapegoated immigrants for California's economic problems in the early 1990s.[32] California is not alone in its concern over illegal immigrants and fiscal consequences; Arizona is also a frontline state wrestling with a growing illegal population. In the 2004 elections, Arizona's Proposition 200 barred illegal immigrants from voting or seeking public assistance.

Revisions to welfare in 1996 gave immigration concerns a national forum. The Personal Responsibility and Work Reconciliation Act fundamentally altered welfare provision in the United States by cutting money to welfare programs, giving states greater control over spending, and enacting work and duration restrictions to programs. Although its impact on the native born was just as significant, welfare reform directly targeted immigrants and their use of programs. Revisions barred most legal immigrants from receiving Supplemental Security Income (SSI) and food stamps, two programs in which immigrants received proportionately more benefits than the native born.[33] At the time, it was estimated that upwards of five hundred thousand aliens lost their eligibility for SSI, and it is estimated that an additional one million lost their eligibility to receive food stamps. Aliens legally admitted to the United States after August 22, 1996 (the date revisions took effect) were also barred from federal means-tested programs during their first five years of residency. States were also eligible to bar qualified aliens from receiving Temporary Assistance for Needy Families,[34] Medicaid, and Title XX social services that funded, among other programs, child care and elderly services. Although he objected to provisions restricting eligibility for public benefits, President Clinton signed the bill. In subsequent years, several directives and new bills worked to soften the impact of the restrictions on immigrants, and many state governments provided additional funding for services.

Ultimately, the first line of defense against illegal entry is the U.S. Border Patrol, which works within the U.S. Citizenship and Immigration Services (USCIS, formally INS) to detect and prevent the smuggling or entry of illegal aliens into the United States. In response to increasing concerns with the number of illegal immigrants entering the country, the Border Patrol increased the scope of its operations in 1994 along the southern border with Mexico, the primary entry point from Central and South America. A series of operations, including Operation Gatekeeper in San Diego, California, Operation Hold-the-Line in El Paso, Texas, and Operation Safeguard in Tucson, Arizona, were meant to control the border in each of these areas by cutting off avenues of illegal entry (see figure 4.3). Most operations included a variety of interventions to deter illegal entry, such as new fencing and the use of new technology, including infrared scopes, underground sensors, and computer tracking of illegal entrants. By USCIS measures, these programs have been highly successful, reducing the number of apprehensions from over 450,000 in 1994, to 284,000 in 1997, to 138,608 in 2004 in the San Diego sector alone.[35] Programs in other sectors have reported

Figure 4.3. The U.S.-Mexico Border. *Source:* Author's photo.

The fence separating the United States and Mexico in San Diego. Would-be illegal immigrants are on the Mexico side, waiting for nightfall, when they will attempt to enter the United States.

similar "successes," although the number of apprehensions jumped between 2003 and 2004 by over 234,000 (see table 4.3).

In reality, these programs may be somewhat less effective than advertised. While reducing the number of crossing attempts at key locations such as San Diego or El Paso, the deterrence effect of increased surveillance and capture has diverted the streams of illegal aliens to areas that have not received the same degree of attention from the Border Patrol.[36] Operation Hold-the-Line, for instance, succeeded only in reducing local border crossings (i.e., local domestic workers who traveled short distances) but failed to deter long-distance illegal-labor migration. Instead, crossings were diverted to Arizona, where the number of apprehensions increased, or elsewhere along the border.[37] The problem is also indirectly illustrated by the **Border Safety Initiative** (BSI), a binational program initiated in 1998 between the United States and Mexico. With increasing risk of apprehension in traditionally high-traffic areas, illegal entry has shifted to hazardous areas such as deserts or mountains, where the number of deaths among illegal entrants rose from 44 in 1999 to 207 in 2005.[38] Meant to reduce injuries and fatalities along the southwestern border, the BSI has made public education with respect to the risks associated with illegal crossings one of

Table 4.3. Yearly Border Patrol Apprehensions, Fiscal Years 1998–2004

Border Patrol Sector	1998	1999	2000	2001	2002	2003	2004
All Southwest	1,516,680	1,537,000	1,643,679	1,235,718	929,809	905,065	1,139,282
San Diego, CA	248,092	182,267	151,681	110,075	100,681	111,515	138,608
El Centro, CA	226,695	225,279	238,126	1072,852	108,273	92,099	74,467
Yuma, CA	76,195	93,388	108,747	78,385	42,654	56,638	98,060
Tucson, AZ	387,406	470,449	616,346	449,675	333,648	347,263	491,771
El Paso, TX	125,035	110,857	115,696	112,857	94,154	88,816	104,399
Marfa, TX	14,509	14,952	13,689	12,087	11,392	10,319	10,530
Del Rio, TX	131,058	156,653	157,178	104,875	66,985	50,145	53,794
Laredo, TX	103,433	114,004	108,973	87,068	82,095	70,521	74,706
McAllen, TX	204,257	169,151	133,243	107,844	89,927	77,749	92,947
All other sectors	**39,096**	**42,010**	**32,759**	**30,496**	**25,501**	**26,492**	**21,113**
Blaine, WA	2,403	2,421	2,581	2,089	1,732	1,308	1,354
Buffalo, NY	1,640	1,666	1,570	1,434	1,102	564	671
Detroit, MI	1,768	1,838	2,057	2,106	1,511	2,345	1,912
Grand Forks, ND	905	656	562	921	1,369	1,223	1,225
Havre, MT	1,145	1,448	1,568	1,305	1,463	1,406	986
Houlton, ME	307	461	489	685	432	292	263
Livermore, CA	11,633	11,198	6,205	5,211	4,371	3,565	1,850
Miami, FL	6,065	6,961	6,237	5,962	5,143	5,931	4,602
New Orleans, LA	8,008	10,777	6,478	5,033	4,665	5,151	2,889
Ramey, PR	1,244	1,405	1,731	1,952	835	1,688	1,813
Spokane, WA	2,176	1,308	1,324	1,335	1,142	992	847
Swanton, VT	1,802	1,871	1,957	2,463	1,736	1,955	2,701

Source: 2003 Yearbook of Immigration Statistics.

its primary aims, especially because illegals who are little prepared for the hardships of these locations are forced to cross in remote areas.

In placing additional resources along the border and proposing other policies aimed at controlling illegal immigration, the U.S. government effectively recast the immigration debate as a national-security issue. George Sanchez,[39] for example, has argued that such politics represent a resurgence of American nativism, which in turn reflects increasing fears of linguistic differences, as well as rising concerns that nonwhites will soon represent the majority within American society,[40] that immigrants will drain public resources, and that whites are increasingly losing political and economic ground to nonwhites with the approval of the government. The immigrant backlash is clearly exclusionary in character. Peter Brimelow's 1995 *Alien Nation: Common Sense about America's Immigration Disaster* expresses the rising nativism among the lay public:[41] he argues that immigrants are responsible for increased crime, the crisis in social security and welfare, and lower educational standards, all of which he believes may ultimately lead to the destruction of America. The academic debate is no less straightforward, with a number of studies identifying immigrants as a drain on taxpayers, despite the bulk of evidence to the contrary.[42] Even if unjustified, these concerns have become dominant themes within the immigration debate. Following the terrorist attacks of September 11, 2001, immigration's status as a potential threat to national security was further solidified when immigration and border issues were consolidated under the Department of Homeland Security. A coherent and sustainable solution to illegal immigration remains elusive, with the number of illegal immigrants in the United States estimated at 10.3 million as of March 2004, a 23 percent increase from just four years earlier.[43]

Amid the current and ongoing discussions of immigration within both the academic and political arenas, we sometimes lose sight of the fact that nothing is new. In fact, the debate and controversies associated with immigration are well trod, having existed in one form or another since the foundation of the United States, albeit reinvented in light of shifting realities, origins, politics, and economies. At various points, the foreign born have been blamed for every possible social problem—crime, urban unrest, environmental degradation, unemployment—largely because they have proven an easy and visible target. Past nativism resulted in the quota system and exclusionary immigration policies. At the time of the American Revolution, Benjamin Franklin and Thomas Jefferson openly expressed their doubts about whether German Protestants could ever become Americans. The massive influx of immigrants in the mid-nineteenth century opened debates over immigration and called for its control, with Americans objecting to the large numbers of arriving Irish Catholics. Later in the century, the arrival of southern Europeans engendered the same responses. Members of the Know-Nothing Party asserted that immigrants were driving the native born into poverty but surprisingly did not call for restrictions on their number,[44] which would not be implemented until the 1920s. The 1850s witnessed an increase in labor militancy as workers demanded greater protection in the face of changing industrial production and the influx of unskilled workers.

Although it has a familiar ring, today's nativism and the resulting changes to immigration policy differ from historical interpretations in three important respects. First, as Sanchez has pointed out, hostility toward immigrants has taken on a new meaning (and urgency) as immigrants are fitted into established white-versus-black racial patterns, making racism against Latin Americans or Asians an extension of the dominant white-black racism. Within the Cuban American community, for example, skin color defines alternate social and economic worlds for "black" and "white" Cubans, with "black" Cubans increasingly co-opted into the African American community and alienated by their "white" conationals.[45] The use of black and white lenses to view immigrants tends to dull awareness of other racial tensions and identities and is made more problematic by its denial of alternate realities. The implication of this renewed nativism is an increasing identification between race and immigration, which could threaten to close the doors to immigration and is likely to be reflected in future policy agendas, particularly if the economy does not perform as well as it did during the 1990s.

Second, the new nativism is rooted in economic restructuring that is transforming America's economic landscape. Unlike in the past, when rising unemployment triggered calls to restrict immigration, the new economy has actually increased the demands for immigrants in low-wage, low-skilled, and part-time jobs, engendering anti-immigrant sentiments. Instead, the new economy is characterized by an increased proportion of workers in the secondary sector and a transformation of traditional, well-paying jobs into part-time positions, reducing wages and eroding economic security.[46] The anxiety associated with economic insecurity and decreasing economic opportunities is directed toward immigrants, even as demand for them remains strong.

Third, political insecurity in the post–September 11 era has driven recent changes to immigration. While revisions to immigration policies and programs, as well as their administration, are not meant to exclude individual countries of origin per se, entrants to the United States face greater scrutiny due to efforts to bar the entry of potential terrorists. Refugee admissions declined significantly in 2002 and 2003, as did immigration flows, which dropped from 1.06 million in 2001 to slightly more than 700,000 in fiscal year 2003, before climbing to 946,000 in 2004. The decline in both refugee and immigration flows likely reflected security concerns and new immigration protocols, such as fingerprinting and running applicant names through intelligence and law enforcement databases. More broadly, American universities are noting a decline in enrollment of foreign students, which is again an outcome of security issues and could have future implications as many of these graduates, including those with advanced degrees, seek employment within the United States after graduation, particularly in science and engineering.[47]

Canada

Canadian immigration policy is similar to U.S. policy at first glance, but on closer examination, important differences emerge, including Canada's attempt to forge a clear economic, demographic, and political agenda and the relatively small gap between policy and reality. Historically, immigration was important in the evolution of Canada's society and economy, helping it move from a resource-based economy to an industrial one via the importation of immigrants who settled and farmed the western provinces. As early as 1868, the Canadian Free Grants and Homestead Act used the lure of free land to encourage agricultural workers to emigrate to Canada and aid in the settlement of western territories. In the decades after confederation, immigration served two purposes. First, it gave the Canadian government control over its western territories, keeping them out of American control. Second, the government of Prime Minister Wilfrid Laurier (1896–1911) viewed immigration as a nation-building tool, laying the infrastructure for Canada's development in the twentieth century as mining, lumber, and railway interests required laborers. Laurier's government particularly encouraged the immigration of agricultural workers from countries that had not traditionally supplied Canada with immigrants, including Russia, Italy, and Austria-Hungary. The policies were so successful that Canada saw its population grow by 40 percent between 1900 and 1914, with approximately 25 percent of the Canadian population in 1914 being foreign born.

Not surprisingly, increased immigration also gave rise to concerns over Canada's ability to assimilate these new arrivals. Drawing heavily on American literature and accepting the preference for northern Europeans, James S. Woodsworth, a Methodist minister and politician, advocated restricting immigration in the early twentieth century and encouraged the rapid assimilation of those already settled.[48] While Canada encouraged European immigration, it restricted or severely limited nonwhite immigration. Deeming the Chinese unable to assimilate into Canadian society, the government passed the Chinese Immigration Act in 1885, which imposed a "head tax" on Chinese immigrants. Further restrictions in 1907 and 1908 limited immigration from Japan and India as well. Laws enacted in 1906 and 1910 placed the diseased and those advocating violent political change on the restricted list as well.

The post–World War II era saw a continuation of these immigration policies, with the government of Prime Minister William Lyon Mackenzie King charting a careful course through concerns over too many immigrants, stressing the need to integrate returning soldiers, increasing immigration for domestic economic development, and assisting Europeans displaced by the war. King's vision of immigration policy encouraged immigration from traditional sources so as not to alter the character of the population, even as he allowed entry of Ukrainians, Russians, Poles, and Jewish survivors of death camps under the auspices of family reunification, a policy that could hardly be contested. By 1953, however, with concerns over immigration again surfacing, revisions to the immigration act allowed the government to prohibit the entry of immigrants based on nationality, national security, and ethnicity. Preference was again given to those of British or French birth, representing Canada's two founding countries, along with those from the United States, with a second preference including Western European countries.

It was not until 1962 that national-origin restrictions were finally lifted. As in the United States, this led to a fundamental shift in the origins of immigrants. Prior to 1962, most immigrants originated in Europe. As of 2004, Asia has represented the largest origin region (47.2 percent), with China contributing 14.5 percent. Africa and the Middle East were the second largest regions of origin (22.0 percent), and Europe and the United Kingdom combined to form the third largest origin (18.4 percent).[49] In 1967, the "**points system**" was established, a policy that has since become an important tool in shaping immigration to Canada in the late twentieth century (see table 4.4). Economic immigration was encouraged through the selection of immigrants of preferred education and age and with desired training, skills, and language abilities. Although immigration policy has been revised numerous times since its most dramatic reorientation in 1962, the policies of nondiscrimination, family reunion, humanitarian assistance, and the promotion of economic and social goals have remained at its core. Amendments to the immigration act in 1976 introduced yearly target levels for immigrants, determined after federal consultation with provinces and other organizations concerning demographic and labor needs, along with social and cultural considerations.

Since 1967, immigration policy has been designed to promote economic development and demographic stability over fears associated with an aging population and its economic consequences. Out of approximately 200,000 to 235,000 entrants per year, family-class entrants represented just 26.4 percent in 2004, down from a high of approximately 45 percent in the 1980s (see table 4.5).[50] While family reunification remains an important

Table 4.4. Canada's Immigration Point System for Skilled Workers, 2005

Factor	Maximum Points	Points Calculation
1. Age	10	21–49 years at time of application, less 2 points for each year over 49 or under 21
2. Education	25	Less than high school diploma: 0 points Various types of postsecondary training: 5–15 points Diploma, trade certificate, or apprenticeship and work experience: 20–25 points
3. Arranged employment	10	Arranged employment: 10 points Confirmed employment or temporary work permit: 10 points
4. Experience	21	Points are calculated based on the number of years worked in the intended occupation after completion of formal training.
5. Language ability	24	First official language: High proficiency: 4 points Moderate proficiency: 2 points Basic proficiency: 1–2 points No proficiency: 0 points Second official language scored same way.
6. Adaptability	10	Spouse's/partner's education: 3–5 points Minimum one year's authorized work in Canada: 5 points Minimum two years' study in Canada: 5 points Received bonus points under Arranged Employment in Canada factor: 5 points Family relationship in Canada: 5 points

Source: Derived from Citizenship and Immigration Canada at www.cic.gc.ca/english (accessed February 6, 2006).

component of immigration policy, Canada has instead attempted to create a more specific agenda that focuses on economic growth, while U.S. policy has fluctuated between humanitarian, economic, and social agendas. Although politicians and academics alike debate the success, logic, and coherence of immigration policies, economic immigrants now represent over 55 percent of admittances, and the Canadian government has sharpened economic immigration as a tool to promote the economic development of Canada. Economic immigrants include skilled workers and business immigrants and their families, as well as "investor" and "entrepreneur" immigrants. Federal immigration policy has also shifted, focusing more on language, education, work experience, and adaptability to a changing labor market.

Like its larger neighbor to its south, Canada has dealt with questions pertaining to the social, economic, and cultural incorporation of new

Table 4.5. Class of Admission of Legal Immigrants to Canada, 2002–2004

	2002		2003		2004	
	Number	Percent	Number	Percent	Number	Percent
Total, all immigrants	**229,036**	**100.0**	**221,352**	**100.0**	**235,824**	**100.0**
Family class	**65,297**	**28.5**	**69,128**	**31.2**	**62,246**	**26.4**
Spouses and partners	35,468	54.3	42,490	61.5	43,985	70.7
Fiancé(e)s	1,415	2.2	936	1.4	213	0.3
Sons or daughters	3,646	5.6	3,621	5.2	3,037	4.9
Parents or grandparents	22,526	34.5	19,376	28.0	12,732	20.5
Other[a]	2,206	3.4	2,705	3.9	2,279	3.7
Economic immigrants	**138,454**	**54.5**	**121,063**	**54.7**	**133,746**	**56.7**
Skilled workers	**123,316**	**85.5**	**105,240**	**86.9**	**113,442**	**84.8**
Skilled workers—principal applicants	53,416	43.3	45,378	43.1	47,889	42.2
Skilled workers—spouses and dependants	69,900	56.7	59,862	56.9	65,553	57.8
Business class	**11,027**	**8.0**	**8,101**	**6.7**	**9,764**	**7.3**
Entrepreneurs—principal applicants	11,178	8.1	783	9.7	671	6.9
Entrepreneurs—spouses and dependants	3,309	35.2	2,201	27.2	1,806	18.5
Self-employed—principal applicants	635	5.8	444	5.5	366	3.7
Self-employed—spouses and dependants	1,268	11.5	978	12.1	824	8.4
Investors—principal applicants	1,232	11.2	972	12.0	1,671	17.1
Investors—spouses and dependants	3,405	30.9	2,723	33.6	4,426	45.3
Other economic class	**4,111**	**3.0**	**7,722**	**6.4**	**8,768**	**6.6**
Provincial/territorial nominees	2,126	51.7	4,418	57.2	6,248	71.3
Live-in caregivers—principal applicants	1,521	37.0	2,230	28.9	2,496	28.5
Live-in caregivers—spouses and dependants	464	11.3	1,074	13.9	1,796	20.5
Refugees	**25,121**	**11.0**	**25,984**	**11.7**	**32,686**	**13.9**
Government-assisted	7,507	29.9	7,504	28.9	7,411	22.7
Privately sponsored	3,046	12.1	3,254	12.5	3,116	9.5
Landed in Canada	10,574	42.1	11,267	43.4	15,901	48.6
Dependants	4,021	16.0	3,959	15.2	6,258	19.1
Other immigrants	**164**	**0.07**	**5,176**	**2.3**	**9,196**	**3.9**

Source: Citizenship and Immigration Canada, 2002–2004.
[a] Applies to orphans under 18, potential adoptees under 13, and other miscellaneous groups.

immigrants. Canada's immigration policy has been described as consensual and open, owing in part to the relatively small gap between policy goals and outcomes,[51] and it has enjoyed relatively unique success with respect to immigration. Indeed, immigrants are still viewed as an asset and an important part of Canada's economic strategy, and it is easy to point out the cultural diversity of metropolitan centers. Culturally and socially, Canada has actively pursued policies aimed at the incorporation of immigrants into society while simultaneously recognizing their diversity. Fundamental to this thinking was the liberalization of immigration policy in 1962, which encouraged immigration from nontraditional source countries, the introduction of the "points" system in 1967, and federal multicultural policies. First enacted in 1971 under Prime Minister Pierre Elliot Trudeau and enhanced in 1988, multicultural policies reshaped thinking associated with the long-term adjustment of immigrants to Canadian society, allowing the expression and preservation of ethnocultural affiliations.

While multiculturalism has given social and economic confidence and expression to various ethnic groups, and episodes of racism or discrimination are relatively infrequent, it has not been without its critics. Critics have accused multicultural policies of fostering social isolation by emphasizing the preservation of cultural traditions.[52] Multiculturalism may in fact work to opposite ends, promoting equal participation that necessarily requires societal integration on the one hand, while simultaneously promoting ethnic distinctiveness on the other. Ambivalence toward multicultural policies and the desirability of retaining ethnic identity is also found within the Canadian public. That is, while multiculturalism is officially promoted, Canadians continue to desire and expect movement by immigrants toward some single (typically middle-class), unifying culture. They expect immigrants to realize that they will need to integrate themselves into a society in which the dominant structures are English and French in order to participate effectively. Multiculturalism may merely provide the veneer of ethnic and racial self-identity and expression within the immigrant community.

The incorporation of immigrants into the fabric of Canadian society has not been seamless. In 1957, 95 percent of all immigrants were from Europe or the United States, with the single largest group coming from the United Kingdom. By 2004, this group accounted for 18.4 percent of new arrivals, with the leading countries of origin shifting to China, India, Pakistan, Philippines, Korea, United States, and Iran (see table 4.6). Groups have experienced different settlement processes and reception. During recessions in the 1970s, 1980s, and early 1990s, their arrival coincided with competition for jobs and the provision of public services, leading to social problems and raising questions regarding Canada's ability to absorb these new immigrants economically and socially. Fears of increased unemployment and ethnic or racial tensions, together with pressure on the welfare

Table 4.6. Immigrants Admitted to Canada by Selected Country of Birth, Top Ten Origins, 2002–2004

Rank	2002 Country	Number	Percent	2003 Country	Number	Percent	2004 Country	Number	Percent
—	All countries	229,036	100.0	All countries	221,352	100.0	All countries	235,824	100.0
1	China, People's Rep. of	33,237	14.5	China, People's Rep. of	36,116	16.3	China, People's Rep. of	36,411	15.4
2	India	28,822	12.6	India	24,560	11.1	India	25,569	10.8
3	Pakistan	14,156	6.2	Pakistan	12,330	5.6	Philippines	13,301	5.6
4	Philippines	11,003	4.8	Philippines	11,978	5.4	Pakistan	12,796	5.4
5	Iran	7,738	3.4	Korea, Republic of	7,086	3.2	United States	7,494	3.2
6	Korea, Republic of	7,324	3.2	United States	5,990	2.7	Iran	6,063	2.6
7	Romania	5,293	2.3	Iran	5,648	2.6	United Kingdom	6,058	2.6
8	United States	5,687	2.5	Romania	5,465	2.5	Romania	5,655	2.4
9	Sri Lanka	4,962	2.2	United Kingdom	5,194	2.4	Korea, Republic of	5,337	2.3
10	United Kingdom	4,719	2.1	Sri Lanka	4,442	2.0	France	5,026	2.1

Source: Citizenship and Immigration Canada.

system, were felt within the political system and expressed by the electorate during national elections in 1993 and 2000, with calls to curb immigration numbers; in 2005, polls reflected a hardening of Canadian attitudes toward immigration.[53]

Other recent expressions of anti-immigrant sentiment further indicate that anxieties associated with immigration have not disappeared. At best, they were simply swept under the carpet by a robust economy in the late 1990s. While the federal government debated immigration policy, Toronto grappled with the economic and social incorporation of Somali and Chinese immigrants, with local politics reflecting negative public opinion from time to time.[54] Likewise, the return of Hong Kong to Chinese control in 1997 saw the arrival of large numbers of Hong Kong Chinese in Vancouver, significantly altering the social, ethnic, and economic makeup of the city. While welcomed in some respects, Hong Kong immigrants and investors faced a mixed reception, including open (but modest) hostility due to their impact on the local housing market via the increase of rents, the construction of "monster homes," and the loss of Anglo-Canadian heritage in older residential neighborhoods. Linguistic and cultural tensions have also arisen, particularly in Quebec, where new arrivals tend to adopt English rather than French. Since the mid-1970s, with the introduction of Bill 101, Chartre de la Langue Française, which limited the use of the English language within the province, the Parti Québécois has targeted the foreign born on numerous occasions. The most prominent case was in 1995, when Jacques Parizeau, then leader of the separatist Parti Québécois, blamed the ethnic vote for the narrow defeat of the sovereignty referendum, alienating Quebec's foreign-born population.

Canadians have also only recently recognized illegal immigration as a problem, even though one would reasonably assume Canada to be a destination. Indeed, upward of two hundred thousand people may be in Canada illegally.[55] Historically, illegal immigration into Canada was assumed to be relatively small, with most arriving as visitors and then **overstaying** once in Canada. This complacency gave way in the 1990s as evidence revealed the presence of larger numbers of illegal immigrants within Canada. One estimate counted as many as fifteen thousand Chinese entering the country illegally over the 1990s. If the alarm bells were not yet ringing, they did in 1999 and 2000 when several boatloads of illegal immigrants from China were intercepted off the coast of British Columbia. Most had paid hefty sums, reportedly up to $100,000 (Canadian), to "snakeheads" who smuggled them into Canada or, ultimately, the United States. Burdened with repaying the cost of the smuggling, along with an additional 18 percent interest, it would take years for illegal immigrants to repay their smugglers. Paid low wages by employers who knowingly take advantage of their illegal status and need for work, they become virtual slaves in the underground economies of cities like Toronto, Vancouver, and Montreal.[56]

The fact that many illegal entrants quickly seek refugee status, a route toward legalization of their status that provides constitutional protections, complicates the issue of illegal immigration into Canada. As such, it is closely associated with refugee issues, a topic discussed in chapter 5. Canadian officials have initiated a clampdown on illegal immigration, but it remains too early to evaluate the success of these policies. Like other developed countries, however, Canada is likely to have a difficult time staunching the flow of illegal immigrants. Instead, economic and social conditions within sending countries like China and the rise of liberal policies that extend rights to these groups explain the difficulty of controlling immigration.

THE EUROPEAN EXPERIENCE: THE RISE OF ANTI-IMMIGRANT SENTIMENTS

In contrast to the experience of North America, where immigrants laid the nation's foundations, most European countries have engaged the immigration debate only recently, becoming, according to several authors, "reluctant" importers of labor.[57] Rather than immigrant destinations, most Western European countries have traditionally been exporters of labor. Germany, for instance, was primarily a source of **emigrants** up until the 1950s, exporting its population to Canada, the United States, or elsewhere, while countries such as Spain have exported their labor to other European destinations. Western European countries became importers of labor in the post–World War II era, increasingly looking outside their borders for labor as their domestic labor forces declined and thereby stimulating large-scale immigration from the periphery of Europe.

The shift from labor export to labor import is a significant one. Although the European Union has moved toward an integrated immigration policy in recent years, the immigration debate remains divisive, capturing the attention of governments, policymakers, and citizens. Moreover, early experiences with immigration were diverse and have had long-lasting effects, in some cases leading to growing nationalism and **xenophobia**. Four nonexclusive realities drive the current immigration debate in Europe, namely, the demographic realities European nations face, the sanctioned importation of labor that has served to legitimize ongoing movements, the increasing political liability of immigrant populations within European countries, and fears of uncontrolled immigration from the developing world.

First, without immigration, the population and labor force of most European nations is expected to shrink. Already, with a total fertility rate

(TFR) of 1.3, which is well below replacement level, and a natural increase of –0.2 percent, Germany's population is declining. More generally, a low TFR (1.6 in Western Europe) and a growing elderly population (17 percent of Western Europe's population is aged sixty-five or over) drive the demographic need for sustained immigration in one form or another. With aging populations, many Western European countries also face a growing shortage of skilled workers entering the labor force, and the economic implications of not importing labor are significant. Most observers believe, for example, that Germany's rise as an industrial power would not have been possible without foreign guest workers. To ease labor shortages, Europe has considered increasing child bonuses and other incentives to encourage fertility, but such programs have had limited success. Alternatively, immigration can bolster population numbers, but using immigration to prevent population decline, maintain Europe's social welfare programs, increase fertility rates, or maintain the ratio of workers to dependents would require a massive increase in immigration numbers. The UN Population Division estimates, for example, that immigration into the European Union would need to increase to 1.1 million per year to maintain the labor force. If saving social welfare programs is the goal, immigration numbers would need to increase an incredible thirty-seven times.[58]

Second, like the United States, many European governments have directly sanctioned the movement of workers, creating linkages between sending and receiving areas that remain strong and continue to provide a willing pool of labor. Employers too have promoted the use of low-cost workers in production. France's history of liberal immigration and naturalization policies has kept that country's door open to immigration. The government sanctioned worker recruitment, but it had very little control or authority. France's immigration policy was complicated by the end of its colonial era in the 1950s and 1960s, creating a special class of immigrants from North Africa who were protected by a society that emphasized the rights of the individual.[59]

After publicly declaring that it was not a nation of immigrants, Germany too faces a gap between its immigration policy and the reality that more than one million newcomers entered the country each year throughout the 1990s, with many arriving from non–European Union countries, such as the Balkans, Eastern Europe, or Turkey.[60] The gap between policy and results has led to widespread dissatisfaction, particularly as Germany's economy has collapsed, and unemployment has increased; 60 percent of Germans want immigration reduced or stopped, leading to increasing support for antiforeigner political parties, as well as violence against the foreign born. This divergence can largely be attributed to Germany's guest-worker program. With economic recovery in the post–World War II era, the need for labor prompted German industry to recruit workers actively from Spain, Italy, Greece, Turkey, and Portugal. The state-sanctioned guest-worker program was based on the assumption that guest workers could be rotated in and out of the country as needed or as economic conditions dictated. Over the long term, the rotation policy did not work: workers needed longer to realize their financial goals, and employers were reluctant to let employees go, given their investment in them. In the interim, guest workers sent for their families. While this benefited employers since wives were also eligible to work, stays were prolonged, and the number of nonworking immigrants rose substantially, further legitimizing the presence of foreigners within Germany.

At the peak of the program in 1972, guest workers made up 12 percent of the German labor force, but problems were emerging as the German public recognized the dilemma of immigrant labor. The German government also acknowledged that the assumed temporary nature of the guest-worker policy had failed, with many of the temporary workers becoming "permanent" residents. Most Germans opposed the reality of a large, settled foreign population, and in the face of mounting concerns, the government stopped further labor recruitment in 1973. At the same time, Germany improved the status of workers currently resident within the country and encouraged family reunification, meaning that the number of foreigners within the country actually increased as workers brought their families into Germany rather than leaving and risking being denied reentry.

Germany's generous asylum law also entitled individuals to public assistance, accommodation, and a German work permit, making Germany an increasingly strong magnet during the 1980s. The upsurge in the number of asylum seekers, from approximately 100,000 per year in the mid-1980s to over 430,000 less than ten years later, fueled anti-immigrant tensions as local taxpayers footed the bill. As the number of asylum seekers rose, so did violence and attacks on foreigners. The collapse of the Soviet Union added to Germany's immigration concerns with a flood of returning ethnic Germans and asylum seekers.

Spain did not draft its first comprehensive immigration policy until 1985 as it prepared to enter the European Union and sought to restrict immigration from non-European countries. With a large number of illegal immigrants relative to its total foreign-born population,[61] Spanish immigration policy has attempted to strike a balance between keeping the doors open to needed legal workers and closing the doors to illegal immigrants, a policy that has had little success. Spain's large underground economy has generated a flow of illegal aliens, a group that is economically important, predominately filling service, construction, or agricultural occupations that many Spaniards avoid because of low pay or poor working conditions. The Spanish government has also granted amnesty to illegal aliens within the country. As with the case with IRCA in the United States, however, amnesty programs actually generated illegal immigration. Despite indicating that it would not support any further legalization programs (there had been three legalization programs between 1985 and 1991), Spain offered amnesty to illegal immigrants again in 1999.[62]

Third, a once sanctioned movement of labor has since become a political liability. Throughout Western Europe, the arrival of workers, particularly non–European Union immigrants and their families, has created deep ethnic and racial divisions within the respective societies. Most European countries view immigration as socially disruptive, yet the European Union receives several hundred thousand immigrants a year, with immigrants primarily entering France, Germany, Italy, and the United Kingdom.[63] Even if foreign workers and their families are in a country as legal guest workers, they are often unwanted as permanent additions to the population. More so than North America, Europe is concerned with the maintenance of national culture, language, and identity in the face of immigration, and the threat it poses to national culture is frequently used to justify restricting immigration. Immigrants are associated with increased crime, face discrimination in housing or labor markets, and are seen as idle or lazy, relying on the state for support (see figure 4.4). Nativism, xenophobia, and violence

Figure 4.4. Laissez-Faire and Lazy Foreigners. *Source:* Kirk Anderson, reproduced with permission.

The developed world condones the use of cheap labor in developing countries as companies like General Motors and Ford, as well as apparel manufacturers, draw upon large pools of inexpensive labor. These same workers, if present in the developed world, may be stereotypically defined as "lazy."

have become common in many countries, fed by fears of a diluted national identity or the collapse of overburdened social welfare institutions. In response, right-wing parties such as the French Front National or Austria's Freedom Party, which speaks of "overforeignerization," have found ample political support, as expressed by such events as the violent riots that rocked Britain's northern cities in the summer of 2001. Even Britain's more mainstream political parties, the Labor and Conservative parties, adopted anti-immigrant tones in the May 2005 general election, given increasing concerns with immigration within the country.

Increases in the expression of nativism and racism reflect Europe's deeprooted concerns regarding the ability to integrate immigrants into host societies. In Germany, the emergence of a strong anti-immigrant backlash and right-wing anti-immigration political parties has led to a tightening of the country's asylum laws and the imposition of a limit on the number of ethnic Germans allowed to return per year. Germany has made the integration of the foreign born a priority of successive governments, but such policies have not been successful. The Turks being the poorest and most visible guest-worker population (25 percent) in Germany, their integration poses a special concern. Although German cities are less segregated residentially than American ones, Germans regard the Turkish population as the most difficult group to integrate, given its members' lower education and skill levels. France, too, has struggled to integrate its foreign-born populations. Its rejection of the European Union constitution in May 2005 was, in part, a reflection of concerns voiced by the far-right that the agreement would have allowed the free movement of immigrants into France.[64] France also moved in late 2004 to ban religious symbols, such as an Islamic veil, a Jewish skullcap, a Sikh turban, or a large Christian cross, from its public schools.[65] Two of its primary concerns—religious differences between Christian European countries and Islamic fundamentalism and being overwhelmed by immigrants from the developing world—are echoed in other European countries.[66] Denmark and Italy have also moved to reject or reduce immigration, with Denmark passing new laws that tighten the criteria for asylum seekers and curtail their rights, while Italy has cracked down on all forms of immigration.

Spain's relatively late entrance into the immigration debate has not yet produced the same degree of political isolation as that seen in Germany or France, perhaps reflecting its previous immigration history. Prior to 1985, most foreigners within the country were retirees or wealthy northern or western Europeans. After 1985, the majority of entrants were workers from Morocco, the Philippines, or elsewhere in the developing world. As recently as the early 1990s, public opinion was tolerant of immigrants, but Spaniards may not have been ready to accept new realities as immigrant numbers increased and they were forced to grapple with the cultural leap entailed in the transition from labor exporter to importer. Their tolerant attitude changed quickly, with increasing violence toward immigrant populations, particularly illegal immigrants.

Fourth, Western Europe fears the demographic and societal implications of massive immigration from non–European Union countries in the face of changing global trading structures and linkages. Fears of increased immigration from Turkey have led Germany to oppose Turkey's entrance into the European Union, which would allow the free movement of workers across Europe. As the southern door into the European Union, Spain keeps an uneasy watch on the poor and rapidly growing populations of North Africa only twenty kilometers from Spain across the Straights of Gibraltar. On a regional scale, the European Union has moved to harmonize immigration policies, with frontline states like Spain screening arrivals.[67]

EMERGENT THEMES AND ISSUES

The demographic realities of low fertility and an aging population mean that European countries face a labor force crisis. Given the difficulties and limitations associated with fertility policies as discussed in chapter 1, increased immigration may be the only option to meet employment requirements, but it is fraught with political, social, and cultural problems. Increased nativism in Europe and the United States and the emergence of anti-immigrant violence and right-wing political parties that have cultivated a fear of foreigners serve as a warning bell. In response, Europe has moved to limit immigration, but attempts to restrict it have often led to increased "backdoor" immigration through family-reunification policies, illegal immigration, or seasonal-worker admission. Failure to control immigration means that European societies prepare to transform themselves into immigrant destinations, something that most states are unwilling to do at this time. In part, doing so raises questions regarding the integration of immigrants into the social, economic, and political structures of the host nations. The problem for all of these states is that they must define who "belongs" within their borders. In Europe, immigration did not provide national foundations as it did in North America, and the cultural shift involved in moving from labor exporter to importer is huge. Consequently, immigration debates are part of the much broader debate of national identity that pervades the economic, social, political, and cultural aspects of a society.

Traditional countries of immigration, such as the United States, Canada, and Australia, cannot sit idly and hope that the emergent storms over immigration and national identity will pass them by. Early warning signs that anti-immigrant sentiment is rising within both American and Canadian societies are already present. Welfare reform, Propositions 187 and 200, increased nativism, illegal-immigration control, and the Balkanization debate provide ample evidence of increasing public concern with legal and illegal immigration alike, fueled by shifts in immigration sources, policies, and rights over the past three decades. Up until the 1960s, white Anglo-Saxon images of society shaped immigration to the United States and Canada. Liberalization of immigration policies during the 1960s broadened the scope of immigration but injected new racial and ethnic tensions into the debate, even as they were defined as white-versus-black differences. But such debates cannot be cast in a black-versus-white or us-versus-them context. In both Canada and the United States, a growing population identifies itself with mixed racial or ethnic heritages, and intermarriage between racial or ethnic groups is increasing. In the 2000 U.S. Census, for example, Americans could choose to identify themselves by more than one race, and responses pointed to an increasingly diverse population. In the face of potentially rising anti-immigrant feelings, selling immigration's humanitarian dimension is an alternative option, albeit one that is unlikely to meet with widespread success.

The recent history of European immigration policies and the pressure caused by domestic and international changes suggest that states have relatively little room to maneuver with immigration policy. Countries might pursue economic development in origin countries, a policy that the European Union is pursuing in North Africa that is roughly equivalent to the **maquiladoras** lining the Mexican-U.S. border. Over the short term, however, the economic restructuring generated by such policies may actually increase immigration as redundant workers search for employment. As a second option, states are relying increasingly on the removal of political rights from immigrants, which flies in the face of decades of advances. Most nations, including France, Germany, and the United States, are now advancing a mix of agendas that remove or reduce access to welfare services among immigrants, including education and health care, reduce employment options, and reduce programs meant to block the integration of immigrants and discourage permanent settlement. Recent policy shifts in the United States highlight this trend. In order to regain control of its borders, the United States has moved to restrict access and, in doing so, has realized that this requires a rollback of civil and human rights for noncitizens. Recent legislation, including welfare reform and Propositions 187 and 200, has either removed or proposed to remove rights and protections given to U.S. immigrants. An additional example is the policy of interdicting Haitian immigrants on the ocean to prevent them from reaching the United States and initiating the refugee process.[68]

Removal of the right to work is particularly problematic. Unless the right to work is withdrawn, curtailing the rights of immigrants is unlikely to reduce immigration since little evidence demonstrates that the provision of social services is an important reason for movement; instead, employment and income are the main determinants. As long as countries demand low-cost labor, immigration will continue. As the native born shun low-paying, manual-labor positions, demand grows for inexpensive illegal labor. Moreover, removing the right to work is hardly a deterrent, given the role of the underground economy and illegal immigration in the developed world. It is estimated, for example, that 50 to 80 percent of U.S. farm workers are illegal immigrants, with an annual entry of an estimated 150,000 illegals into the United States.[69]

Given the experiences of the United States and other countries, closing the doors to immigrants is unlikely to stem the flow, given the strength of push and pull factors in both the origin and destination areas. Realizing that state control over immigration is limited and incomplete, labor unions have voiced support for more open and moderate immigration policies.[70] Fearing that immigrants would compete with the native born for employment and reduce wages, unions historically sought to limit immigrant numbers, making them strange bedfellows in the current immigration debate. In recent years, however, unions in Europe and America have supported liberalized immigration policies and courted immigrant workers. In the United States, the American Federation of Labor and Congress of Industrial Organizations withdrew its support for employer sanctions and called for amnesty for illegal immigrants in February 2000. Similarly, one proposal that would benefit the agricultural sector would increase the number of seasonal workers in the United States from forty to two hundred fifty thousand per year, a measure that some unions have supported since unions would represent these workers.[71] In Los Angeles, unions have focused their organizational efforts on immigrant workers and have added members more quickly than anywhere else in the United States.[72] Promoting moderate labor immigration is seen as one way to protect workers, ensure a safe work environment, reduce illegal immigration, and maintain union strength at a time of dwindling membership.

Countries are slowly awakening to the realization that immigration policy is truly problematic. Whichever way they turn—be it to restrict immigration or to promote particular components of immigration—there is no guarantee that they will achieve their desired results. Attempts to decrease immigrant flows have proven largely unsuccessful in the face of economic restructuring and globalization. Increasing immigration is problematic in its own way, threatening ethnic, racial, or social instability while creating a cadre of low-paid workers that would reduce wages and compete for positions with the native born. Opening the doors might be a slippery slope from which governments could not back away, with immigration further spiraling out of their control. Both measures carry the risk of sending mixed messages that condone immigration on the one hand while reducing it on the other. Ultimately, the future shape of immigration policy is unclear.

NOTES

1. For a discussion of the measurement and definition of migration, see David Plane and Peter Rogerson, *The Geographical Analysis of Population* (New York: Wiley, 1994).

2. Following the collapse of the Soviet Union and its satellite states, ethnic Russians who had been relocated to other republics to secure political and economic control have been returning to Russia. Interestingly, providing housing and employment for returning Russians poses a difficulty for the Russian government at a time of economic restructuring. Failure to meet citizens' expectations has the potential to create civil unrest.

3. For summaries of these theories, see Douglas Massey, Joaquin Arango, Graeme Hugo, Ali Kouaouci, Adela Pellegrino, and J. Edward Taylor, "Theories of International Migration: A Review and Appraisal," *Population and Development Review* 19, no. 3 (1993): 431–66; Douglas Massey, Joaquin Arango, Graeme Hugo, Ali Kouaouci, Adela Pellegrino, and J. Edward Taylor, "An Evaluation of International Migration Theory: The North American Case," *Population and Development Review* 20, no. 4 (1994): 699–752.

4. Wayne A. Cornelius, Philip L. Martin, and James F. Hollifield, "Introduction: The Ambivalent Quest for Immigration Control," in *Controlling Immigration: A Global Perspective*, ed. Wayne A. Cornelius, Philip L. Martin, and James F. Hollifield, 1–22 (Palo Alto: Stanford University Press, 1994).

5. Cornelius, Martin, and Hollifield, "Introduction," 1.

6. The term was borrowed from the ethnic fragmentation observed in the Balkans. See, for example, Mark Ellis and Richard Wright, "The Balkanization Metaphor in the Analysis of U.S. Immigration," *Annals of the Association of American Geographers* 88 (1998): 686–98; William Frey, "Immigrant and Native Magnets," *American Demographics* 18 (1996): 37–53; James G. Gimpel, *Separate Destinations* (Ann Arbor: University of Michigan Press, 1999).

7. Cornelius, Martin, and Hollifield, "Introduction," 1.

8. Julie R. Watts, *An Unconventional Brotherhood: Union Support for Liberalized Immigration in Europe* (La Jolla, CA: Center for Comparative Immigration Studies, 2000).

9. Cornelius, Martin, and Hollifield, "Introduction," 1.

10. Manuel Garcia y Griego, "Canada: Flexibility and Control in Immigration and Refugee Policy," in *Controlling Immigration: A Global Perspective*, ed. Wayne A. Cornelius, Philip L. Martin, and James F. Hollifield, 119–42 (Palo Alto: Stanford University Press, 1992).

11. Recent trends in U.S. opinion can be found in Thomas J. Espenshade and Charles A. Calhoun, "An Analysis of Public Opinion toward Undocumented Immigration," *Population Research and Policy Review* 12 (1993): 189–224; Rita J. Simon and Susan H. Alexander, *The Ambivalent Welcome: Print Media, Public Opinion, and Immigration* (Westport, CT: Praeger, 1993).

12. James P. Smith and Barry Edmonston, *The New Americans* (Washington, DC: National Academy Press, 1997). In Canada, a similar review of the costs and benefits of immigration was carried out in the late 1980s: Review of Demography, *Charting Canada's Future* (Ottawa: Health and Welfare, 1989).

13. See results of the 2000 Census.

14. John Isbister, *The Immigrant Debate: Remaking America* (West Hartford, CT: Kumarian Press, 1996); K. Bruce Newbold, "Immigration: Prospects and Policy," *Policy Options* 15, no. 8 (October 1994): 42–45; Smith and Edmonston, *The New Americans*.

15. Smith and Edmonston, *The New Americans*. Similar conclusions have been found in Canada. See Roderic Beaujot, *Population Change in Canada* (Toronto: McCelland Stewart, 1991).

16. Michael Janofsky, "Illegal Immigration Strains Services in Arizona," *New York Times*, April 11, 2001, 10A.

17. Barbara Boyle Torrey and Carl Haub, *Diverging Mortality and Fertility Trends: Canada and the United States* (Washington, DC: Population Reference Bureau, 2003).

18. Stanley Lieberson and Mary C. Waters, "The Location of Ethnic and Racial Groups in the United States," *Sociological Forum* 2, no. 4 (1987): 780–810.

19. For an expanded discussion of the history of U.S. immigration policy, numbers, and origins, see Kitty Calavita, "U.S. Immigration and Policy Responses: The Limits of Legislation," in *Controlling Immigration: A Global Perspective*, ed. Wayne A. Cornelius, Philip L. Martin, and James F. Hollifield, 55–82 (Palo Alto: Stanford University Press, 1994); Roger Daniels and Otis L. Graham, *Debating American Immigration, 1882–present* (Lanham, MD: Rowman & Littlefield, 2001); Isbister, *The Immigration Debate*; Philip Martin and Elizabeth Midgley, "Immigration to the United States," *Population Bulletin* 50, no. 2 (June 1999); Philip Martin and Elizabeth Midgley, "Immigration: Shaping and Reshaping America," *Population Bulletin* 58, no. 2 (June 2003).

20. Immigrant flows in 2004 from Canada, which has traditionally been a major exporter of immigrants to the United States, totaled just 1.6 percent. Therefore, the majority of flows from the Americas were from South and Central America and the Caribbean.

21. Kitty Calavita, "U.S. Immigration and Policy," 55.

22. Cornelius, Martin, and Hollifield, "Introduction," 1.

23. Calavita, "U.S. Immigration and Policy," 55.

24. Keith Crane, Beth Asch, Joanna Zorn Heilbrunn, and Danielle C. Cullinane, *The Effect of Employer Sanctions on the Flow of Undocumented Immigrants to the United States* (Lanham, MD: University Press of America, 1990).

25. Philip Martin, "Labor and Unauthorized U.S. Migration" (Washington, DC: Population Reference Bureau, May 2005).

26. Jeffery S. Passel, "Unauthorized Migrants: Numbers and Characteristics," Pew Hispanic Center, June 14, 2005, at http://pewhispanic.org/reports/report.php?ReportID=46 (accessed July 28, 2005).

27. Philip Martin, "Proposition 187 in California," *International Migration Review* 29, no. 1 (Spring 1995): 255–63; William A. V. Clark, *The California Cauldron* (New York: Guilford Press, 1998).

28. In 1882, anti-Chinese sentiments in California led to the National Exclusion Act. See Alexander Saxton, *The Indispensable Enemy: Labor and the Anti-Chinese Movement in California* (Berkeley: University of California Press, 1971).

29. Clark, *The California Cauldron.*

30. Deborah L. Garvey and Thomas J. Espenshade, "State and Local Fiscal Impacts of New Jersey's Immigrant and Native Households," in *Keys to Successful Immigration: Implications of the New Jersey Experience*, ed Thomas J. Espenshade, 139–72 (Washington, DC: Urban Institute Press, 1997).

31. Clark, *The California Cauldron.*

32. George J. Sanchez, "Face the Nation: Race, Immigration, and the Rise of Nativism in Late-Twentieth Century America," in *The Handbook of International Migration: The American Experience*, ed Charles Hirschman, Philip Kasinitz, and Josh DeWind, 371–82 (New York: Russell Sage Foundation, 1999).

33. Smith and Edmonston, *The New Americans.*

34. Temporary Assistance for Needy Families, or TANF, replaced Aid for Families with Dependent Children, or AFDC, benefits.

35. USCIS, *Yearbook of Immigration Statistics*, at http://uscis.gov/graphics/shared/statistics/yearbook/index.htm (accessed February 6, 2006).

36. Understandably, apprehensions are the only measure of the success of Border Patrol operations. They are only a rough approximation of the number of individuals who try to cross the border and may include multiple attempts by the same persons.

37. Frank D. Bean, *Illegal Mexican Immigration and the United States/Mexico Border: The Effects of Operation Hold-the-Line on El Paso/Juarez*, Report Prepared for the U.S. Commission on Immigration Reform, July 1994.

38. Dennis Wagner, "Illegals Dying at Record Rate in Arizona Desert," *USA Today*, August 19, 2005, 1A. See also James Sterngold, "Devastating Picture of Immigrants Dead in Arizona Desert," *New York Times*, May 25, 2001, 1A.

39. Sanchez, "Face the Nation," 371.

40. U.S. Census 2000 indicated that white, non-Hispanics were no longer the majority in California.

41. Peter Brimelow, *Alien Nation: Common Sense about America's Immigration Disaster* (New York: Random House, 1995).

42. See Isbister, *The Immigrant Debate*; Smith and Edmonston, *The New Americans.*

43. Jeffrey S. Passel, *Estimates of the Size and Characteristics of the Undocumented Population* (Washington, DC: Pew Hispanic Center, 2005), at http://pewhispanic.org/reports (accessed June 9, 2005).

44. Joseph P. Ferrie, *Yankeys Now: Immigrants in the Antebellum U.S., 1840–1860* (New York: Oxford University Press, 1999).

45. Mirta Ojito, "Best of Friends, Worlds Apart," *New York Times*, June 5, 2000, 1A; Emily Skop, "Race and Place in the Adaptation of Mariel Exiles," *International Migration Review* 35, no. 1 (2001): 449–71.

46. Calavita, "U.S. Immigration and Policy Responses," 55.

47. Council of Graduate Studies, at www.cgsnet.org/index.htm (accessed June 9, 2005). Competition for graduate students by other countries has also contributed to declining enrollment. Foreign students in science and engineering applying for visas must also be cleared by the FBI and CIA.

48. James S. Woodsworth, *Strangers within our Gates* (1909; Toronto: University of Toronto Press, 1972).

49. See the annual report published by Citizenship and Immigration Canada (CIC) at www.cic.gc.ca (accessed June 28, 2005).

50. Statistics Canada, *1996 Canada Year Book* (Ottawa: Statistics Canada, 1997).

51. Manuel Garcia y Griego, "Canada."

52. See discussions by Beaujot, *Population Change in Canada*; Raymond Breton, "Ethnic Stratification Viewed from Three Theoretical Perspectives," in *Social Stratification in Canada*, ed. James E. Curtis and William G. Scott, 51–72 (Toronto: Prentice Hall, 1979).

53. Bill Curry and Marina Jimenez, "Canadian Attitudes Harden on Immigration," *Globe and Mail*, August 12, 2005, 6A.

54. See articles by Daniel Hiebert, Alan Nash, and Niall Majury in the special focus section of *The Canadian Geographer* 38, no. 3 (1994): 254–70.

55. Peter Cheney and Colin Freeze, "200,000 May Be in Canada Illegally," *Globe and Mail*, May 26, 2001, 1A.

56. Tom Fennell, "The Smuggler's Slaves," *Macleans* 113, no. 5 (2000): 14–19.

57. Cornelius, Martin, and Hollifield, *Controlling Immigration*.

58. Allison Tarmann, "The Flap over Replacement Immigration," *Population Today* (May/June 2001): 7.

59. James F. Hollifield, "Immigration and Republicanism in France: The Hidden Consensus," in *Controlling Immigration: A Global Perspective*, ed. Wayne A. Cornelius, Philip L. Martin, and James F. Hollifield, 143–76 (Palo Alto: Stanford University Press, 1992).

60. Philip L. Martin, "Germany: Reluctant Land of Immigration, in *Controlling Immigration: A Global Perspective*, ed. Wayne A. Cornelius, Philip L. Martin, and James F. Hollifield (Palo Alto: Stanford University Press, 1992), 189–226.

61. Estimates place Spain's illegal population at approximately half its legal immigrant population of nearly seven hundred thousand, or 1.3 percent of the total population.

62. Roger Cohen, "Europe's Migrant Fears Rend a Spanish Town," *New York Times*, May 8, 2000, A1.

63. Philip Martin and James Widgren, "International Migration: Facing the Challenge," *Population Bulletin* 57, no. 1 (March 2002).

64. Doug Saunders, "France Shatters EU Unity," *The Globe and Mail*, May 30, 2005, 1A.

65. Elaine Sciolino, "France Turns to Tough Policy on Student's Religious Garb," *New York Times*, October 22, 2004, 2A.

66. Martin, "Germany: Reluctant Land," 189.

67. Stefan Teloken, "Europe: The Debate over Asylum: It's a Long Way to . . . Harmonization," *Refugees* 113 (1999): 3–7.

68. Cornelius, Martin, and Hollifield, "Introduction," 1.

69. Ginger Thompson and Steven Greenhouse, "Mexican 'Guest Workers': A Project Worth a Try?" *New York Times*, April 3, 2001, 1B.

70. Watts, *An Unconventional Brotherhood*.

71. Thompson and Greenhouse, "Mexican 'Guest Workers.' "

72. Steven Greenhouse, "Los Angeles Warms to Labor Unions as Immigrants Look to Escape Poverty," *New York Times*, April 9, 2001, 7A.

5

✒︎

Refugees, Asylees, and Internally Displaced Persons: The Growing Crisis

As a subset of migration flows, refugees and other displaced persons represent a growing population. Defined by the United Nations' 1951 Convention Relating to the Status of Refugees and the 1967 Protocol Relating to the Status of Refugees,[1] refugees (and **asylees**[2]) are people outside of their countries who are unable to return owing to fear of persecution for reasons of race, religion, nationality, membership in a particular social group, or adherence to a political opinion.[3] In 2004, more than sixty countries produced uprooted populations. According to the United Nations High Commissioner for Refugees (UNHCR), the leading coordinator and protector of refugees, estimates placed the total number of refugees at over 9.7 million in 2004 (see table 5.1).[4] Major generators included Afghanistan, Sudan, Burundi, Democratic Republic of Congo, the former Palestine, Somalia, Angola, Vietnam, Iraq, and Liberia.

Despite the legal definition in UN documents, who is or is not a refugee has significant implications with respect to the degree of support and protection an individual receives, along with the priority given to the long-term resolution of his or her status. Refugee status confers the fundamental right that these individuals will not be returned to their countries of origin against their will. Legally, this is termed **nonrefoulement**, and nations that ratify the convention and protocol are obligated not to expel individuals without due process. Defining individuals as refugees also obligates the host country to provide the medical care, schooling, and basic civil rights enjoyed by other legal immigrants. In cases of large-scale refugee flows, the international community or agencies such as the UNHCR may fill gaps in the care of refugees.

Chapter 5

Table 5.1. Refugees and Internally Displaced Persons by Major Source Countries, 2004

Internally Displaced Persons			Sources of Refugees		
Rank	Country	Number	Rank	Country	Number
1	Sudan	4,800,000[a]	1	Former Palestine	3,000,000[a]
2	Congo-Kinshasa	3,200,000[a]	2	Afghanistan	2,500,000[a]
3	Colombia	2,730,000[a]	3	Sudan	600,000
4	Uganda	1,400,000[a]	4	Myanmar	586,000[a]
5	Angola	1,000,000[a]	5	Congo-Kinshasa	440,000
6	Iraq	800,000–1,000,000[a]	6	Liberia	384,000[a]
7	Jordan	800,000	7	Burundi	355,000
8	India	650,000	8	Angola	323,000[a]
9	Myanmar	600,000–1,000,000[a]	9	Vietnam	307,000
10	Indonesia	600,000–1,000,000[a]	10	Iraq	280,600[a]
11	Azerbaijan	571,000	11	Eritrea	280,000[a]
12	Liberia	500,000	12	Somalia	277,000
13	Sri Lanka	500,000	13	Colombia	233,600
14	Cote d'Ivoire	500,000[a]	14	Croatia	209,100
15	Burundi	400,000[a]	15	Western Sahara	190,000[a]
16	Russia	368,000	16	China	157,500
17	Somalia	350,000[a]	17	Bosnia and Herzegovina	142,200
18	Turkey	350,000–1,000,000[a]	18	Bhutan	128,700
19	Bosnia and Herzegovina	327,200	19	Sri Lanka	105,700
20	Lebanon	300,000	20	North Korea	101,700[a]

Source: U.S. Committee for Refugees and Immigrants at www.refugees.org (accessed June 13, 2005).
[a]Sources vary widely in number reported.

Given the economic and political obligations associated with refugees, governments may dispute refugee claims to avoid these responsibilities.[5] The United Nations and other countries do not, for example, accord refugee status to those who flee for economic reasons, largely out of fear in the developed world that doing so would open the floodgates and refugees would pour into a system already strained by the existing number of political refugees. In essence, for example, recognizing economic refugees would legalize Mexican immigration into the United States as entrants would simply need to claim economic refugee status to gain legal entry. Proving the legitimacy of a refugee claim is difficult, especially when it is clouded by ideological, social, or economic concerns. The United States, for example, has been accused of having a double standard. With its acceptance of Mariel Cubans in the early 1980s, most of whom did not meet the international standards for refugee status, the U.S. government was accused of altering its definition of a political refugee for political expediency. At roughly the same time, it denied entry to Haitians who claimed political asylum; the government defined them as voluntary and economic migrants, even in light of evidence of political persecution by the Haitian government. Likewise, "fear" may not be defined, for example, as a sharply defined fear of individual persecution; it may, however, be fear of getting caught in the crossfire, which has little to do with individual traits. This is not meant to belittle the fear of the individual since this fear is no less real. Consequently, the definition of refugee generally extends beyond persecuted individuals to whole groups of people fleeing danger.

With the end of the cold war, the nature of conflict changed from large-scale confrontations backed by superpowers to smaller, internal struggles. Old alliances were disrupted, and the totalitarian regimes that had kept the social order were toppled. The former Yugoslavia is a case in point as Serbian leadership struggled to maintain control of Yugoslavia in the face of unilateral declarations of independence by Slovenia and Croatia in 1991. Later, in its wars in Bosnia and Kosovo, Serbian leadership would attempt to carve out a "greater Serbia." In the process, an estimated 863,000 refugees were generated during the Bosnia conflict in the early 1990s, and an additional 900,000 were generated in Kosovo in 1999. Similar situations have evolved, or threaten to evolve, in the former Soviet Union, including conflict in Soviet Georgia, Chechnya, Armenia, and Azerbaijan. Former republics such as Tajikistan and Uzbekistan also teeter near the brink of civil disorder, with the latter producing hundreds of refugees in May 2005 owing to internal struggles, while thousands of Aghani refugees fled the country to neighboring Pakistan to avoid conflict between pro- and anti-Taliban forces. In Africa, decades of political turmoil following the end of the colonial era continue to generate a seemingly endless list of conflicts and refugees.

The growing number of conflicts and evolving political landscape have also increased the number of internally displaced persons (IDPs). Unlike refugees, IDPs are unable to leave their countries of nationality and typically cannot avail themselves of the protection and assistance of international agencies, meaning that they face an uncertain future. It is estimated that 21.3 million individuals were internally displaced in 2004,[6] the fallout of civil strife, ethnic unrest, or disasters in countries including Sudan, Columbia, Congo, Uganda, Iraq, Sri Lanka, Azerbaijan, Kosovo, Bosnia, Afghanistan, Liberia, and Rwanda. Because IDPs tend to fall through the cracks and receive no international recognition or assistance, the United Nations has engaged a debate on who should be responsible for their care, a difficult situation given the importance associated with state sovereignty.

Rather than focusing on the individual generators of refugees and displaced persons and how or why they were generated, this chapter focuses on the implications and options of displaced populations. The chapter begins by exploring the alternatives available to deal with refugee populations, including their return to the country of nationality, settlement in the country of asylum, or resettlement to a third country. No one option is politically expedient or costless, and the following discussion examines each alternative before considering North American and European responses to refugees. Historically, Canada and the United States have played an active role in the resettlement of refugees. As with issues of immigration policy discussed in chapter 4, Canada and the United States have been left grappling with, and ultimately tightening, refugee policies as a result of the terrorist attacks of September 11, 2001, and the resulting focusing of policies on terrorism. Europe, on the other hand, has not been a major resettlement destination and has, in some cases, actively tried to avoid the resettlement of refugees within its borders. Instead, it has dealt with large numbers of asylum seekers, who are also seen as abusers of the system. European response has been to tighten refugee and asylum policies as well. This chapter then considers the internally displaced population, the most rapidly growing segment of displaced peoples. It concludes with a discussion of emerging issues and trends with respect to the displaced population.

ALTERNATIVES FOR REFUGEES: NO EASY WAY HOME

Once refugees have left their home countries, the international community faces three broad alternatives in assisting them, including voluntary repatriation, settlement in the country of first asylum, or resettlement in a third country.[7] Of these, voluntary return to the home country is the ideal solution, particularly for the refugee. It is perhaps also the most difficult of the three alternatives since a minimum requirement for return is the resolution of the problem that created the refugee flows in the first place. Additional material and financial support for the refugees may also be needed until they can reestablish their livelihoods after their return. Despite its difficulties, voluntary repatriations have succeeded, the most recent being the ongoing return of Afghanis to Afghanistan in the post-Taliban era. However, their return and continued security have depended heavily on assistance from nongovernmental organizations such as the Red Cross, donations and support from other nations, and the continued presence of peacekeeping forces, which may yet prove a long-term requirement.

Permanent settlement outside of the home country, which is typically referred to as the *country of first asylum*, is a poor second alternative but frequently the only practical one. The welcome that a country extends to refugees depends on a complex set of considerations, including economic strength, the political stability of the host government, and the compatibility of refugees with the host society. Given that many countries of first asylum are in the developing world, most have difficulty meeting the needs of refugees. Even provision of basic needs, including water, sanitation, food, and shelter, may prove difficult given poor infrastructure or the lack of financial resources to deal with the refugee population. By necessity, host governments are forced to put their native-born populations first. Any attempts to do otherwise may increase tensions between the native-born populations and the refugees. As such, most countries rely heavily on organizations like the Red Cross or UNHCR to provide assistance in meeting the basic needs of the refugees in the short term.

Support of refugees is not necessarily a short-term effort. Over the longer term, refugee populations may continue to require external support and may or may not be fully incorporated into their host countries, a problem exemplified by Palestinian refugees.[8] Spread throughout Jordan, Lebanon, and Syria, as well as the West Bank and Gaza Strip in Israel, Palestinians became refugees after they fled Israel in 1948 (when the state of Israel was established) or later during the 1967 Six-Day War. The United Nations Relief and Works Agency for Palestine refugees in the Near East provides education, health, relief, and social services to Palestinians. With the exception of Jordan, where more than half of the population is Palestinian, the admission and integration of Palestinians by other Arab countries has been less than enthusiastic, largely due to host governments' fear that removing the refugee label will destroy chances of recreating a Palestinian state.

In other cases, the presence of refugees may inflame tensions between countries or ethnic groups. In Lebanon, the delicate balance between Muslims and Christians has prevented Palestinian refugees from naturalizing for fear of upsetting the political balance. In other cases, fighters or militia members often use refugee camps as bases, promoting instability both within and outside the camps. For instance, Rwandan refugee camps in Zaire became the base for rebel Hutu fighters who conducted border raids into Tutsi-dominated Rwanda.[9] Complicating matters, soldiers who were often guilty of genocide in Rwanda at the start of the crisis frequently controlled food and other supplies within the camps, and the UNHCR was accused of feeding and protecting those accused of genocide. The safety of Hutu refugees within the refugee camps was hardly guaranteed. Later, in the face of a relatively powerless UNHCR, the predominately Hutu refugees became the target of Tutsi rebels in Zaire, who eventually overthrew the Zairian government of Mobutu Sese Seko and established the Democratic Republic of Congo, furthering the bloodshed.

Racially or ethnically heterogeneous societies face further pressures as an influx of refugees may upset the delicate balance between groups. In the 1999 Kosovo conflict, for example, approximately one million ethnic

Albanians sought refuge in the neighboring countries of Albania, Macedonia, and Montenegro.[10] In an already politically unstable region, the sheer number of refugees endangered the political stability of Kosovo's neighbors and threatened to embroil the region in a larger civil war.[11] For example, Albania, the poorest country within Europe, had a weak political system that was already reeling from internal conflict and anarchy following the collapse of its government in 1997. Refugees were arriving in a remote and economically undeveloped part of the country, and its financial and economic ability to cope with the influx was limited.[12] In Macedonia, where ethnic Albanians represented 25 percent of the population, it was feared that a large influx of Kosovar Albanians, estimated at 239,000, could radicalize Macedonian nationalism and Albanian separatism, upsetting the existing ethnic balance and increasing the likelihood of an expanded regional war. These were not minimal concerns. With an estimated ethnic Albanian population of 506,000, the Macedonian Albanian population was inflated by approximately 50 percent. Since Macedonia's emergence as an independent state in 1992, internal conflict between ethnic Albanians and Macedonians (Slavs) had threatened the state's existence on numerous occasions. Although most refugees eventually returned to Kosovo, and the conflict did not expand during 1999, this fear seemed to come to fruition in the spring of 2001 as Kosovar Albanians fought with Macedonian security forces for control of the Albanian-dominated areas in Macedonia.

The strain associated with Kosovar refugees was felt elsewhere in Western Europe.[13] Although Germany, France, and Italy were all concerned with the number and location of refugees, Germany was perhaps the most vocal, openly expressing its belief that refugees should stay in the Balkans and out of northern or western Europe. This clearly meant that poor neighboring states would have to deal with refugees, but it also demonstrated the ability of the Kosovo conflict to destabilize and politically charge the European continent. However, the fears of Western European countries also reflect European concerns with state identity and the influx of foreigners discussed in chapter 4, with European countries becoming increasingly concerned about the social, economic, and political implications of the influx of large numbers of foreigners.

As demonstrated by Indochinese boat people in the late 1970s and by Kosovo Albanians in the late 1990s, resettlement to a third country such as Canada, the United States, or Australia is a long-term option, but for many, it is also the only option.[14] According to the UNHCR, some 55,600 refugees were resettled in 2003 globally, with the major countries of resettlement in 2003 including the United States, which accepted approximately 28,420 individuals, which was down considerably from previous years given security concerns arising in the post–September 11 era. Canada, Australia, and Norway were also major resettlement regions (resettling 10,730, 11,860, and 1,630 refugees in 2003, respectively), but the total number of refugees resettled within any one year is small relative to the total number. Although there was a dramatic fall in the number of new refugees,[15] some 290,000 individuals were newly registered as refugees in 2003 alone, relocating from countries including Liberia, the Democratic Republic of Congo, Burundi, Somalia, and the Central African Republic.[16] In other words, less than 1 percent of the refugee population was relocated to a third country in 2003. If the total displaced population of seventeen million is counted, only 0.33 percent was resettled. The remaining refugees were far less fortunate, experiencing life in desolate refugee camps, threatened with violence, and frequently marginalized by the host society. Even among those who are resettled, however, life is not easy. Refugees must adjust to their host country and frequently suffer from depression or posttraumatic stress disorder in the months immediately after their arrival.

Unlike those who emigrate legally for economic opportunities or family reunification, refugees are often the least successful of all entrants, frequently entering the host country with a poor or variable set of skills relative to other legal immigrants. Over a longer term, as has been the case with *Marielitos* or Southeast Asian refugees, most become legal, permanent residents in their host countries. Although technically no longer labeled refugees, use of the term *refugee* raises interesting questions and possibilities. For example, do former refugees attain similar benchmarks or levels of adjustment in the host country relative to legal immigrants or other refugees? In what direction do they assimilate? What is the time frame?

Existing evidence suggests that refugees continue to have divergent experiences after arrival, reflecting such differences as the endowed human capital they bring with them and their period of arrival (i.e., economic conditions in the resettlement country or whether they were among the first to flee, a group typically characterized by higher socioeconomic status). By definition, the refugee population is characterized by a broader diversity of human capital (i.e., skills or education) than the immigrant population, whose members select themselves for entry into the immigration process (i.e., the better educated and those with more skills are more likely to immigrate) and are screened by the host country. The endowed human capital or skills that refugee groups bring with them will influence the adjustment process, allowing quicker socioeconomic advancement among those with greater skills. Among Southeast Asian refugees, for example, differences in the adaptation of Sino- and ethnic Vietnamese refugees have been noted,[17] with the Vietnamese tending to be more economically integrated than other Southeast Asian refugees, despite similar periods of residency within the United States.[18] An emerging Vietnamese business class contrasts with other Southeast Asian refugees, best reflected by the Laotian population, whose members continue to have lower rates of business ownership and are more likely to depend on public assistance programs and minimum wage labor.[19]

Yet, the process of adjustment into the host society is only partially dependent on the abilities and experiences that refugees bring with them.[20] Instead, broader issues contextualize their opportunities and relative success or failure within the host country. Refugees often lack the networks and ties in the destination country that can help with locating jobs or accommodations, making them more likely to require state assistance during the transition period. This poses a fiscal burden on the host country. In recent decades, government policies have played a key role in the admittance of refugees, with public assistance available to refugees that is not available to other legal immigrants. But the availability of public aid may interact with other characteristics and lead to different outcomes. Dependence on government or other sources for assistance may either prove beneficial or slow their adaptation into the host society.[21] National and ethnic origin and the level of public and private reception also influence refugee groups' postarrival success. Hungarians have successfully adapted to life in the United States and Canada, but their success depended not only on their skills but also on the fact that they were white and fleeing a communist country at the height of the cold war. Although Mariel Cubans have fared relatively well, assisted by an already economically and politically strong Cuban community, differences between "white" and "black" Cubans have been noted.[22] Even recent arrivals are forced to conform to American expectations (and stereotypes) of race and its consequences for social mixing, residential location, and employment opportunities. Together, these instances suggest a complex and unequal process that transforms "refugees" into "immigrants" and, ultimately, into naturalized citizens of the host country.

NORTH AMERICA: WELCOMING REFUGEES?

Although relocating refugees to a third country is difficult and less than ideal, Canada and the United States both have long histories of admitting refugees for permanent resettlement,[23] including the resettlement of European refugees in the immediate post–World War II years, along with Hungarian refugees in 1956.[24] Although the number of refugees granted settlement in the United States dropped in the post–September 11 era, the United States expected to resettle seventy thousand refugees in 2003, resettling more refugees than all other countries combined. Similarly, Canada targeted over thirty thousand refugees for resettlement in 2005, a somewhat higher per capita rate of resettlement than that of the United States.[25] Despite their records of accomplishment, the evolution of refugee policies in both countries was relatively slow, and both adopted ad hoc policies for refugee admission throughout much of the postwar era. The admission of Hungarian refugees came at the height of the cold war, and both countries viewed the admission of this group as a foreign policy tool to control communism. Later, the absorption of some 132,000 Cuban refugees by the United States following the Cuban revolution in 1959 reflected the same foreign policy agenda.

In fact, not until the 1960s was refugee legislation codified in both countries.[26] The 1965 Immigration and Nationality Act formalized U.S. refugee policy by establishing that 6 percent of all immigrants (the so-called seventh preference category) could enter as refugees if they satisfied certain conditions. These included that (1) they had departed from a communist country or the Middle East, (2) their departure was caused by fear of persecution on account of race, religion, or opinion, (3) they had departed in flight, and (4) they were unwilling or unable to return. In essence, the United States had adopted the UN definition of "refugee" but attached geographical and ideological caveats. It finally recognized the UN Convention in 1968 but did not amend its immigration and refugee statutes to reflect its new obligations. Canada ratified the UN convention and its protocol in 1969.

Only in 1980 did the United States pass the Refugee Act and fully ratify the UN Convention, regularizing refugee admissions and institutionalizing resettlement assistance. Still, the act failed to change the political considerations underlying refugee admission and selection, and the refugee system remains highly politicized even now. Each year, the president and Congress determine the number of authorized admissions (in 2003 and 2004, the ceiling was seventy thousand) broken down by region of origin. The president and Congress also define who is of special humanitarian concern to the United States, a category that may be manipulated to bar entry to those from countries friendly to the United Sates, even in the face of observed persecution, as has been the case with Haitian entrants. Some critics have gone as far as to suggest that refugee flows from the former Soviet Union and its satellite states were more about family reunification in the 1990s than about being true refugees. At the same time, needy refugees in Africa were overlooked, although there has been improvement in recent years.[27] Out of the 52,835 refugees admitted in 2003, 55 percent sourced from Africa, including Somalia, Sudan, Ethiopia, Sierra Leone, and Liberia (see table 5.2).[28]

Echoing immigration trends, as shown in table 5.2, post–September 11 concerns have led to a reduction in the number of refugees admitted to the United States on a yearly basis. In 2001, for instance, nearly sixty-nine thousand refugees were admitted, a number that dropped to less than twenty-seven thousand the following year. These shifts reflected increased

Table 5.2. U.S. Refugee Arrivals by Top Ten Origins, Fiscal Years 2002–2004

	2002			2003			2004		
Rank	Country	Number	Percent	Country	Number	Percent	Country	Number	Percent
—	All countries	26,839	100.0	All countries	28,306	100.0	All countries	52,835	100.0
1	Ukraine	5,219	19.5	Ukraine	5,065	17.9	Somalia	13,331	25.2
2	Bosnia and Herzegovina	3,463	12.9	Liberia	2,957	10.5	Liberia	7,140	13.5
3	Vietnam	3,081	11.5	Iran	2,471	8.7	Laos	6,005	11.4
4	Russia	2,100	7.8	Sudan	2,140	7.6	Sudan	3,500	6.6
5	Cuba	1,925	7.2	Somalia	1,993	7.0	Ukraine	3,482	6.6
6	Serbia and Montenegro	1,860	6.9	Serbia and Montenegro	1,839	6.5	Cuba	3,959	5.6
7	Afghanistan	1,677	6.3	Ethiopia	1,704	6.0	Ethiopia	2,710	5.1
8	Iran	1,525	5.7	Afghanistan	1,453	5.1	Iran	1,787	3.4
9	Moldova	1,021	3.8	Russia	1,394	4.9	Moldova	1,711	3.2
10	Sudan	895	3.3	Sierra Leone	1,378	4.9	Russia	1,446	2.7

Source: 2004 Yearbook of Immigration Statistics.

screening of applications, a decrease in the number of applications for refugee status, and a decreased approval rate, dropping from 77 percent approval in 2001 to just 49 percent approval in 2001. By 2002, approval rates had increased to 60 percent, and the number of refugees admitted in 2004 exceeded 52,000, although the approved ceiling of seventy thousand was not approached.

Although following a similar timeline, Canada's refugee policy has differed in important respects from American policy, taking a more liberal and humanitarian interpretation of the 1951 UN Convention.[29] Over the past thirty years, for example, Canada resettled large numbers of refugees from Chile, Uganda, El Salvador, and Guatemala, groups that the United States did not welcome for various (largely political) reasons (see table 5.3). Canada also led the United States by incorporating the principles of the convention into Canadian statutory law in 1976, four years before the United States did, and more recently by recognizing those at risk of torture or cruel and unusual treatment as legitimate refugees. The 1976 act also defined two classes of refugees. First, *convention refugees* follow UN guidelines. Individuals seeking resettlement must be convention refugees and are subject to medical, security, and criminal screening. Approximately thirty-two thousand refugees were received in 2005; the major sources included Sri Lanka, Pakistan, Columbia, and China.[30] Second, Canadian refugee law recognizes people in *designated classes*, including those who do not entirely qualify for entrance as refugees but who need protection and are admitted with private sponsorship.

While both countries accepted refugees specifically chosen for resettlement in the post–World War II era, neither dealt with large numbers of asylum seekers until the last two decades of the twentieth century, which pressured them to reform their refugee systems. In the United States, the 1980 Refugee Act provided a statutory asylum policy. Importantly, the asylum provision did not establish a limit on the number of **aliens** who could apply for or be granted asylum in a year, meaning that any alien who arrived in the United States could request asylum, which allowed the individual to remain in the country until the review was completed and entitled that individual to benefits.

The number of asylum cases ranged from over 147,000 in 1995 to slightly more than 32,500 in 2004, with the major origins including China, Venezuela, Columbia, and Haiti. Asylum cases are heard before an asylum officer who determines the validity of the claim.[31] As with the resettlement of refugees, political considerations appear to influence the granting of asylum, emphasizing control of the border rather than protection of individual rights, even though State Department involvement in asylum cases was supposedly reduced in the 1990 revisions to the Refugee Act, with regional variations in approval rates remaining in 1998.[32] On average,

Table 5.3. Canadian Refugee Arrivals by Top Ten Origins, 2002–2004

		2002			2003			2004	
Rank	Country	Number	Percent	Country	Number	Percent	Country	Number	Percent
—	All countries	25,494	100.0	All countries	22,809	100.0	All countries	18,226	100.0
1	Pakistan	2,455	9.6	Pakistan	2,882	12.6	Columbia	2,724	14.9
2	China	2,025	7.9	Mexico	1,930	8.5	Mexico	2,040	11.2
3	Columbia	1,870	7.3	Columbia	1,484	6.5	China, People's Rep of	1,429	7.8
4	Mexico	1,599	6.3	China, People's Rep of	1,429	6.3	Sri Lanka	884	4.9
5	Sri Lanka	1,324	5.2	Costa Rica	1,322	5.8	India	880	4.8
6	Costa Rica	1,173	4.6	Sri Lanka	984	4.3	Pakistan	670	3.7
7	India	1,050	4.1	India	964	4.2	Costa Rica	490	2.7
8	Turkey	835	3.3	Bangladesh	541	2.4	Nigeria	441	2.4
9	Peru	746	2.9	Nigeria	538	2.4	Peru	270	2.0
10	Nigeria	550	2.2	Guyana	408	1.8	Congo	279	1.5

Source: Citizenship and Immigration Canada. Refugees aged 18 and over.

32 percent of asylum cases were approved in 2004, which is substantially less than in years preceding the terrorist attacks of September 2001 but, again, reflects increased screening of applicants. Not surprisingly, there was large regional variation in rates of approval, which were well below average for many Central American countries.[33] For example, the 2004 approval rate was 10 percent for Guatemala, 7 percent for Honduras, and 8 percent for El Salvador. In contrast, approval rates were generally higher among many Asian, North African, and Eastern European states. Refusal of asylum can result in detention and deportation.

U.S. law also provides for a number of "refugeelike" situations, giving the government and president latitude in allowing entry or residency in a number of situations; this latitude can be seen in the U.S. government's differential and ambiguous responses to Haitian and Cuban entrants. Haitians, most of whom arrived by sea, claimed political asylum, but were defined by the government as economic migrants searching for a way to leave the poorest country in the Western Hemisphere.[34] Despite ample evidence of persecution by the Haitian government, the U.S. government refused entry to most Haitians so as not to undermine the Haitian regime. Fearing a large and uncontrollable influx of Haitian refugees should the door appear open, the U.S. government has also vigorously pursued a policy of **interdiction** on the high seas, with detainees returned to Haiti. Differentiating between political and economic refugees is often difficult, and the situation is compounded when ideological considerations cloud definitions.

Arriving shortly after the 1980 Refugee Act was signed, Mariel Cubans received a decidedly different reception, and only a minority met the conventional requirements of asylum.[35] Rather than processing the Marielitos under the new system, the U.S. government bypassed the Refugee Act and "paroled" Cubans directly into the United States. Eventually, the government regularized their status, allowing them to become immigrants in 1986.[36] The United States has also used a number of devices, including extended voluntary departure and temporary protected status (TPS) to grant safe haven to groups in the United States when a return to their country of nationality would be dangerous for political or other reasons, including natural disasters. The TPS statute provides aliens with employment authorization but does not convey residency status.[37] Decisions to provide these measures have typically been based on humanitarian grounds, and they have been extended to the Chinese following the Tiananmen Square massacre in 1989 and to Hondurans and Salvadorans following the devastating earthquakes in those countries in the late 1990s.

Canada has also dealt with an increasing number of asylum claims; an average of twenty-five to thirty thousand were made each year in the late 1990s, increasing to over forty-four thousand in 2001 before dropping slightly, sourcing largely from China, Sri Lanka, Pakistan, Hungary, India, and Mexico.[38] In Canada, asylum claims are heard before the Immigration Review Board, an independent administrative tribunal charged with determining the veracity of refugee claims. In the recent past, approximately 45 percent of cases have been approved, although this number is lower than it was just a few years ago.[39] While waiting for their hearings, refugees are eligible to apply for employment authorization (if it can be shown that they cannot subsist on public assistance) and for student authorization to go to school. Emergency and essential health services are also provided.

While Canada has not experienced widespread abuse of its immigration system in general, its refugee system has been problematic, forcing the government to adjust refugee policy on a number of occasions in response to specific concerns.[40] The arrival of boatloads of Chinese from Fujian Province during the summers of 1999 and 2000, en route to the United States or Canada, reignited a long-running debate over Canada's immigration and refugee laws. Those apprehended immediately claimed refugee status, raising public concerns over backdoor illegal immigration and the abuse of the refugee system. Their arrival also contrasted markedly with the warm reception given to Kosovar refugees just months earlier, underlining the ambiguity of refugee policy, public opinion, and the definition of who is or is not a refugee.

Reforms tabled in the Canadian House of Commons in February 2001 were meant to close this backdoor via increased screening of potential refugees in their countries of origin, as well as detention, interdiction, and increased penalties for smugglers.[41] New measures to screen refugees (and immigrants) were also introduced following the September 11 terrorist attacks in the United States. In an effort to increase border security, both Canada and the United States have moved to harmonize immigration and refugee requirements by implementing the Safe Third Country Agreement on January 1, 2005. Under this agreement, certain asylum seekers in Canada and the United States will be required to make their refugee claim in the country where they were last present, meaning that asylum seekers arriving in Canada at the land border from the United States will not be eligible to have their refugee claims determined in Canada. Similarly, the agreement allows the United States to return to Canada asylum seekers attempting to enter the United States from Canada.[42] However, critics argue that the law is more about security, will lead to increased illegal entry, and will decrease the flow of legitimate refugees. Statistics tend to bear the final argument out: over the first three months of 2005, the number of individuals seeking asylum in Canada had fallen by as much as 40 percent compared to the same period a year before.[43]

The United States has also moved to tighten its refugee and asylum process and to insulate itself from becoming the primary destination for asylum applicants. The 1980 Refugee Act did not limit the number of aliens who could apply for or be granted asylum in any year, making asylum an unknown quantity in immigration. Although the United States has long used measures such as interdiction and detention to deter the arrival of asylum seekers, the Illegal Immigration Reform and Immigrant Responsibility Act of 1996 directly responded to the perceived abuse of the asylum system.[44] People entering the United States without documentation or with false identification become subject to immediate detention and can be deported. If asylum is requested, a screening process determines the credibility of the applicant's claim and whether the full asylum process should be initiated. Nor has the act been without its critics. Pointing to the policy of interdiction and detainment, the system has been accused of mistreating those it is meant to protect.

EUROPE: A LUKEWARM RECEPTION

Most European countries have not been resettlement destinations, although Norway, Sweden, Denmark, and Finland accepted limited numbers of refugees through the 1990s, and the United Kingdom and Iceland have recently agreed to accept a limited number of refugees. With little opportunity to immigrate legally to Western Europe, would-be immigrants have sought entry through asylum. Until the early 1980s, the number of asylum seekers arriving in Western Europe was approximately one hundred thousand per year, with most arriving from Eastern Europe. By the mid-1980s, the number of refugees had grown rapidly, and their influx fueled antiforeigner violence that threatened the political stability of European governments as they dealt with rising nationalism, part of the larger unease with immigration discussed in chapter 4. Rather than being viewed as legitimate refugees fleeing persecution, entrants from North Africa, Turkey, or Eastern Europe were frequently viewed as illegitimate economic refugees. Interestingly, the growth of nationalism coincided with Western Europe's move toward a common currency and market, consequently surrendering of a portion of their sovereignty and allowing the free movement of European Union members throughout the community. This apparent contradiction is explained by antiforeigner sentiments—anyone outside the European Union is foreign and a threat. Discussions of asylum are consequently cast in terms of national security, with implications for the shape and outlook of European society.

Although the pressure to deal with refugees was felt throughout Western Europe, it has been particularly acute in Germany, where generous asylum laws were associated with an upsurge in the number of asylum seekers from approximately 100,000 per year in the mid-1980s to over 430,000 by 1992. Most would-be asylees arrived from Turkey, Yugoslavia, Poland, Bulgaria, and Romania.[45] Although Germany's approval of asylum applicants was less than 5 percent, many of those denied legal status either slipped into the underground or moved elsewhere. Germany's attempt to deal with the rush of asylum seekers was ad hoc and limited. To discourage asylum seekers from traveling to Germany, the government moved to deny work permits. The response was immediate and predictable: idle refugees made for highly visible targets, fanning antiforeigner sentiments that were already high due to the cost of supporting arrivals to local taxpayers. Numerous examples of violence against foreigners were reported in the early 1990s, leading to questions regarding the integration of foreigners and asylum laws. In response, Germany reformed its asylum laws in 1993 such that asylum seekers could be turned back without a hearing if they had transited through a safe third country that also offered asylum and unilaterally declared all immediate neighbors "safe" countries. For those who illegally slipped into the country, Germany followed a complex system for determining asylum.

Germany's move to reform its asylum laws was later reflected throughout the European Union. In light of a growing numbers of asylees seeking residency within Europe, governments faced the difficult task of interpreting who was a legitimate refugee. Building on the Dublin Convention of 1990, which marked the first attempt to coordinate asylum policies, the Amsterdam Treaty of 1997 moved the European Union toward a harmonization of policies.[46] The treaty introduced a variety of measures to limit asylee flows, including the detention of asylum seekers and reduced social benefits, meant to reduce the differences in facilities and benefits between northern Europe, where benefits have been traditionally better, and the south.[47] Europe has also imposed a narrow interpretation of the UN Convention on refugees. Germany's courts, for instance, ruled that people fleeing Afghanistan's Taliban regime did not qualify for refugee status since the Taliban was not a recognized government. This allows countries to recognize people persecuted by a government or its agents but not, for example, at the hands of a rebel movement. Even if a state's authority has completely broken down in the country of origin, a request for protection can be refused.[48] Bosnian Muslims, Somalis, and others have run into this legalistic barrier as well, but there is nothing in the UN Convention that excludes refugee status for people persecuted by nonstate agents. Finally, the European Union has followed the principle that would-be refugees must seek asylum in the first country where they are able. The so-called safe-third-country policy is legally binding, designed to prevent asylum seekers from "shopping" for the best place of refuge.

INTERNALLY DISPLACED PERSONS:
A GROWING CONCERN

Similar to refugees in that they have been forced to flee their homes for fear of persecution, conflict, or human rights abuses, IDPs differ from refugees in that they do not reside outside of their countries of nationality. Many are trapped in war zones, unable to cross international borders into safer areas. By 2004, IDPs represented over twenty-one million individuals according to the U.S. Committee for Refugees and Immigrants, the result of multiple wars and conflicts. In Sudan alone, two decades of war between the Islamic government of the north and the Christian south has produced over five million displaced individuals.[49] Other major displaced populations at the end of 2004 were found in Columbia, Afghanistan, Iraq, Uganda, Sri Lanka, Azerbaijan, and Sierra Leone. In Indonesia, the IDP population exceeds five hundred thousand. In many cases, a large percentage of the displaced were originally *transmigrants*, products of a long-standing government program that relocated Indonesians from the island of Java to less populated areas by offering economic and land incentives. But the causes of forced displacements in the late 1990s were deep and spatially variant across the island state. In some locations, conflict between the government and rebels caused displacement; in others, religious conflicts between the country's majority Muslim population (90 percent) and Christians grabbed headlines but were underlain by economic control and power, **transmigration**, and the control of resources, leading to displacement. Since 2002, the number of IDPs in Indonesia has declined, with the UNHCR reporting that some thirty-two thousand individuals have been voluntarily repatriated.

IDPs often face an insecure future. They may confront ongoing internal conflict or be without a safe place to stay, and domestic governments may view them as enemies of the state or as enemy sympathizers. Unprotected by international refugee laws and with little access to international assistance, IDPs typically fall between the cracks in current humanitarian laws. In part, this reflects Western interests and the ability of certain conflicts to "grab the headlines," including conflicts that threaten the national security of developed countries or that are defined as interesting. In other cases, there is only indifference toward long-running disputes. Three of the world's most protracted conflicts, those in Sudan, Angola, and Columbia, are largely internal conflicts ignored by the Western media.

The failure to protect IDPs reflects much more than Western awareness of events; it also reflects the current viewpoint that state sovereignty is sacrosanct, making it extremely difficult to work with a displaced population in the country responsible for its displacement. Can the United Nations and international law, for instance, override issues of state sovereignty to provide humanitarian assistance? This issue was central to policy in both Bosnia and Kosovo long before NATO became involved. Although assistance was ultimately provided in these cases, victims of many other low-profile or long-term crises, such as that in Sudan, do not receive this benefit, with donor money or assistance instead directed toward visible refugee crises. Nongovernmental organizations and other aid groups have had some success but still reach only a small segment of the total displaced population. The UNHCR has increasingly become involved in assisting IDPs, but it still deals with only a small proportion of the total displaced population in places like Chechnya, Yugoslavia, and Indonesia, and it will only intervene when so asked by the UN secretary general and given consent by the state or parties involved.

Changing political circumstances, independent and sovereign states versus rebel armies, and control of territory complicate the provision of assistance. In response to the growing numbers of IDPs, the United Nations has established a set of guiding principles to protect displaced populations.[50] These guiding principles call for the protection of a person's basic rights, outline the responsibilities of the state, and provide the individual with the right to leave a state. Although ignored by most governments with displaced populations, the principles have gained some acceptance, paving the way for increased involvement by organizations such as the UNHCR and the United States Committee for Refugees and Immigrants (USCRI).

EMERGENT THEMES AND ISSUES

With an increasing world population, conflict will become increasingly common, spurred by conflicting ideologies, as well as desire for land and control of resources, ultimately leading to population displacement. Widespread poverty also provides a fertile breeding ground for tensions that can erupt in violence. The ongoing potential for political instability means that the total number of displaced persons (refugees, asylees, and IDPs) will not likely decrease soon. In response to the relatively unrestricted flow of asylum seekers, countries will increasingly move to close their borders at a time when greater access is needed. In the United States, Canada, and other countries of resettlement, the overseas admission of refugees has traditionally rested on a humanitarian basis. Given the events of September 11, however, receiving countries such as Canada or the United States revisited domestic refugee policies, restricting refugee admissions and tightening the screening process of refugee claimants. Over the short term, this has resulted in a decrease in the number of refugee admissions to both countries, although both have also publicly indicated that the number of refugees will be allowed to increase.

In Europe, the asylum crisis in the 1990s led to a streamlining and harmonization of procedures and policies across the European Union, reflecting an increasing reluctance to offer refugee status. The reduction in benefits granted to asylees, the imposition of a narrow definition of UN Convention refugees, and binding third-country policies have ultimately led to a partial closing of the doors. While the European Union has mounted a response to asylum seekers that maintains the spirit of the 1951 UN Convention, each country wants to take as few refugees as possible and to shift the problem elsewhere. The poor recognition of refugee claims raises troubling questions, highlighted by Western Europe's fear of becoming the destination for Kosovar refugees. First, low rates of recognition (i.e., a recognition rate in 2004 of just 16 percent throughout Europe) could further erode public support for refugees.[51] Rather than viewing them with compassion, public opinion could perceive all asylum applicants as abusers of the system. In North America, both Canada and the United States have moved to tighten asylum laws through a variety of measures. Second, the implementation of safe-third-country policies by the European Union, Canada, and the United States has been one technique implemented to slow the flow of asylum seekers. Yet, there is no clear consensus on what constitutes a "safe" country. Should countries such as Romania be declared "safe" when their democracies are still young and fragile?

Third, if Europe, Canada, and the United States are unable to implement generous asylum practices, how can poorer countries be expected to allow large numbers of refugees entry? Many smaller states have refused to acknowledge refugees, fearing the economic, political, and social implications of doing so. At the height of the Kosovo crisis, Macedonia closed its doors to some refugees and physically removed others. In short, in backing away from refugee resettlement, the developed world has set a dangerous and shortsighted precedent, one that the developing world has simply followed. These governments have increasingly relied on aid and nongovernmental organizations to safeguard the rights of refugees and IDPs. Rather than providing their fair share of assistance, they leave it to the richer, developed world to do more. The challenge lies in states' finding the balance between protecting their own interests and allowing for the legitimate claims of refugees, something that is itself difficult.

The reluctance of developing countries to accept refugees must be partially attributed to the failure of the developed world to accept greater numbers of refugees, along with a hesitancy to become involved in humanitarian issues. Fears associated with a large influx of asylum seekers have host countries concerned about the control of their national borders as they have grown fearful of the economic, political, and social instability that frequently accompanies large refugee flows. Compassion for refugee claimants has turned to fatigue, underlain by a feeling that refugees are simply abusing the system. The difficulty of distinguishing bona fide refugees from economic, voluntary migrants, combined with national political, social, and economic concerns, clouds the picture. Refugee flows have therefore been redefined as a national-security threat to receiving countries, with many looking to impose greater restrictions on asylum seekers and tighter refugee policies that include detention and interdiction.

Attempts to restrict asylum may, of course, be only partially success-ful. Like the attempts to restrict legal immigration discussed in chapter 4, closing the doors on refugee movements may only serve to increase illegal entry. Already, European governments have a poor record of removing individuals not granted asylum. Instead, they slip into the underground economy. Refugees may also increasingly turn to smugglers as a means of reaching safety. Reports of refugees trying to get into England via the Channel Tunnel (smuggling themselves onto trucks or under trains, risk-ing death by crushing, electrocution, or exposure) or traveling by sea to Canada and the U.S. in boats that are barely oceanworthy point to the desperation of these people. Once they reach a safe haven, their ordeal is hardly over, with most struggling for years in poor working conditions to repay smugglers under threats of violence to themselves or family mem-bers. Others are lured into prostitution. According to one estimate, human smuggling is a US$7 billion annual business, linked to the arms trade, drugs, prostitution, and child abuse.[52] Most governments in the developed world are trying to address problems associated with human smuggling, a growing phenomenon that preys on the impoverished and desperate in the developing world. Both Canada and the United States are considering new legislation to slow the flow, including stiff penalties and life impris-onment for traffickers.[53] But these policies, including reforms to Canada's Immigration and Refugee Act, also victimize the victims. Policies allowing detention mean than many would-be asylees are held for months pending a refugee hearing. In the case of illegal immigrants from China, most have been deported at the end of the process to face an uncertain future. The UNHCR and other human rights groups have criticized this policy.

Closing the doors on refugee movements may also simply shift the refugee problem to one of dealing with an internally displaced popula-tion. If settlement in a second or third country is barred, then the number of IDPs must increase. So, while it may appear that the number of refugees has decreased (as the evidence to date would suggest), individuals are simply redefined as internally displaced. Their lack of protection under international law and lack of access to resources magnifies the problem.

Not only is the forced displacement of individuals the result of politi-cal instability, but it can perpetuate instability as well. As is the case with Kosovo Albanians in Albania and Macedonia or Palestinian refugees in

Lebanon and other Arab countries, the presence of refugees may upset the political and ethnic balance within a state or strain its abilities to meet the needs of a refugee population. Radicalism caused by population imbalances may result in members' calling for the separation of the state or increased nationalism that further oppresses the minority group. In Israel, the peace process is complicated by Palestinian and Jewish demographics as noted in chapter 1. The Palestinian population, which, at 3.7 million, is the world's largest refugee population, is characterized by high **fertility** in contrast to the relatively low rates of fertility and population growth among Israeli Jews.[54] The scattered Palestinian population and its right to return complicate the peace process. Israel opposes the Palestinians' return because of its democratic implications, while a Palestinian return would tax the existing infrastructure in Gaza and the West Bank heavily.

On a different note, the actual demography of displaced populations is an inexact science, one that needs to be refined.[55] UNHCR and USCRI figures illustrate this problem: the UNHCR estimates the refugee population to be some 10.5 million, while the USCRI estimates it to be 11.5 million. Estimating the size of the displaced population is difficult, hampered by the conditions in which the events that generate occur. Further, refugees may not stop in designated camps but filter into the larger population. Yet, aid organizations rely on demographic data and estimates of the size of the displaced population to determine the amount and type of food, shelter, and other assistance needed. Detailed estimates of the age and sex distribution of the population would provide information about the need, for example, for immunizations or prenatal care. Regardless of the perspective, much more can and must be done to assist refugees and IDPs.

NOTES

1. The 1951 UN Convention was meant only to deal with European refugees associated with pre-1951 events at the end of World War II. The 1967 protocol removed the provisions associated with geography and the requirement that only victims of pre-1951 events be defined as refugees.

2. Asylees are individuals forced out of their countries of origin who seek refuge in the new country in which they are living.

3. See www.unhcr.ch/cgi-bin/texis/vtx/basics/opendoc.htm?tbl=BASICS&id=3b6917cf4 (accessed June 24, 2005).

4. The spring 2001 (vol. 35) issue of *International Migration Review* is a special issue that deals with the UNHCR: "UNHCR at 50: Past, Present and Future of Refugee Assistance."

5. Kathleen Newland, "Refugees: The New International Politics of Displacement," in *Perspectives on Population*, ed. Scott W. Menard and Elizabeth W. Moen, 314–21 (New York: Oxford University Press, 1987).

6. See www.refugees.org (accessed June 24, 2005).

7. Newland, "Refugees," 314.

8. Farzaneh Roudi, "Final Peace in the Middle East Hinges on Refugee Population," *Population Today* 29, no. 3 (April 2001): 1. Readers can also find information applicable to Palestinian refugees through the UN Relief and Works Agency for Palestine Refugees in the Near East at www.un.org/unrwa (accessed June 24, 2005).

9. Ray Wilkinson, "The Heart of Darkness," *Refugees* 110 (winter 1997): 3–8.

10. Holly Reed, "Kosovo and the Demography of Forced Migration," *Population Today* 27, no. 6 (June 1999): 4–5.

11. Carlotta Gall, "Crisis in the Balkans: In Macedonia; at Wit's End, a Neighbor Turns Back the Refugees," *New York Times*, March 31, 1999, 1A.

12. Misha Glenny, "When Victims Become a Threat," *New York Times*, April 6, 1999, 2A; Anthony DePalma, "Crisis in the Balkans: Neighbor; Kosovo Crisis Strains Already Struggling Albania," *New York Times*, May 26, 1999, 4A.

13. Roger Cohen, "Crisis in the Balkans: The Europeans; Already Burdened, Western Europe Is Reluctant to Take in Kosovo's Outcasts," *New York Times*, April 2, 1999, 3A.

14. Following the resolution of the war in Kosovo, many refugees who had been resettled in North America chose to return home. Many others stayed.

15. In 1999, for instance, some seven million individuals were newly uprooted.

16. UNHCR, *Refugees by the Numbers*, 2003 ed., at www.unhcr.ch/cgi-bin/texis/vtx/basics/opendoc.pdf?tbl=BASICS&id=3c149b007 (accessed June 24, 2005).

17. Jacqualine Desbarats, "Ethnic Differences in Adaptation: Sino-Vietnamese Refugees in the United States," *International Migration Review* 20, no. 2 (1986): 405–27. See also K. Bruce Newbold, "Refugees into Immigrants: Assessing the Adjustment of Southeast Asian Refugees in the U.S., 1975–1990," *Canadian Studies in Population* 29, no. 1 (2002): 151–71.

18. David W. Haines, *Refugees as Immigrants* (Totawa, NJ: Rowman & Littlefield, 1986).

19. Alejendro Portes and Reuben Rumbaut, *Immigrant America: A Portrait* (Berkeley: University of California Press, 1996).

20. K. Bruce Newbold and Matthew Foulkes, "Geography and Segmented Assimilation: Examples from the New York Chinese," *Population, Space and Place* 10 (2004): 3–18.

21. Sara Corbett, "The Long Road from Sudan to America," *New York Times Magazine*, April 1, 2001, 1–6. For an academic discussion of the adjustment of refugees to the host society, see Reginald P. Baker and David S. North, *The 1975 Refugees: Their First Five Years in America* (Washington, DC: New TransCentury Foundation, 1984); Haines, *Refugees*; Alejendro Portes, "Economic Sociology and the Sociology of Immigration: A Conceptual Overview," in *The Economic Sociology of Immigration*, ed. Alejendro Portes, 1–41 (New York: Russell Sage, 1995).

22. Emily Skop, "Race and Place in the Adaptation of Mariel Exiles," *International Migration Review* 35, no. 1 (2001): 449–71.

23. I use this term with caution. Both the United States and Canada have resettled large numbers of refugees in the past from a variety of sources. However, U.S. refugee policy has frequently been a tool of foreign policy, as is discussed later in

this section. Moreover, while both countries have resettled refugees, they could do much more.

24. Not all groups have shared equally in the generosity of Canada and the United States, with both countries blocking the admission of European Jews during the 1930s and 1940s. See, for example, Irving Abella and Harold Troper, *None Is Too Many: Canada and the Jews of Europe 1933–1948* (Toronto: Lester and Orpen Dennys, 1983).

25. Citizenship and Immigration Canada, *Annual Report to Parliament on Immigration*, 2004. Per-capita statistics can be found at www.refugees.org (accessed June 24, 2005).

26. Hania Zlotnik, "Policies and Migration Trends in the North American System," in *International Migration, Refugee Flows and Human Rights in North America*, ed. Alan B. Simmons, 81–103 (New York: Center for Migration Studies, 1996).

27. Ray Wilkinson, "Give Me... Your Huddled," *Refugees* 119, no. 2 (summer 2000): 5–21.

28. *Yearbook of Immigration Statistics, 2004*, at http://uscis.gov/graphics/shared/statistics/yearbook/index.htm (accessed February 4, 2006).

29. This should not be interpreted as implying that Canada has always followed a strict humanitarian agenda. At the beginning of the Indochinese refugee crisis in the 1970s, Canada was initially slow to offer resettlement to refugees.

30. See www.cic.gc.ca (accessed June 24, 2005).

31. Each year, the number of applications for asylum exceeds the number granted, following the determination of the veracity of the refugee claim. Calculating an average approval rate would be misleading since approval rates vary significantly by country, being higher in the 1980s and 1990s for aliens from the former Soviet Union and lower for Central Americans.

32. T. Alexander Aleinikoff, "United States Refugee Law and Policy: Past, Present and Future," in *International Migration, Refugee Flows and Human Rights in North America*, ed. Alan B. Simmons, 245–57 (New York: Center for Migration Studies, 1996).

33. *2004 Yearbook of Immigrant Statistics*, at http://uscis.gov (accessed June 24, 2005). See also *Refugees, Asylees, Fiscal Year 1998* (Washington, DC: Immigration and Naturalization Service, 1998).

34. Lucas Guttentag, "Haitian Refugees and U.S. Policy," in *International Migration, Refugee Flows and Human Rights in North America*, ed. Alan B. Simmons, 272–89 (New York: Center for Migration Studies, 1996).

35. Newland, "Refugees," 314.

36. Aleinikoff, "Refugee Law and Policy," 245.

37. Aleinikoff, "Refugee Law and Policy," 245.

38. UNHCR, "Asylum Levels and Trends in Industrialized Countries," 2004, at www.unhcr.org/cgi-bin/texis/vtx/home/opendoc.pdf?tbl=STATISTICS&id=422439144&page=statistics (accessed June 24, 2005).

39. Wilkinson, "Give Me," 5.

40. Manuel Garcia y Griego, "Canada: Flexibility and Control in Immigration and Refugee Policy," in *Controlling Immigration: A Global Perspective*, ed. Wayne A. Cornelius, Philip L. Martin, and James F. Hollifield, 119–42 (Palo Alto: Stanford University Press, 1992).

41. See www.cic.gc.ca/english/irpa/index.html (accessed June 24, 2005).

42. Approximately eleven to twelve thousand per year seek protection in Canada after passing through the United States. The flow in the opposite direction, into the United States, is much smaller, at about two hundred asylum seekers per year.

43. See www.cbc.ca/story/canada/national/2005/07/27/refugee-claims050727. html (accessed July 28, 2005).

44. See www.ins.usdoj.gov/graphics/index.htm (accessed June 24, 2005); see also Wilkinson, "Give Me," 5.

45. Philip L. Martin, "Germany: Reluctant Land of Immigration," in *Controlling Immigration: A Global Perspective,* ed. Wayne A. Cornelius, Philip L. Martin, and James F. Hollifield, 189–226 (Palo Alto: Stanford University Press, 1992).

46. Stefan Teloken, "Europe: The Debate over Asylum: It's a Long Way to . . . Harmonization," *Refugees* 113 (1999): 3–7.

47. Judith Kumin, "Europe: The Debate over Asylum: An Uncertain Direction," *Refugees* 113 (1999): 8–13.

48. Teloken, "It's a Long Way," 3.

49. See www.refugees.org (accessed June 24, 2005).

50. Ray Wilkinson, "IDPs: The Hot Issue for a New Millennium: Who's Looking after These People?" *Refugees* 117 (1999): 3–8.

51. UNHCR, "2004 Global Refugee Trends," at www.unhcr.ch/statistics (accessed June 24, 2005); see also Kumin, "An Uncertain Direction," 8.

52. Judith Kumin, "A Multi-Billion Dollar Trade in Humans," *Refugees* 119 (2000): 18–19.

53. At the time the first edition of this book was published, both countries were discussing new legislation to deal with human trafficking. By winter 2006, no significant changes in policy had occurred, with most amendments sidestepped by increased security concerns.

54. Farzaneh Roudi, "Final Peace," 1.

55. Reed, "Kosovo," 4.

6

%

Population, Economic Growth, Resources, and the Environment

E arly on in this book, we established that the continued growth of the human population is inevitable. Even if the demographic transition results in lower fertility and growth rates, population momentum and above-replacement fertility levels will ensure that the population reaches 7.5 or 8 billion by 2025, with potentially significant societal and economic consequences. The remaining question, however, is whether a growing population has had positive or negative implications for resources, food production, and economic growth. The debate has a long history, dating to Thomas Malthus's 1798 "Essay on the Principle of Population" and later writings by Karl Marx and Friedrich Engels. Writing during a period of poor harvests and food shortages, Malthus argued that food supply would increase in a linear fashion (1, 2, 3 . . .), while population would increase exponentially (2, 4, 16 . . .).[1] Ultimately, population would exceed agricultural output unless population growth was somehow checked. Historically, Malthus argued that so-called positive checks, including famine, plague, and war decreased the population. Alternatively, population growth could be controlled through "preventative checks," with individuals imposing their own limits on reproduction. Malthus held out little hope that humanity would be able to control its sexual and reproductive needs and forecast a dismal future of population decline and widespread poverty. In opposition to Malthus, Marx and Engels argued that people were poor because economies and societies were organized in such a way that they had no opportunity to be anything but poor. Influenced by the social and economic conditions of Europe during the industrial revolution, they advocated social and political change (often through revolution) and believed that a just and equitable distribution of resources, aided by technology, would allow unlimited population growth.

Time has proven the basic perspectives of the **Malthusian** and **Marxist** theories both right and wrong—our mere presence on this planet points to the failings of Malthus's ideas. While fertility has been reduced largely by personal choice as standards of living have risen and new ideas have filtered through society, technology, the **green revolution**, and biotechnology have allowed the world to accommodate a population far larger than Malthus ever saw possible. Agricultural production has grown tremendously, allowing per capita food supplies to increase despite population growth. Marx's position, on the other hand, seems to have been vindicated in China, which, with a population in excess of 1.3 billion, has proven that it can provide for the basic needs of a large and rapidly growing population. At the same time, China has recognized that there are limits to growth and moved to reduce fertility through its one-child policy.

Even now, however, the United Nations Food and Agricultural Organization (**UNFAO**) estimates that over 852 million people were malnourished between 2000 and 2002. While the majority of these were people lived in the developing world, including some 204 million (33 percent) in sub-Saharan Africa, 221 million in India (26 percent), and 142 million (17 percent) in China, some 9 million were also found in the developed world.[2] Millions more consume sufficient calories but fail to get the necessary proteins. Consequently, the world continues to grapple with the basic question of whether it can feed itself, both now and in the years to come. At the same time as agricultural production has increased, degradation of cropland through erosion, desertification, salinization, and urbanization have reduced the amount of land available for agriculture.[3] Erosion, for example, created by poor farming practices, deforestation, and the use of ecologically marginal land, can decrease average yields by reducing the soil's ability to retain moisture, carrying away nutrients, and degrading its physical qualities. The unequal distribution of food due to distributional difficulties, conflicts, or politics within and among countries compounds the problem.[4] With the world's population growing at a rate of 1.3 percent per year, and with over eighty million new souls each year requiring food and clothing and other resources, questions as to whether the earth can feed and sustain such a large population continue to arise.[5]

While Malthus's dire predictions remain a focal point of the debate over population growth, and while our ability to feed the world's population remains an important question,[6] the debate has expanded from the original correlation between population and food to include linkages between population, resources, environmental degradation, and economic development and to encompass three competing perspectives. The debate, currently defined by **neo-Malthusians** (those who are accepting of the

Malthusian position), **distributionists (Marxists)**, and economic optimists (those who believe that population growth stimulates economic development), has splintered, generating two lines of argument, with one focusing on population (resource linkages, such as food, water, and cropland) and the other considering the potential connections between population and economic growth. Such a division creates an artificial divide within the population debate, when, in reality, resources, economic growth, and population are all tightly related. First, neo-Malthusian, economic-optimist, or distributionist perspectives underpin both divisions. Second, the degradation, depletion, or denial (i.e., through legislation or conflict) of resources will have a direct impact on economic growth and the livelihoods of populations. Conversely, economic growth or population growth directly influences the level, type, and quantity of resources consumed within a society.

In the coming decades, population growth, rising per capita resource consumption of food and resources, and inequalities in resource access guarantee that scarcities of **renewable resources** will become an issue. The need for resource substitution and conservation will be urgent and complex, increasing the need for political and scientific leadership able to find solutions without aggravating existing problems and group conflicts. This chapter focuses on the linkages between population growth, resource scarcity, and economic opportunity. The intent is to draw on ideas developed in previous chapters and to evaluate their relationships relative to broader resource and economic-development issues. Doing so, however, requires an explanation of alternative approaches that link population growth with these issues. This chapter discusses these opposing approaches, including their merits and problems, along with current perspectives and how the differences between each may be reconciled. The chapter moves on to discuss linkages between population growth, economic development, and resource scarcity, considering whether renewable resources are truly renewable, and it concludes by looking at emerging issues.

SETTING THE STAGE: THE DEBATE AND CURRENT PERSPECTIVES

Growing from the initial Malthusian-Marxist distinctions within the literature, three perspectives underlie the current debate and influence public policy and commentary.[7] Pointing to growing carbon dioxide concentrations, the declining health of oceans, reductions in biodiversity, and the degradation of land, neo-Malthusians argue that finite resources place strict limits on the growth of the human population and its consumption.[8] If limits are exceeded, social breakdown occurs.[9] Writing in the 1960s, in *The Population Bomb*, Paul Ehrlich alerted the public to the population crisis, giving it a sense of urgency.[10] Economic optimists like Julian Simon see few limits to population growth and prosperity, provided the economic system and market mechanisms work correctly.[11] Following their reasoning, few societies face strict limits to growth or consumption, with optimists pointing to improvements in human health, life expectancy, and increasing food production to support their position. Finally, the distributionist viewpoint favored by Marxists focuses on inequalities in the distribution of wealth and power within a society and argues that poverty, inequality, and the poor distribution of resources are the causes, not consequences, of population growth and resource depletion.

While the neo-Malthusian, economic-optimist, and distributionist perspectives are still identifiable within the literature, the debate has essentially become two-sided, with neo-Malthusians on one side and optimists on the other. Each argument has some basis but neither accounts for the whole picture. So, what went wrong and where do we currently stand? First, returning to the neo-Malthusian perspective, empirical and anecdotal evidence has failed to support the assumption that population growth is limited by resource barriers. In very general terms, the human population has grown beyond most of the barriers that neo-Malthusians assumed. Over the past two centuries, agricultural technology and capital have increased agricultural productivity tremendously, allowing agricultural output to increase. Similarly, neo-Malthusians forecasted energy shortfalls, predicting that energy prices would grow over fivefold between 1973 (the first oil crisis) and 2000. Today, however, energy and other **nonrenewable resources** remain arguably as abundant and inexpensive as they were thirty years ago.[12]

Economic optimists have done much better at explaining the ability of the world to overcome these apparent barriers. They see the operation of economic institutions, particularly free markets, as key. Properly functioning institutions can facilitate the conservation, substitution, innovation, and global trade of goods. Induced-innovation theory argues that changes in endowments of land or labor, for example, are reflected in market price signals.[13] Through their ability to generate profits, markets stimulate innovations that loosen or remove constraints on population growth, and price changes encourage people to tap new resources or to substitute. Ester Boserup, for example, shows that scarcity of cropland stimulates greater labor specialization, increased productivity, and changes in agricultural practices.[14] Likewise, new lands may be opened to agriculture, conservation may be stimulated, or resource substitution may promote the increased use of fertilizers to increase agricultural output. Similarly, scarcities of nonrenewable resources can be overcome through resource substitution, conservation, improved production efficiencies, and enhanced resource extraction technologies. Economic optimists also argue that population growth has a key advantage in that it produces more geniuses, providing society with the means to resolve scarcities. For Simon, resources are only limited by humanity's ability to invent. Thus, innovation and technical fixes allow societies to move beyond constraints to growth. Resource scarcity and degradation are therefore not due to population growth or increased consumption but are instead due to market failure.

Like the neo-Malthusian perspective, however, the optimist framework is also flawed. A larger population does not, for instance, necessarily mean more discoveries or more Einsteins; perhaps it means only that more people make the same discovery. Instead, the supply of scientists and other thinkers is constrained by the level and accessibility of education, the brain drain out of many countries in the developing world, limited capital, poor and incompetent bureaucracies, corruption, and weak states. The brain drain from developing countries into the developed world may have an especially pernicious effect. As discussed in chapter 4, much of the developed world has tailored immigration policies to accept the educated or those with skills. This institutionalized brain drain poses further long-term difficulties for the developing world in terms of maintaining social capital and its ability to generate, retain, and use the highly educated members of its populations, which will be necessary to solve impending problems.

Moreover, optimists' arguments rest on the free operation of the market, an assumption that is stretched in many cases. Free markets are far from universal. Even in America, the quintessential free market economy, regulations at various government levels (state, national, and international) interfere with its free operation. In the developing world, the markets frequently become murkier. Institutional limitations, including market failure associated with unclear common property rights and inappropriate pricing for scarce resources (i.e., undervaluing) limits the creation or substitution of alternatives. In addition, institutional biases may be present within markets such that institutions tend to favor some actors over others, leading to the marginalization of segments of the population. Consequently, a key caveat of the optimist viewpoint is the *quality* of institutions, policies, and technologies that is inherent within a society. Together, these effects, which are in turn modified by cultural, historical, and ecological factors, have direct bearing on a society's ability to respond to resource scarcity. If markets cannot identify or effectively incorporate the costs of scarcity so that resources or goods are undervalued, resources will be exploited and solutions to scarcity will not be forthcoming. Furthermore, it is unlikely that population growth can promote increases in agricultural output that will keep pace with population growth rates in Africa and parts of Asia.

For the most part, the debate between these three groups has stopped there. It is a debate that Thomas Homer-Dixon characterizes as sterile and with relatively little advancement.[15] Science, however, has better revealed the complexity and interconnectivity of ecological systems with implications for the population. In the past, the earth's environmental systems were regarded as stable and resilient to our tampering. Instead, there is mounting evidence drawn from observation of ocean currents, ozone depletion, and fish stocks that environmental systems are not stable in the face of human action. Changes to systems that were previously considered slow or incremental might be better described as nonlinear, changing in character when some threshold is exceeded, making "chaotic" and "anarchic" better descriptors of environmental systems.[16] Humanity is taxing the earth's resources to such a degree that complete ecosystems are disappearing. Global warming and the loss of biodiversity may, at some point, cascade to produce dramatic changes that humanity is ill prepared to deal with.

Extreme events, interdependency, and the interactivity of environmental systems further complicate our understanding of ecosystems, with implications for our ability to manage scarce resources. Even if global environmental systems change only slowly, the frequency of extreme events, such as flooding, drought, and so forth, will increase. The interdependency and interactivity of environmental systems mean that degradation or damage to one resource produces effects that reach through neighboring systems. Clear-cut logging, for example, removes habitats in the immediate area and the ability to sequester carbon dioxide, a greenhouse gas, but the effects are much more widespread. The reduced or altered ability of the land to absorb rainwater alters drainage patterns and increases soil erosion. This, in turn, may lead to the siltation of streams and rivers, destroying fish habitats and local fisheries and reducing our ability to manage river flows for the purposes of irrigation, navigation, or the generation of hydroelectric power, a situation faced by the government of Panama, which is working to ensure the long-term viability of the Panama Canal.[17] Moreover, multiple human impacts on environmental systems could produce damaging outcomes far greater than the sum of their individual effects so that agricultural output could be stressed by local deforestation, erosion, and changing rainfall patterns associated with climate change.

Given threshold effects, interdependence, and interaction, societies will need increased ingenuity and innovation to deal with these problems and with resource scarcity. As Homer-Dixon has argued, however, one of the key questions is whether societies will be able to provide the necessary ingenuity to tackle new and emergent problems.[18] Countries will respond differentially to scarcities and will, as a result, provide various qualities and quantities of ingenuity. Innovation or ingenuity is more likely to come from those with the resources, including time, capital, and properly functioning institutions that enable the development of new concepts or technology. Simon, for instance, argued that if population growth was to be beneficial, it must occur within a democratic, capitalist system.[19] Yet, democracy may be just what the doctor didn't order. If democracy is forced on a society in which it has no history or foundation, the appropriate checks and balances essential to a democratic system will not likely be in place. Under conditions where corruption maintains power and wealth within a small circle of elites, existing scarcities and ethnic or religious differences could aggravate problems and produce further societal discord. Obviously, such a line of reasoning would be a difficult sell in Washington, which has long trumpeted the power of democracy, despite recent setbacks in the democratization of countries such as Iraq and Afghanistan and in pressure for democratic reforms in other Middle Eastern countries.[20] Unfortunately, democracy is no better at ensuring equality of resource distribution or income within a population than any other form of government. In fact, it may only institutionalize inequality between groups, particularly in countries where corruption is rampant. The evidence is widely available in countries like Chad, Angola, Kazakhstan, Nigeria, and Angola, where wealth provided by booming oil prices has failed to lift the population out of poverty and instead has lined the pockets of the elite within corrupt societies mired in conflict. In addition, it is already apparent that poorly functioning markets and other institutions may limit a society's ability to respond to resource scarcity.

If the ability to generate ingenuity is missing or its supply is insufficient, it is reasonable to assume a country's ability to respond to resource scarcity will be diminished. The "ingenuity gap," or the difference between the need for ingenuity and a society's ability to supply it, becomes an important variable in a society's ability to deal with resource scarcity.[21] If a society can supply the needed ingenuity, it can overcome the limits to growth, but a society may lack the infrastructure, or economic and political institutions may block a country's ability to overcome resource scarcities and limits. Those societies that lack the ability to generate ingenuity will be increasingly unable to deal with rising scarcities and their implications. Instead, a gap between the supply and required amount of ingenuity will develop, and societies may be faced with increasing resource scarcity, with implications for social organization, social dissatisfaction, and violence. Resource scarcity may, for example, stimulate competition to protect and secure existing resources, a process known as **resource capture**, which is further examined in the coming pages. Social friction between groups, engendered by ethnic, ideological, or religious differences, also reduces societies' ability to adapt by diminishing their capacity to supply the ingenuity needed to resolve resource scarcity. In other words, rather than creating technological change, as optimists would argue, the lack of ingenuity and social capital may exacerbate resource scarcity. Resource scarcity may also force actors, such as state governments, to secure resources through legislative or military means. Doing so places severe pressures on marginalized groups and fails to resolve the long-run difficulties of resource scarcity.

Given the advances on the scientific side of the debate, Homer-Dixon argues that the concepts of ingenuity supply and adaptation enable the bridging of the various perspectives of population growth.[22] Improved markets and greater equality in the distribution of wealth, both optimists and distributionists argue, will assist in reducing the negative effects of a scarcity. The ability of a society, however, to make improvements will be partially determined by the scarcity itself, which is also determined by its physical context, including economic resources. The neo-Malthusian perspective can also be addressed by focusing on the supply and demand for ingenuity. Rather than focusing on strict limits to population, which neo-Malthusian perspectives do, Homer-Dixon argues that it is better to consider the ability of a society to supply ingenuity in the face of increasing requirements. If a society can supply the needed ingenuity, limits can be overcome. If it cannot, a gap between the supply and required amount of ingenuity will develop, and societies may be faced with increasing resource scarcity, with implications for social organization, social dissatisfaction, and violence.

POPULATION AND ECONOMIC DEVELOPMENT

As the economies of the developing world, particularly the poorest sub-Saharan countries, started to stagnate in the 1980s, social scientists scrambled to unearth the linkages between rapid growth and economic development.[23] After all, foreign investment and aid had poured into the developing world for years, yet there was little to show for it. Instead, per capita incomes had declined, and an increasing proportion of the population lived in poverty. At the heart of the debate is the question of whether population growth favors economic development or hinders it, with the available data supporting a number of interpretations.[24] On the surface, it is readily apparent that the richest countries are also those with slow population growth characterized by low rates of fertility and low mortality levels, while some of the poorest countries have high rates of population growth. The relationship is, however, not perfect; for example, the oil-producing countries in the Middle East have high population growth (the rate of increase in Saudi Arabia and other gulf states remains at over 3 percent per year), as well as strong economic growth, although this reflects the demand for oil. The opposite is also true, with slow population growth and low economic growth rates.

Muddying the waters are counterarguments that population growth promotes economic development. Recalling Boserup's argument (first presented in chapter 1), optimists have long asserted that population growth promotes economic development, assuming that it is a motivating force in the adaptation of societies, including the uptake or innovation of new technologies and techniques or economic reforms.[25] The notion that population growth is in fact good for economic growth is well grounded. In Europe and North America, population growth and declining mortality levels are thought to have stimulated economic development and the industrial revolution. However, a different perspective is seen in the developing world. Building on a much lower standard of living than Europe or the Americas at similar stages in their economic development, and having far greater rates of population growth, this group of countries is not, on average, following the lead of developed countries. In fact, due to the HIV/AIDS epidemic and its social and economic ramifications, they may be slipping further into economic crisis.

Although the linkage between population and economic development is complex, emerging evidence reinforces the negative linkage between rapid population growth and economic development. The U.S. National Research Council reinforced population's negative effect on economic growth, concluding that rapid population growth damages economic growth.[26] For economic development to occur, capital must be invested in such things as education, health, or infrastructure, a difficult proposition in much of the world, where poverty impedes governments' and individuals' ability to invest. For economies to grow, the level of capital investment must also grow, with higher rates of population growth necessitating higher rates of capital investment. Following a Malthusian line of reasoning, if the population growth rate exceeds the investment rate, countries will be trapped in poverty, unable to invest in themselves and provide the needed infrastructure. Although economic growth will take place under these conditions, population growth is so high that economic growth is distributed throughout a larger population, meaning that individuals will receive a smaller share.

This negative linkage can be viewed through a number of relationships connecting rapid population growth and high fertility to economic growth.[27] First, rapid population growth tends to dampen the growth of per capita gross domestic product (GDP), the total value of goods and services produced in a country. This relationship first appeared in the 1980s and appears strongest in the poorest countries.[28] The growth of GDP can be limited by high young dependency rates (where the proportion of youth aged zero to fourteen is high relative to the size of the labor force), a result of high fertility rates. With a young population profile, the attendant costs associated with health and education for children is high, reducing household savings and increasing government expenditures. In turn, the growth of GDP is reduced, with the investment providing only long-term economic payoffs.[29] The impact on economic growth is also seen in the creation of new jobs. In countries with rapid population growth, labor markets are frequently unable to provide sufficient employment opportunities for the young, leading to underemployment or unemployment. This negative relationship has continued, ensuring that inequalities between the developed and developing worlds remain and providing little hope for their rapid amelioration.

Second, population growth and high fertility tend to aggravate poverty and promote its institutionalization from one generation to the next. In particular, population growth will likely reduce or slow wage growth among the least-skilled and lowest-income groups. India, for example, has accommodated high population growth, but economic-development policies have favored or improved the status of only 15 to 20 percent of the population. The poor in India have paid the highest price. Much of India's public education system, which is predominantly attended by lower socioeconomic classes, is underfunded and inadequate. The poor are progressively marginalized and are increasingly unable to participate in the economy because of poor health, lack of nutrition, or illiteracy.[30] In addition, a cadre of low-skilled, low-wage workers may slow the adoption of more efficient technologies.

Third, high fertility inhibits household savings, instead forcing household expenditure on basic goods and services for a larger number of people, while savings for or expenditures on education are postponed or neglected. Conversely, declining population growth and fewer children mean that households are able to invest in education and place more of their earnings in savings, a necessary condition for economic growth. The economic literature has, for example, largely attributed the growth of Asian economies such as South Korea during the 1980s to increased household saving rates as fertility dropped and incomes grew.[31] As families saved more, domestic savings increased and were invested both within the country, as well as exported elsewhere.

Fourth, higher fertility rates mean that parents have less to invest in each child than those with smaller families. Similarly, children from larger families have less schooling on average than their counterparts from smaller families. In countries with rapid population growth, increased pressure is placed on education and health care facilities, requiring increased financial commitments. Unless rapid growth of government revenues is also occurring, or governments are willing to shift spending priorities, expenditures on education and health are depressed.[32] Again, evidence in support of this can be drawn from Asia. In South Korea, decreasing fertility levels and young dependency rates meant that the government was able to quadruple real per-student educational expenditure between 1970 and 1989, even as it spent an approximately equivalent proportion of its national budget on education. If South Korea's share of school-aged children had grown as fast as Kenya's during the same period, it would have needed to spend more than double what it did.[33]

Finally, population growth threatens resources by placing increased pressure on them, whether resource use is associated with increased per capita consumption (i.e., through increasing incomes and demand) or increased demand generated by a growing population, even if per capita demand remains the same. Forest products, fisheries, cropland, and freshwater resources, along with the services that they provide, are all vulnerable to human-induced pressures.

Rapid population growth and high fertility seemingly have the greatest negative impact in the poorest countries where national institutions are weak.[34] In these cases, population growth reinforces a downward economic spiral, reflective of several sub-Saharan countries with high fertility rates and lower average per capita incomes today than two decades ago.[35] Poorly developed markets or ineffectual government programs and leadership fail to protect, invest in, or build the basic infrastructure that is needed. Without strong institutions to assist national programs associated with education, fertility and family planning, and infrastructure development, rapid population growth will decrease the supply of ingenuity, exacerbating resource scarcity and environmental degradation. In turn, failure to invest in infrastructure and the degradation of assets can cripple institutions and markets. Moreover, governments in developing countries often lack the financial or political ability to invest in institutions that will promote labor force development.

POPULATION AND RESOURCE SCARCITY

The debate over the relationship between population growth and resources parallels that of population and economic development, pitting neo-Malthusians against economic optimists, with both groups claiming evidence to support their positions. One point seems intuitive: the collective impact of six billion people on the Earth's ecosystems, measured through resource use, consumption, or pollution, is tremendous. Whether the current rate of resource consumption is sustainable we do not know, but we suspect that current consumption patterns and human impacts are not sustainable over the long run. Already, many regions face environmental scarcity, including scarcities of cropland, water, and forests.

In his 1999 book, Homer-Dixon identified three forms of resource scarcity: supply-induced, demand-induced, and structural scarcities. *Supply-induced scarcity* occurs when a resource is depleted in quantity or has become degraded, perhaps through overexploitation or pollution. *Demand-induced scarcity* occurs when population growth and changes in consumption patterns boost the demand for a resource. Such scarcities occur only when a resource is **rivalrous**, meaning that its use by one economic actor reduces its availability for others, with examples including fisheries, water, or forests. *Structural scarcity* occurs when there is an imbalance in the distribution of a resource or in power and wealth within a society, such that certain groups get a proportionately larger share of the resource. If a resource is excludable (i.e., cropland), such that its use can be restricted or blocked through property rights or other institutions, some groups may be prevented from accessing it.

Not surprisingly, population growth is a key factor driving all three types of resource scarcity. Rather than operating independently, they may interact with and reinforce one another, either through resource capture or **ecological marginalization**.[36] *Resource capture* occurs when a scarce resource forces actors (i.e., governments or ethnic groups) to assert control over resources through legislation or other means. Land scarcities in Chiapas, Mexico, encouraged wealthy landowners and ranchers to seize lands from the indigenous population by exploiting weak land laws. The marginalized peasants were forced deeper into poverty and off their traditional lands, a process that eventually resulted in violence as they rebelled against the Mexican government. The indigenous population of Chiapas was also ecologically marginalized, the outcome of population growth and the maldistribution of resources (structural scarcities), which forces individuals into ecologically marginal areas such as rainforests and steep hillsides, increasing the risk of resource degradation through erosion, siltation, or desertification.[37] Poverty, desperation, and a lack of environmental knowledge to protect resources magnify the problem.

It is questionable whether some countries, such as China, Egypt, and India, have the resources and economic ability to sustain their populations indefinitely, even if population growth were to cease immediately. Writing for the World Watch Institute in 1995, Lester Brown questioned China's ability to feed itself in the coming decades.[38] Drawing from the experiences of other Asian countries, Brown forecasted that due to a combination of rising standards of living, which tend to move people "up the food chain" from staples to more complex diets, increased consumption, loss of cropland, and declining water resources, among other factors, China would not be able to feed itself. Its inability to grow a sufficient food supply domestically would force China to turn to world markets to purchase the necessary grains and other foodstuffs. The problem lies in the country's expected demand for grains, which Brown projected would exceed total world output, driving up prices globally and weakening the ability of smaller, poorer countries to purchase their requirements.

Whether the discussion is global or national, the debate is not just a question of feeding a large population but also of providing health care, education, and infrastructure while finding employment and increasing the standard of living over the longer term in a sustainable fashion. Population growth also influences such diverse issues as increased energy consumption, global warming, ozone depletion, deforestation, loss of cropland and biodiversity, and shrinking fresh-water resources. Together, the requirements of a growing population may exact a huge toll on limited resources, which may only cripple future sustainability, a situation compounded by unequal access to resources and the marginalization of populations.

The Fallacy of Renewable Resources

> When the well's dry, we know the worth of water.
> —Benjamin Franklin

When discussing resources, most authors distinguish between nonrenewable (finite) resources, such as oil and gas reserves, and renewable resources, such as timber, fish stocks, and water. Renewable resources can be harvested and used up to some threshold without threatening their long-term viability. As long as that threshold is maintained, long-term use of the resource can be ensured. The question is, however, whether our use of renewable resources is sustainable over the long term. In many places where people rely on them, renewables are being degraded or depleted faster than they can be renewed. Population growth amplifies many of the effects of human activity on renewable resources simply through increased demand (demand-induced scarcity).[39] Renewable resources can also be directly or indirectly depleted or degraded by direct consumption or harm to that resource (i.e., pollution), which in essence makes them nonrenewable. Likewise, thresholds are not always known or acknowledged, inadvertently leading to the degradation of the resource. Therefore, although the distinction is useful, it is arguable whether renewable and nonrenewable resources should be seen as belonging to necessarily exclusive categories. Much of the world is in danger of learning this the hard way as renewable resources are wasted, mismanaged, or overused (see figure 6.1).

A number of brief examples serve to highlight the point that resources are not necessarily renewable. Water, for example, is an abundant resource but one that is unevenly distributed. Despite its renewal through the hydrological cycle, significant shortages loom on the horizon. From 1900 to 1995, global water consumption increased six times, more than double the rate of population growth, and over five hundred million people live in countries with water shortages; that number is expected to grow dramatically to between three and seven billion over the next two decades.[40] Many

Figure 6.1.   Now Serving. *Source:* Joe Sharpnack, reproduced with permission.

areas, including the southwestern United States, the Middle East, Central Asia, and northern Africa, already face insufficient water resources at the same time that increasing populations, urbanization, and industrialization are increasing demand. This means, therefore, that per capita supplies drop as population increases. Israel faces an annual deficit of water (i.e., more water is used than is supplied through renewable sources on a yearly basis), which is covered by the overwithdrawal of aquifers, including those under the West Bank. Consequently, aquifer levels have dropped, some wells have been exhausted, and others have been tainted with seawater, limiting their future use. The situation is only expected to worsen with the continued growth of Israel's population.[41]

Water scarcity in Israel and elsewhere has implications for violence, especially since many water resources (especially rivers) are transnational, meaning that a scarce resource is shared by many states with potentially differing claims and needs. Israel, for example, moved to protect its water resources by limiting water use by Jewish settlers and Arabs alike on the West Bank (see figure 6.2). With Arabs receiving far less water than their Jewish counterparts, the limits were far from equitable. The number and

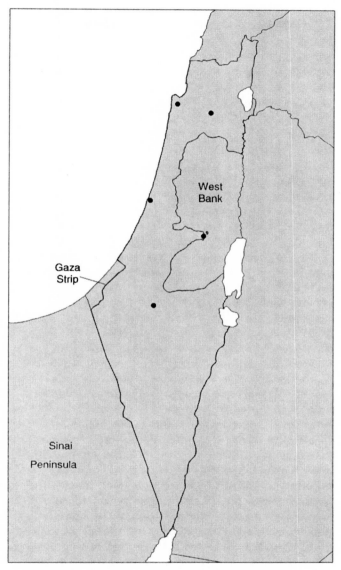

Figure 6.2.   **Israel.** *Source:* **Map courtesy of Roger Stump.**

depth of new Arab wells was also limited, resulting in a reduction in the amount of agricultural land irrigated by Arab farmers. Abandoning the land for lack of water, Arab farmers were forced to rely on day labor or move into crowded cities in the West Bank or Gaza. Although the links and processes that have generated unrest within the occupied territories are complex and reflect multiple social, religious, political, and economic factors, it seems reasonable to assume that water scarcity and its economic implications have contributed to violence in these areas. Some critics have asserted that water has been a cornerstone of the Israeli political and military agenda. While moving to create a security zone to protect northern Israel, Israel invaded southern Lebanon in 1982, placing the waters of the Litani River within Israel's borders for the duration of the occupation. Nor is the possibility of securing water rights through military actions far-fetched since there have been repeated calls, some dating back as far as 1919, to make the Litani the border of a new Jewish state.[42] In short, while water is a renewable resource, its increasing scarcity threatens the livelihoods and ultimately the security of groups and states within the region.

Similar pressures are felt in Central Asia, where Uzbekistan, Turkmenistan, Kazakhstan, Tajikistan, and Kyrgyzstan compete for the limited resources of the Amu and Syr rivers. The government of the former Soviet Union dammed and diverted the rivers, turning an arid desert into a huge cotton-growing region.[43] Since the collapse of the Soviet Union, competing rivalries between the five countries, capitalism, and waste have all but destroyed the system, leading to water shortages and increasing salinization of cropland. In addition, regional total fertility rates exceed 2.1, and the population growth rate is 15 percent per decade, meaning that governments face the challenge of providing more food and employment, even as the water is spread more thinly across the region. As these areas are already ruled by oppressive governments and dealing with Islamic insurgencies, some regional observers suggest that without better use of the water, economic and social crises, perhaps even open war, are not far off.[44]

Cropland scarcity is another issue, one already arising in diverse locations such as Chiapas, Haiti, the Philippines, and Bangladesh. When it was first colonized, Haiti was heavily forested. Since then, logging for commercial activities, as well as fuelwood, has dramatically reduced forest cover, with less than 2 percent of the forest remaining;[45] poor economic institutions and slow economic growth have perpetuated this process. With the loss of the protective forest cover, soil erosion has increased, and UN estimates show that a majority of the farmland is now permanently lost or degraded. In the poorest country in the Western Hemisphere, poor land-management policies and the farming of hillsides, together with fragmented and small land holdings, have reinforced deforestation and erosion. Peasants have tried to augment their small incomes by using wood for charcoal production, and the army, which has benefited from high fuel-wood prices, has ripped up seedlings, further contributing to deforestation. The government has also played a key role through its failure to provide capital for agricultural improvement.

Canada's Atlantic cod fishery provides another example of the depletion of a renewable resource to the point where its future is questionable. Once dominated by small, individual fishers and so plentiful that fishers only had to drop a bucket into the water, the fishery was self-sustaining. Improved technology, including the introduction of offshore trawlers and factory ships, allowed increased catches of cod beyond a level that the fishery could support. While the cod fishery fell victim to overfishing, it also lacked awareness of the threshold or sustainability of the industry, as well as ignorance of the reproductive cycle of the codfish and an inability to forecast stock sizes correctly. Although the Canadian government has continuously (and perhaps optimistically) argued that the cod fishery will be reopened, fish stocks have not recovered since the moratorium was first imposed in 1992, and there is speculation that it has been irreparably damaged and will never again support the same level of fishing and employment that it did in the past.[46]

The Atlantic cod fishery is not unique, with depletion or degradation of fishing stocks occurring on a variety of spatial scales due to exploitation, eutrophication, pollution, or the destruction of nursery grounds. On the local scale, dams, the discharge of pollutants, and siltation have reduced the potential of fisheries. The construction of a dam on India's Naramda River will likely eliminate coastal fisheries by the mouth of the river and cause permanent damage upstream due to the loss of forests, cropland, and biodiversity.[47] The UNFAO noted in 1997 that a majority of the world's fishing stocks have been depleted, exploited, or overexploited, with over 69 percent of stocks in need of urgent management.[48] Similarly, a 2003 report in *Nature* argued that large predatory fish biomass is only 10 percent of preindustrial levels, with declines observed in all geographic areas.[49] Over both the short and long terms, the situation is not sustainable and will exact ecologic and economic damage if not corrected. At the same time, millions are dependent on fishing to provide economic and food security.[50]

It is now generally acknowledged that population growth has a deleterious effect on renewable resources. Therefore, while resources such as fish stocks, soil, and water are all technically renewable, an increasing human population and per capita consumption have removed the word "renewable" from label through degradation and overtaxation. In many parts of the world, scarcities of these resources are appearing. With approximately half of the world's population relying on local renewable resources for some aspect of day-to-day living, these scarcities have an immediate impact on the well-being of a large number of people. Millions are already directly affected by the depletion and degradation of cropland, water, fuelwood, and fishing stocks. Optimists would argue that these issues can be corrected through technology, input substitution, properly functioning markets, or democracy. Input substitution does not necessary offer alternatives. For instance, water is a difficult (if not impossible) resource to substitute, meaning that technology must be relied on to "fix" the problem. This perhaps can be accomplished through appropriate wastewater treatment, desalinization, or efficient irrigation technologies, but implementing these fixes is often prohibitively costly. Desalinization, for example, is an expensive and energy-intensive option. Capturing and treating polluted water (including surface runoff and industrial and domestic water sources) is also expensive. Other tactics, such as market reform, improved irrigation technology, and conservation techniques, are available but may not remove the underlying problem of resource scarcity in the face of a growing population. Instead, such technologies may merely postpone resource scarcity. As discussed earlier in this chapter, it is also important to realize that the ability to generate solutions and overcome problems may not be available in many cases.

EMERGENT THEMES AND ISSUES

The position of neo-Malthusians, often referred to as **doomsters**, contrasts with that of economic optimists, or **boomsters**. Intuitively, we can find relationships between population growth, resource use, and environmental scarcity. For example, in regions where population growth is high, resources like food, fuel, and water are often scarce, and the risk of environmental degradation is increased; we need look no further than Haiti for confirmation. But these relationships are not exact. In fact, the linkages between population growth, the environment, and resources are sketchy at best.[51] However, even if the most alarmist predictions are discounted, most commentators now believe that population growth slows economic growth and multiplies the damage created by other problems. That is, it is difficult not to conclude that population growth exacerbates land degradation and that resource depletion promotes violence and conflict, placing pressure on institutions and governments. This is not to say that population growth is solely responsible for these problems. Environmental degradation, for example, is not just a function of the number of people, but how much and what they consume and how that consumption damages the environment. Nevertheless, population growth is an issue.

The not-so-trivial question that both neo-Malthusians and economic optimists consider is whether the world can provide sufficient food, water, and other resources to the existing population, in addition to the eighty million that are born each year, at the same time that the standard of living is increasing, necessarily raising the consumption of resources. Given the record of increasing agricultural production over the past fifty years, a number of commentators have proclaimed that food shortages have been largely solved.[52] A recently released UNFAO report, for example, concludes that agricultural output will continue to grow more quickly than the world population over the next two to three decades.[53] Even as the report cautioned that in several areas of the world, including portions of Asia, the potential for further agriculture is exhausted, it concluded that a population of 8.9 billion could be fed. Most of the increase in food production would come from multicropping and improvements in inputs and technology (e.g., irrigation, aquaculture, and the application of pesticides and herbicides), particularly in the developing world, along with the addition of some cultivatable cropland.[54] Assuming that there is modest increase in agricultural output through biotechnology and genetic engineering and that future population predictions are reasonably correct (the Population Reference Bureau estimates a continued slowing of population growth over the next five decades, with a total population of 9.0 billion by 2050), the world might just squeak through. Additional improvements in storage and distribution would also help alleviate the problem.

Yet, it remains unclear whether the world can feed its growing population, both now and in the future, and the UNFAO's rosy speculation may be premature.[55] Food production might continue to grow faster than the population, and the world will likely be able to feed a much larger population, but it may yet have difficulty feeding its population given various restrictions on or barriers to ensuring equitable access to food resources. At the risk of invoking the neo-Malthusian responses criticized earlier, we must realize that critical resources, including "renewable" resources such as land, water, and fish, are finite. Their degradation or depletion has lead to continued uncertainty about our ability to provide for both the current and future populations, particularly if society wishes to improve the standard of living of the majority of the world's population. At some point, it is likely that humanity will simply exhaust earth's capacity to produce, particularly as the world's standard of living improves, a finding voiced by the World Wildlife Foundation in its annual *Living Planet* report and based on the concept of our **ecological footprint**.[56] The geographer Vaclav Smil, for example, estimates that we would have already exceeded the **carrying capacity** of the earth if all six billion people were fed a diet similar to that of the average American.[57] Fortunately, Americans tend to be overfed, the American diet is wasteful, and there are global inefficiencies in the way food is produced, distributed, and consumed. Correcting these inefficiencies and altering the diet, for example, by decreasing or removing animal protein (which tend to be less efficient users of agricultural resources in that they require food inputs themselves), Smil estimated that a population of 8.4 billion could be supported, requiring no new land for cultivation and no new technologies to increase agricultural output dramatically.

While dietary changes are possible, they are unlikely, meaning that the world must look to remove inefficiencies in storage and distribution, as well as to increase crop yields, in order to ensure an adequate food supply in the future. Such expectations are also problematic. Despite the green revolution, it is unrealistic to expect future increases in crop yields and agricultural output similar to those observed during its peak. In fact, declining rates of growth in agricultural output and increasingly marginal returns on the application of additional inputs, such as fertilizers, have recently been observed: the green revolution is ending. Concerns are also being raised that new patent restrictions in agriculture and biotechnology are limiting the free exchange of seeds and technology.[58] The implication is that research into crop improvements has been delayed or abandoned, and new developments may not be introduced into widespread use quickly because of patent restrictions. If biotechnology or gene research ultimately yields advances, their large-scale application could be decades away. At the same time as private investment is increasing, growth in government spending on agricultural research, which has traditionally provided a large proportion of agricultural advances, has slowed. Worldwide, the amount of arable land has decreased 42 percent from 0.45 hectares per person in 1961–1963 to 0.21 hectares in 2002,[59] with increasing amounts of cropland lost to nonagricultural uses through urbanization or industrialization.[60] While erosion of the amount of cropland per capita does not mean decreasing output or decreasing ability to coax food out of the ground, there are long-term problems. Average figures of the amount of cropland or food resources, for example, are misleading since inequalities frequently mean weaker or marginal groups will be subjected to greater scarcities than revealed by averages. Similarly, there may be long-term problems of maintaining the productivity of irrigated cropland as water becomes scarce or soils become saline. Loss of topsoil through erosion and the movement of people up the food chain cast further doubt on our long-term ability to feed the world's population, while the effects of global warming remain unknown. More generally, the problems of feeding, providing shelter and employment, and improving standards of living will have just begun. Importantly, however, the ability to support a population in excess of eight billion does not imply sustainability over longer terms.

What of the broader resource and economic issues? Can the same logic be extended to include the impact of a growing population and increasing consumption on other resources? Are current levels of resource consumption sustainable? The emerging consensus is that rapid population growth and high young **dependency ratios** relative to the labor force reduce economic growth by increasing poverty and underemployment, weakening investment in human and physical assets (i.e., education, institutions, family planning, household savings), decreasing ingenuity, and degrading resources. Worse, rapid population growth and poor economic growth appear to be self-reinforcing, making it exceedingly difficult for countries to pull themselves out of this downward spiral given the lack of well-developed institutions in many of the poorest countries. Although rates of poverty have shown some improvement in areas recently, the number of countries that the United Nations defines as "**least developed**"—those with incomes less than US$900 per year and little investment in health, nutrition, and education—nearly doubled from twenty-five to forty-nine between 1991 and 2001, despite decades of global economic growth and development aid.[61] More than half of the population of 630 million in these countries, predominantly found in sub-Saharan Africa and Asia, but also in Haiti, lives on less than US$1 a day, and aid money to these countries has dropped by 45 percent since 1990. With rapid population growth and average per capita incomes less than they were two decades ago, sub-Saharan Africa has been hit particularly hard.

Expressing hope for the future of sub-Saharan Africa, Richard P. Cincotta and Robert Engelman note that health and economic indicators in the region are remarkably similar to those observed in Southeast Asian countries in the 1950s, just prior to the boom that transformed their economies.[62] In Asia, slower population growth created opportunities for sustained economic growth. Applying this same logic to sub-Saharan Africa is problematic, given the lack of investment, poor institutions, unstable governments, poor health, and HIV/AIDS epidemic. Slowing population growth in sub-Saharan Africa cannot solve all the problems related to economic growth, resource scarcity, environmental degradation, or violence, but it can contribute to their solution. The best hope for solving many of these problems lies in early intervention: act early and act quickly. Programs targeting the prevention of resource scarcities and population growth and fostering economic development will be more effective now than after the fact. In other words, the world should not be forced to adapt to a scarcity but rather should prepare for it. For sub-Saharan Africa and other regions, this means that attention is required on a number of fronts, including market reform to remove institutional biases or limitations, externally generated public and private investment, increased education and literacy (particularly among women), and continued investments in family-planning services.[63] Perhaps then countries will be able to generate the necessary ingenuity and momentum to overcome barriers to growth and to extract themselves from economic stagnation. Pinning hopes on just one or two options is not sufficient. Indeed, there is no magic bullet for the problems of population growth, economic stagnation, or resource scarcity.

Many of the potential solutions are also problematic. Slowing population growth is a difficult but worthwhile long-term pursuit. Technology, ingenuity, resource substitution, and free markets offer solutions commonly espoused by economic optimists. Yet, the value or applicability of such concepts may be limited. Input substitution does not necessarily offer alternatives, particularly if the alternative is scarce itself or prohibitively expensive. Ingenuity and technical fixes that allow populations or countries to overcome Malthusian limits are also possible. However, as Homer-Dixon has argued, ingenuity is not without cost or ubiquitous itself; instead, ingenuity is fostered in locations where resources like time and capital are abundant. These may not be available in many poor developing countries and cannot simply be provided through free markets or democracy. Markets and other institutions may be poorly developed, and resources may not be correctly priced to reflect their scarcity. If the ability to generate ingenuity is missing, countries may face an ingenuity gap, and their ability to respond to resource limits or other threats will be diminished.

As chapter 7 discusses in detail, the available evidence also suggests that population growth and its impact on resource scarcities, especially of critical resources such as cropland or water, contribute to violence. This should not be taken to mean that they cause wars or violence but rather that they contribute to social stress and stimulate ethnic violence within populations. In countries faced with a gap between their requirement for ingenuity and ability to generate it, social disruption and environmental degradation are likely to occur. Although marginalized groups will tend to be the most affected, gaps may result in the undermining of agricultural or economic productivity and mass population migrations. There is a potential then for the competency and legitimacy of governments to be questioned or undermined, leading to increased conflict. In turn, conflict or civil disobedience will further erode societies' ability to supply ingenuity and solve resource issues as human and financial capital will flee, reinforcing the crisis.[64] Rather than "haves" and "have-nots" or "developed" and "developing" worlds, Homer-Dixon argues, there may be an increasing division between societies that can generate ingenuity and those that cannot. Resource scarcities will therefore be local and regional, occurring within countries that are unable to generate sufficient ingenuity to adapt to changing environments.

To complicate matters, scarcity of resources will affect the world with greater severity, speed, and scale, meaning that effects will not be confined to a spatially small area. Instead, effects will be regional (e.g., water scarcity), perhaps even global. Violence and civil unrest will not be felt in the developing world alone. Instead, their consequences will ripple across the globe, promoting (among other things) international migration, the displacement of populations, and the destabilization of governments, threatening trade relations and economic development, and inducing further environmental degradation. While many scarcities and environmental problems are observable now, the effects of global warming or ozone depletion are long term, large scale, and not completely understood, becoming a wildcard in the population debate. Although a growing consensus now agrees that global warming is occurring and will result in an increase in temperature of between 1°C and 3°C over the next hundred years, the implications of warming are relatively unknown. There is the very real possibility that global warming will exacerbate environmental scarcities by shifting precipitation patterns, altering growing seasons, and causing coastal flooding or more extreme weather events. These changes are likely to affect agricultural production worldwide, the effects of which may be multiplied if other resources, such as cropland or water supplies, are degraded or depleted.

Finally, this chapter has argued that either resource scarcities prompt actors to secure the resources in question or they prompt the ingenuity that allows a society to adapt. A third possibility, and one that Homer-Dixon does not really consider, is that scarce resources may also become a bargaining chip within peace processes, equal to or greater than land and territory, which have frequently been a part of previous peace agreements. Indeed, water has figured in peace treaties in the Middle East. With the signing of the peace accord between Israel and the Palestine Liberation Organization (PLO) in 1995, Israel pledged to increase the Palestinians' share of West Bank water as well as to search for new sources.[65] In a 1994 agreement with Jordan, Israel was to increase the diversion of water from the Jordan River to benefit Jordan. Previously, the water that Jordan received from the river was far below the country's allocation. In addition, both sides agreed to build dams on the Yarmouk and Jordan rivers to boost water supplies. The anticipated benefits and payoffs of these peace agreements remain a distant hope. Indeed, the peace agreement between Israel and the PLO has largely broken down, and restrictions on water supplies remain. Nevertheless, water and other scarce resources have the potential to become a source of cooperation rather than antagonism and conflict.

NOTES

1. Thomas Robert Malthus, *An Essay on the Principle of Population*, in *Perspectives on Population*, ed. Scott W. Menard and Elizabeth W. Moen, 74–77 (New York: Oxford University Press, 1987).

2. Based on 2000–2002 data, drawn from the UNFAO website at www.fao .org/sof/sofi/index_en.htm (accessed July 26, 2005). See also William Bender and Margaret Smith, "Population, Food, and Nutrition," *Population Bulletin* 51, no. 4 (February 1997).

3. Bender and Smith, "Population, Food, and Nutrition"; Paul Ehrlich, Anne H. Ehrlich, and Gretchen Daily, "Food Security, Population, and Environment," *Population and Development Review* 19, no. 1 (1993): 1–32; Robert Livernash and Eric Rodenburg, "Population Change, Resources, and the Environment," *Population Bulletin* 53, no. 1 (March 1998).

4. Frances Lappe and Joseph Collins, *Food First* (Boston: Houghton Mifflin, 1977).

5. Digby J. McLaren, "Population and the Utopian Myth," *Ecodecision* 21 (June 1993): 59–63.

6. See, for example, Ehrlich, Erlich, and Daily, "Food Security."

7. In particular, the popular press and green movement have adopted neo-Malthusian perspectives, while the viewpoints of economic optimists inform the governments of most developed nations and are reflected in the policies of the World Bank.

8. In his original writings, Malthus did not believe in birth control. Neo-Malthusians are distinguished from true Malthusians in their belief that birth control can be used as a check against population growth.

9. Numerous authors have contributed to this debate. Among the most famous are Paul Ehrlich and Anne Erlich, *The Population Explosion* (New York: Touchstone, 1991).

10. Paul Ehrlich, *The Population Bomb* (New York: Ballantine Books, 1968).

11. Julian L. Simon, *The Ultimate Resource.* (Princeton, NJ: Princeton University Press, 1981).

12. Despite the fact that oil prices exceeded US$50 a barrel in 2005, gasoline prices remained lower than they were in 1973 after accounting for inflation. However, there are increasing concerns that major new discoveries of oil and natural gas are unlikely and that world reserves have peaked.

13. John Richard Hicks, *The Theory of Wages* (London: Macmillan, 1932).

14. Ester Boserup, *The Conditions of Agricultural Growth: The Economics of Agrarian Change under Population Pressure* (Chicago: Aldine, 1965).

15. Thomas Homer-Dixon, *Environment, Scarcity, and Violence* (Princeton, NJ: Princeton University Press, 1999). Much of the following discussion is derived from Homer-Dixon's writing.

16. See, for example, Wallace Broecker, "Unpleasant Surprises in the Greenhouse?" *Nature* 328, no. 6126 (July 9, 1987): 123–26; William Clark, *On the Practical Implications of the Carbon Dioxide Question* (Laxenburg, Austria: International Institute of Applied Systems Analysis, 1985).

17. Cornelia Dean, "To Save Its Canal, Panama Fights for Its Forests," *New York Times*, May 24, 2005, 1S.

18. Thomas Homer-Dixon, *The Ingenuity Gap* (Toronto: Alfred Knopf, 2000).

19. Simon, *The Ultimate Resource.*

20. Thomas Homer-Dixon, *Environment, Scarcity, and Violence.* See also Lynda Hurst, "The Global Guru," *Toronto Star*, July 19, 1995, 1C. The U.S. government has pushed democracy on Middle Eastern nations, although progress has been slow. Saudi Arabia has held free elections, but critics suggest that this is merely window dressing to satisfy Washington.

21. Homer-Dixon, *The Ingenuity Gap.*

22. Homer-Dixon, *Environment.*

23. Jane Menken, "Demographic-Economic Relationships and Development," in *Population—the Complex Reality: A Report of the Population Summit of the World's Scientific Academies,* ed. Francis Graham-Smith, 123–54 (Golden, CO: North American Press, 1994).

24. John R. Weeks, *Population: An Introduction to Concepts and Issues,* 7th ed. (Belmont, CA: Wadsworth, 1999).

25. Ester Boserup, *Population and Technological Change: A Study of Long-Term Trends* (Chicago: University of Chicago Press, 1981); Boserup, *The Conditions of Agricultural Growth.*

26. National Research Council, Committee on Population, *Population Growth and Economic Development: Policy Questions* (Washington, DC: National Academy Press, 1986).

27. Richard P. Cincotta and Robert Engelman, *Economics and Rapid Change: The Influence of Population Growth* (Washington, DC: Population Action International, 1997).

28. Allen C. Kelley and Robert M. Schmidt, *Population and Income Change: Recent Evidence* (Washington, DC: World Bank, 1994).

29. Edward M. Crenshaw, Ansari Z. Ameen, and Matthew Christenson, "Population Dynamics and Economic Development: Age-Specific Population Growth Rates and Economic Growth in Developing Countries, 1965 to 1990," *American Sociological Review* 62, no. 6 (1997): 974–84.

30. Cincotta and Engelman, *Economics and Rapid Change.*

31. See, for example, Kenneth H. Kang, "Why Did Koreans Save So 'Little' and Why Do They Now Save So 'Much,'" *International Economic Journal* 8, no. 4 (1994): 99–111. See also World Bank, *The East Asian Miracle* (Oxford: University of Oxford Press, 1993).

32. Allen C. Kelley, "The Consequences of Rapid Population Growth on Human Resource Development: The Case of Education," in *The Impact of Population Growth on Well-Being in Developing Countries,* ed. Dennis Ahlburg, Allen C. Kelley, and Karen Oppenheim Mason, 67–137 (New York: Springer, 1996); T. Paul Schultz, "School Expenditures and Enrollments, 1960–1980: The Effects of Incomes, Prices and Population Growth," in *Population Growth and Economic Development: Issues and Evidence,* ed. D. Gale Johnson and Ronald D. Lee, 413–36 (Madison: University of Wisconsin Press, 1985).

33. Cincotta and Engelman, *Economics and Rapid Change.*

34. Cincotta and Engelman, *Economics and Rapid Change.*

35. United Nations Development Program (UNDP), *Human Development Report 2000* (New York: UNDP, 2000).

36. Homer-Dixon, *Environment.*

37. While they support lush rain forests, the soils themselves are poor and thin. The transformation of forests for agricultural uses, such as growing crops or grazing, is not sustainable over the long term and may only support a family for a few years before it is forced to relocate and repeat the process, pushing deeper into the rain forest.

38. Lester R. Brown, *Who Will Feed China? Wake-up Call for a Small Planet* (New York: W. W. Norton, 1995). See also Lester Brown, "Averting a Global Food Crisis," *Technology Review* (November/December 1995): 44–53.

39. Lester R. Brown, *Outgrowing the Earth* (New York: Norton, 2004).

40. Alanna Mitchell, "The World's 'Single Biggest Threat,' " *Globe and Mail*, June 4, 2001, 8A–9A. Shortages are compounded by access to safe drinking water. In 2005, more than one billion people lacked access to safe drinking water, and polluted water contributed to the death of about fifteen million children under the age of five. William J. Broad, "With a Push from the UN, Water Reveals Its Secrets," *New York Times*, June 25, 2005, 1S.

41. Hussein Amery and Aaron T. Wolf, *Water in the Middle East: A Geography of Conflict* (Austin: University of Texas Press, 2000).

42. Terje Tvedt, "The Struggle for Water in the Middle East," *Canadian Journal of Development Studies* 13, no. 1 (1992): 13–33.

43. In doing so, it also largely drained the Aral Sea, once the world's sixth-largest inland ocean, causing a huge environmental disaster.

44. For a geographical perspective, see Sara O'Hara, "Central Asia's Water Resources: Contemporary and Future Management Issues," *International Journal of Water Resource Development* 16 (2000): 423–41; Sara O'Hara, "Lessons from the Past: Water Management in Central Asia," *Water Policy* 2 (2000): 365–84; Philip Micklin, *Managing Water in Central Asia* (Washington, DC: Brookings Institute, 2000).

45. Laurence Lewis and William Coffey, "The Continuing Deforestation of Haiti," *Ambio* 14, no. 3 (1985): 158–60.

46. See http://cbc.ca/cgi-bin/templates/view.cgi?category=Canada&story=/news/2001/04/10/cod_stocks010410 (accessed June 14, 2005). The Canadian Fisheries Resource Conservation Council (FRCC) has been charged with oversight of the cod stocks. See www.dfo-mpo.gc.ca/frcc (accessed June 14, 2005).

47. Bradford W. Morse and Thomas R. Berger, executive summary of "Sardar Sarovar Projects: Independent Review," *STEPS Quarterly* 2, nos. 3 and 4 (1992): 28–34.

48. See the UNFAO website at www.fao.org/documents/show_cdr.asp?url_file=/docrep/003/w4248e/w4248e00.htm (accessed June 14, 2005).

49. The industrialization of the fishing fleet has aided in the overfishing of large fish. Even as staples like cod, tuna, and marlin have been depleted, so have other less popular fishes. Moreover, commercial fishing is able to reduce community biomass within fifteen years of the exploitation of a particular species. See Ransom A. Myers and Boris Worm, "Rapid Worldwide Depletion of Predatory Fish Communities," *Nature* (May 2003): 280–83.

50. See the UNFAO website at www.fao.org/newsroom/en/news/2005/102911/index.html (accessed June 14, 2005).

51. For an up-to-date review, see Roger-Mark De Souza, John S. Williams, and Frederick A. B. Meyerson, "Critical Links: Population, Health and the Environment," *Population Bulletin* 58, no. 3 (September 2003).

52. The UNFAO has essentially proclaimed that food shortages are no longer of concern. See also Andrew Pollack, "The Green Revolution Yields to the Bottom Line," *New York Times*, May 15, 2001, 1D; Andrew Pollack, "Changing Times Challenge World Hunger Organization," *New York Times*, May 15, 2001, 2D.

53. UNFAO, *Agriculture: Towards 2015/2030, Technical Interim Report* (New York: United Nations, April 2000). Excerpts from this report can be found at www.fao .org/ag/magazine/0012sp1.htm (accessed June 14, 2005).

54. The report used a generous definition of the potential for cultivation. The most productive agricultural land is already under production. For the remaining "cultivatable" land, portions were defined as marginal or ecologically sensitive. Expansion runs the risk of accelerating land degradation. Land availability in South America and Africa, the two regions with the largest potential for increased cropland, are far from markets. Developing this land requires infrastructure.

55. John Bongaarts, "Can the Growing Human Population Feed Itself?" *Scientific American* 270, no. 3 (March 1994): 36–42.

56. World Wildlife Foundation, *Living Planet Report, 2004,*" Gland, Switzerland: WWF 2004.

57. Vaclav Smil, "How Many People Can the Earth Feed?" *Population and Development Review* 20, no. 2 (1994): 225–92.

58. Pollack, "The Green Revolution Yields," 1D; Pollack, "Changing Times" 2D.

59. UNFAO, FAOSTAT data, 2005, at http://faostat.fao.org/faostat/collections? subset=agriculture (accessed June 14, 2005).

60. One U.S. estimate placed amount of cropland lost each year equal to the size of Connecticut. Between 1970 and 1990, the population of the Chicago Census Metropolitan Statistical Area (CMSA) grew by just over 4 percent, but the amount of land consumed by the urban region grew by over 50 percent, with most lost to low-density urban sprawl, including transportation routes and growth along the periphery in "edge cities." Once this land is lost or "paved over," it is very difficult to recover.

61. Constant Brand, "Poor Countries Demand More Help, Trade from Rich," *Globe and Mail*, May 15, 2001, 12A. Poverty statistics are available through the World Bank at www.worldbank.org (accessed July 28, 2005).

62. UNDP, *Human Development Report 2000.*

63. Cincotta and Engelman, *Economics and Rapid Change*, 1997.

64. Although violence and decreasing capital investment may provide a sufficiently strong impetus to leave, the departure of countries' best and brightest does not occur only under these conditions. Instead, the best and brightest are wooed to other countries by promises of higher pay and higher standards of living.

65. Serge Schmemann, "Israel and PLO Reach Accord to Transfer West Bank Areas," *New York Times*, September 25, 1995, 1A.

7

The Potential for Conflict

In his 1994 article "The Coming Anarchy," journalist Robert Kaplan paints a dire picture of the world's future in which peripheral states, robbed of their economic power by globalization, poor leadership, and environmental decay, disintegrate into smaller units defined by ethnicity or culture and ruled by warlords and private armies.[1] Kaplan held out Africa and its seemingly endless list of war-ravaged countries, including Rwanda, Burundi, Sierra Leone, Angola, Sudan, and Ethiopia, as symbolizing the decay of the current world order, having already succumbed to environmental and demographic distress, leading to the breakdown of traditional civil government. Violence and conflict have become the norm.

While perhaps sensationalized, the basic question Kaplan's article asks is whether resource scarcity can prompt conflict. A short answer would be yes, with conflict potentially arising from scarcities of, and disputes over, cropland, water, forests, and other resources, which are themselves underlain by population issues. Resource scarcity may have harmful social effects, including constrained economic or agricultural production, migration, segmentation of society along ethnic or religious lines, and the disintegration of social institutions, all of which can lead to conflict.[2] Effects are regularly linked causally, oftentimes with some feedback measure that tends to reinforce the initial negative consequences such that resource capture arising from scarcity may induce further environmental degradation or greater scarcity of the resource.

Previous chapters have discussed demographic events, such as fertility, mortality, and immigration, and their outcomes. It is understood, for instance, that below-replacement fertility leads to an aging population. Likewise, it is relatively simple to forecast the demographic implications of HIV/AIDS in sub-Saharan Africa. Indeed, projections of decreased life expectancies and slowing economic growth are already visible in many countries in the region. While this chapter highlights how and why population growth could lead to conflict, forecasting the implications of population growth is a bit like gazing into a crystal ball. Resource scarcities generally do not cause conflict, but they can stimulate it by exacerbating underlying ethnic unrest, creating societal stress, or interacting with other contextual effects, including the physical setting and political and social structures. Although the predictions are becoming clearer as the subject generates greater interest, the best we can do is learn from existing conflicts, recognize the problems a growing population creates, and project the implications for the coming years.

POPULATION, RESOURCE SCARCITY, AND CONFLICT

Although the effects of resource scarcity are still poorly understood, there is a strong possibility, and a growing body of evidence, that they will impact social stability and ultimately underlie conflict. This is an intuition, however, and questions remain as to what the exact relationship between these elements is and how it works. How, for example, does resource scarcity contribute to conflict? Most likely, it does so through a complex of interactions. Given that continued population growth and scarcities of renewable resources caused by depletion or degradation are relatively certain in the coming decades, it is reasonable to suppose that supply, demand, or structural scarcities could result in negative social effects, including reduced agricultural and economic output, migration and displacement, **social segmentation**, and institutional disruption. In turn, each of these could, independently or collaboratively, induce conflict.[3] In addition, resource scarcity can produce resource capture when actors seek to change the distribution of resources in their favor owing to a decline in the quality or quantity of a resource, leading to the ecological marginalization of weak groups. Both processes further environmental degradation, reinforce poverty, and increase the potential for conflict as groups seek to control resources or address imbalances in their distribution. Resource scarcity is particularly problematic in the developing world, which relies heavily on local resources for day-to-day survival. Even now, many developing countries face a bleak future resulting from large-scale demographic, environmental, economic, and societal stresses.

Resource Scarcity and Negative Social Effects

On their own, population growth and resource scarcity are unlikely to trigger conflict directly. Instead, a series of mediating social effects, including reduced agricultural and economic output, migration and displacement, social segmentation, and the disruption of institutions, independently or in tandem, have the potential to induce social stress and conflict. Of these effects, reduced agricultural output associated with resource scarcity may be the most problematic. Despite the impact of the green revolution and agricultural advances observed over the last decades of the twentieth century, per capita agricultural output has dropped in many African, Latin American, and Asian countries. At the same time, growth rates for agricultural yields have been declining, as we have reached the limits of benefits to be derived from the green revolution, foreshadowing a declining potential for dramatic increases in agricultural output. Likewise, advances through biotechnology or genetic engineering are likely decades away, if they ever reach the market. Poor food-distribution networks, insufficient knowledge of sustainable agricultural techniques, poor institutions, inequitable land distribution, conflict, and poverty compound wide disparities in food availability. Ultimately, for those facing land and water scarcities and poor institutions, agricultural output will decrease. The poor and marginalized, who derive much of their income from the land or have relatively little to spend on foodstuffs, will be affected most.

Increased resource scarcities can also reduce economic productivity, with economic productivity closely aligned with agricultural productivity since many developing countries are highly dependent on agriculture for income generation, economic growth, and stability. A number of resource scarcities could affect economic production, including a shortage of water, limiting not only agricultural productivity but also industrial production. In Gaza, Israel, the overpumping of coastal aquifers has resulted in their increased salinization, which is in turn associated with adverse health effects, as well as declining quality and yields associated with agricultural production as cropland becomes increasingly saline. While resource scarcity will generally constrain local or national economic development, these constraints will also widen the gap between the elite of a society, who are able to take advantage of the opportunities created by resource scarcity, and the less-advantaged portion of society through resource capture and ecological marginalization.

Economic or ecological marginalization may prompt migration or population displacement, including the forced relocation of populations, creating what some authors have called "environmental refugees," a label that implies that resource scarcity is directly responsible for their relocation.[4] Rather than a direct cause of displacement, however, resource scarcity is only a partial motivator. Instead, population relocation is a function of both "push" and "pull" factors.[5] Migrants, including Haitians and Bangladeshis (see the later discussion in this chapter in the section titled "Group-Identity Conflict"), are motivated by income opportunities in potential destinations, with resource scarcities or lack of economic opportunities contributing to the decision to move. If large-scale population displacement occurs, migration may aggravate divisions within a society among religious, ethnic, or linguistic groups. This social segmentation encourages competition among groups for control of resources and sharpens the distinction between winners and losers. Scarcity also produces insularity as groups work to protect their own interests, reducing social interaction. Ultimately, social segmentation erodes civil society and the network of nongovernmental organizations and associations that mediate between the state and individuals, impeding the society's ability to function cooperatively by reducing the availability of protective social capital within a society.

Together, these effects are able to disrupt the state and its legislative, judicial, military, and banking institutions in a complex, frequently self-reinforcing process. Mass migrations, for example, can disrupt local power structures and labor markets, as well as alter the relationship between ethnic or other groups. Likewise, social segmentation can result in competition between groups for scarce resources, prevent new institutions from developing, or limit the ability of institutions to respond to changing needs. By weakening the state and its institutions, resource scarcities limit the state's ability to generate and deliver social and technological ingenuity, which in turn reduces its national and international autonomy, engenders competition among elites over resources, and produces social segmentation as groups struggle for dominance and power. While complex, the process raises the possibility of conflict as power is shifted from the state to challenger groups.

Egypt provides a useful example of the linkages between these processes.[6] Confined to less than 3 percent of the country's territory, Egypt's population of seventy-four million is strung out along the Nile River. Heavily dependent on its waters, Egypt has been taxed economically by population growth (the total fertility rate remains greater than 3.0, and the country's population will double in approximately thirty-five years under current conditions), contributing to low-level, but ongoing, conflict between Muslim fundamentalists and the more secular government. Egypt's weak economic position, along with local scarcities of land and water,[7] has reduced its ability to pursue economic and agricultural development, making it unable to provide institutions and services like health care and education for its population, reducing the reach and legitimacy of the state. As a result, the fundamentalist Muslim Brotherhood has stepped in, a group that has openly and violently challenged the authority of the Egyptian government.[8] Opposing Egypt's secular government, it has cultivated grassroots support by operating social institutions, such as schools, clinics, hospitals, and charities, providing otherwise unavailable services to the poor. Simultaneously, fundamentalist groups have sought to weaken Egypt's government by attacking tourist operations, a key income-generating industry, such as the July 2005 bombing of Red Sea resorts. Finally, differences in religious viewpoints have also promoted social segmentation as some of the more radical fundamentalist groups have isolated themselves from mainstream social and religious institutions. The development of fundamentalist views has placed increasing pressure on Coptic Christians, who, representing approximately 10 percent of the population, face discrimination.

The Nature of Resource Conflict

In the past, national and international conflicts have frequently been predicated on the territorial ambitions of governments and the concept of the nation-state.[9] In the twenty-first century, the nature of conflict will likely represent the new realities of resource scarcity and population growth, especially where local institutions are weakest, population growth is greatest, and resources are scarcest. Consequently, the number of conflicts linked to resource scarcity will likely increase in the coming decades, with the developing world at greatest risk. Having greater dependency on local resources for economic and agricultural production and prosperity, frequently lacking the financial resources to buffer themselves from the negative effects of resource scarcity, and having fragile institutions, they are also less able to adapt.

If the emergence of resource scarcity potentially leads to conflict, what types of conflict are most likely to occur? Thomas Homer-Dixon identified five potential types of conflict:[10]

- Disputes directly related to environmental degradation;
- Ethnic conflicts due to migration and population displacement caused by environmental scarcities;
- Civil disorder and conflict caused by environmental scarcity that affects economic productivity and livelihood and, in turn, people's economic livelihoods and governments' ability to meet new demands;
- Resource scarcity induced by wars between states; and
- Conflicts between the developed and developing worlds over resources and environmental issues.

Distillation of these five points, regardless of their spatial scale, means that population or resource-scarcity issues will increasingly underlie conflicts in the coming years. Of these five, Homer-Dixon discounted resource-scarcity conflicts between the developed and developing worlds as being relatively unlikely, limited by the military, technological, and financial advantages of the developed world. Likewise, he argued that disputes related directly to environmental degradation would produce little more than local, small-scale violence. Rather, the disputes more likely to occur—those over resource scarcity, group identity, and civil strife or insurgency—would occur in the developing world, where environmental scarcities would interact, contextualized by existing economic, cultural, political, or social factors, perhaps even reinforcing conflict and the decline of institutions.

In their simplest instances, resource conflicts are easily understood within the traditional paradigms of territory, power, and interstate relations, as states or other actors have commonly moved to secure nonrenewable resources like oil. Conflicts related to oil include the civil wars in Sudan and Angola, as well as Iraq's invasion of Kuwait in 1990, which was partially based on Iraq's desire to control major oil fields in the region.[11] With projections that known world oil supplies will likely peak within the next twenty years, oil is likely to remain a "prize" resource much fought over in the coming years.[12] This form of resource capture—the decreasing quality or quantity of a resource interacts with population growth and increasing consumption, encouraging groups to control that resource through trade or military conquest—can also be extended to renewable resources, such as cropland, forests, or fresh water.[13] Scarcities of some of these resources are increasing rapidly in places, leading to their potential seizure through military or other means, in the process marginalizing groups and increasing resource scarcity or degradation.

The distinction between conflicts related to renewable and nonrenewable resources is important. While we can attribute several conflicts, including the Gulf War, to the need to access oil or mineral resources, in fact relatively little evidence supports the notion that scarce renewable resources have caused interstate conflict. In part, the long payoff time to incorporate resources like forests or cropland does not translate quickly or easily into increased state power and influence. In contrast, states can quickly use resources like oil or diamonds to finance military operations or to expand industry, trade, and commerce. In addition, countries that depend heavily on renewables tend to be poor and, indeed, the very ones that do not have the military ability to attack their neighbors.

The exception might be fresh-water resources, which are critical for the survival of both individuals and the state. While water is a renewable resource, its increasing scarcity, due to not only consumption but degradation through pollution and salinization, threatens the livelihood and security of states, with the shortage termed "water vulnerability."[14] Rather than directly causing conflict, however, water scarcity tends to limit economic development, promote resource capture, or lead to social segmentation, which in turn produces violence. Moreover, its transnational character, with rivers or underground aquifers crossing state borders, means that one country's use and actions affect neighboring states. Various observers, including the United Nations,[15] have not missed the strategic importance of water. In 1995, the World Bank cautioned that wars in the coming century would be fought over water,[16] a statement that echoed an earlier prediction by Jordan's King Hussein in 1990, who declared that only water issues could incite a war between Jordan and Israel. Years earlier, Egypt's former president Anwar Sadat indicated that he was prepared to use force if Ethiopia blocked or reduced Egypt's access to waters from the Nile, while Ethiopia chided Egypt for placing water from the Nile on the negotiating table during peace negotiations between Egypt and Israel in 1976.[17] At other times, water in the Middle East has been described as more valuable than the oil pumped out of the ground. Still, conflict over scarce water resources is only valid in a limited number of circumstances where the downstream country is dependent on the water, and the upstream country restricts its flow. Similarly, conflict is only likely to occur when the water supply is essentially finite (i.e., has limited renewal), as it is in many Middle Eastern countries, so that an increasing population means a decreasing per capita supply.

Despite the constraints of downstream and upstream geography, there are multiple examples of water's ability to incite conflict. When water resources and the relationship between states are contextualized in terms of religious differences and historical animosities, such as those between Israel and its Arab neighbors or between Turkey and Syria, the potential for conflict between states is further increased (see figure 7.1). As discussed in chapter 6, water resources may have promoted Israel's military campaigns in southern Lebanon. Likewise, water has colored relations between Egypt, which is dependent on the Nile River for fresh water, and its upstream neighbor, Ethiopia. Relations between Turkey, Syria, and Iraq have also been strained by issues of control over and access to the Euphrates and Tigris rivers, with Turkey's Great Anatolia Project, a massive complex of dams and irrigation systems in eastern Turkey, promising to reduce the flow of the Euphrates significantly when it is completed. What water does reach Syria will be contaminated with runoff laden with fertilizer, pesticides, and salts. Syria is already short of water, and its population growth (2.4 percent, doubling in approximately twenty-nine years) complicates its need for water. Although Syria is weak relative to Turkey and therefore does not pose a likely military threat as a provoked downstream neighbor, these two countries have already exchanged threats over water resources. However, Syria has allegedly sanctioned Kurdish guerillas fighting the Turkish government for control of eastern Turkey for the creation of a Kurdish state, the same area in which the Great Anatolia Project is located.[18]

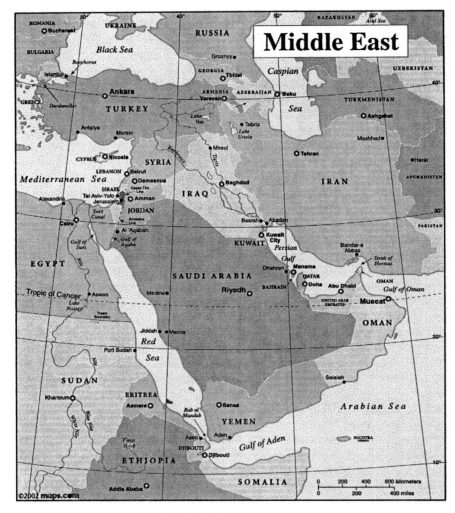

Figure 7.1.   Israel and Neighboring States. *Source:* Maps.com.

Elsewhere, water has been linked to conflict. South Africa's support of a coup in Lesotho in 1986 has been linked to its desire to divert water out of Lesotho and into South Africa.[19] Elsewhere, the Senegal, Zambezi, and Niger rivers all flow through several countries, with the Senegal River the focus of conflict between Mauritania and Senegal. In the Lake Chad basin in North Africa, geophysicists have warned of the shrinkage of Lake Chad.[20] Since the 1960s, it has shrunk by 95 percent, with irrigation and drought being the major causes. This loss of water in a region with a population of over seven hundred fifty thousand that continues to grow, even as the diminished water supply threatens fish stocks and crops, could result in increased tensions between the four countries (Nigeria, Niger, Cameroon, and Chad) that use the lake's water. Finally, the former Soviet republics of Uzbekistan, Turkmenistan, Kazakhstan, Tajikistan, and Kyrgyzstan are competing for water rights to the limited resources of the Amu and Syr rivers, as noted in chapter 6.

Group-Identity Conflict

Of the five potential sources for conflict identified by Homer-Dixon, group-identity conflicts involving religion, ethnicity, or nationalism may be the most common due to large-scale population movements caused by resource scarcity.[21] Discrimination, group status, access to limited resources, and other issues promote a sense of group identity at the same time that they result in social segmentation and cleavages within the society as leaders look to exploit these differences to increase their own political power. Two examples serve to illustrate group-identity conflict. First, the breakup of the former Republic of Yugoslavia can largely be attributed to the efforts of Slobodan Milošević, the former leader of Yugoslavia who mobilized Serb identity and nationalism by defending Serb ethnic and political interests. His actions, along with the general decline of the Yugoslav economy through the 1980s, largely shaped the disintegration of the federation, spawning multiple group-identity conflicts at various spatial scales between Serbs, Croats, Albanians, and Muslims. The movement of Kosovar Albanian refugees into Macedonia during the Kosovo war in 1999 (see chapter 5) raised tensions between Macedonians and ethnic Albanians and elevated the potential for armed conflict between the two groups. These fears were realized in the spring of 2001 when Albanian insurgents operating out of Kosovo sought to carve out an ethnic Albanian state by securing territory dominated by ethnic Albanians within Macedonia. The insurgency pressured the Macedonian government, placed the country on the brink of civil war, and strained the fragile peace between Serbs and Albanians.[22]

The situation in India, where the migration of an estimated twelve to seventeen million Bangladeshis into the Indian states of Assam, Tripura, and West Bengal has generated social segmentation and conflict, is also a good example.[23] Population growth in Bangladesh has contributed to increased (demand-induced) land scarcity,[24] pushing migrants out of the country. At the same time, better income potential and living conditions in India, along with a welcoming political environment that empowers immigrants, have attracted large numbers of cross-border migrants. Their arrival has produced significant changes in land distribution, and Bangladeshi immigrants have been accused of taking the best cropland, co-opting local politics, and altering economic relations in the destination states. Furthermore, in the context of colonialism and its vestiges, which altered the balance of political power in India and sensitized locals to the loss of political control, the immigrants' arrival ultimately triggered violence between the groups.

Insurgencies and Civil Strife

On smaller spatial scales, insurgencies and civil strife within states pose additional challenges to national security. Rooted in group-identity or resource-scarcity issues, rebellion and guerilla wars may be explained through traditional theories of grievance, deprivation, and opportunity to act on grievances.[25] If, for example, resource scarcities result in deprivation, perhaps reducing a group's economic opportunities will lead to an increase in the level of grievance. Given the opportunity to challenge the state and the current status quo, groups may resort to violence and confrontation to rectify the situation. The likelihood of civil strife is greatest when multiple pressures interact, advancing grievances and opportunity together by increasing social segmentation, weakening state institutions, and contributing to economic problems. As before, contextual factors, including leadership, degree of social segmentation (grievances will find a larger audience when shared by groups organized by identity), local concepts of justice, power structures (whether the deprived group speaks from a position of strength or weakness), and the pervasiveness of the problem, will alter the outcome.

Examples of the linkages between environmental scarcity and violence include the events in Chiapas, Mexico, and with the New Peoples Army (NPA) in the Philippines. In the Philippines, violence flared up in the 1980s and early 1990s in response to ecological marginalization and long-standing grievances against landowners and the government.[26] Desperation with the lack of economic opportunity in lowland agricultural or **urban** areas forced peasants into ecologically marginal upland areas to earn a living. There, soils were easily degraded and lost through erosion associated with poor agricultural practices (i.e., slash and burn), ignorance of appropriate practices, and uncertain land-tenure systems, which meant that they did not care for the land. Strict economic policies in the early 1980s further depressed incomes, increased unemployment, and encouraged migration into marginal areas as peasants sought to make a living. Their desperation eventually led to the peasants' finding a voice through the NPA.

Urbanization and Conflict

The worldwide growth of the urban population means that the potential for conflict arising from resource scarcity is also an urban problem, with large, dense, and poverty-stricken populations escalating the potential.[27] With the urban population expected to grow dramatically in the coming decades, the implications associated with the growth of large urban areas are enormous. Problems, including poverty, pollution, crime, class tension, and transportation, will reach scales never before seen. The situation is frequently worse in cities that have been strained by rapid population growth, little investment, and government ineptitude. Infrastructure systems, such as water, roads, or electricity, have decayed as governments have been unable to keep up with the demand posed by continued in-migration from rural areas and smaller centers. The magnitude of urban growth in the developing world has generated an intense and ongoing debate about whether the developing world can accommodate the anticipated growth of cities and whether there is a potential for conflict in areas with few resources and slow economic growth,[28] echoing the earlier discussion of limits to growth at the start of this chapter. Optimists claim that good governance, proper management, and investment can overcome population constraints, although these are themselves often in short supply. Others, following neo-Malthusian reasoning, are more concerned. Higher mortality, low standards of living, poor living environments, depletion of resources, and increasing poverty and inequality are all urban problems that could weaken the state.

In the developing world, urban migrants are typically from rural areas, driven by the large gap in the standard of living, along with poor rural conditions caused by environmental degradation and a skewed distribution of resources favoring the elite. With rural-to-urban migration fueling much of the growth of urban areas in the developing world, the migration flow could prompt conflict through a number of channels. Based on the assumption that urbanization and poverty could lead to conflict, the relationship between urban population, poverty, and political change is of growing concern. For example, with poverty remaining one of the most pressing issues in urban areas, migration could breed economic frustration given insufficient employment opportunities and unfulfilled expectations. Perhaps as many as 42 percent (if not more) of the world's urban population can currently be classified as living below the poverty level, with urban poverty increasing in much of the developing world. In 1970, for example, urban areas contained just 36 percent of Latin America's poor. By 1990, the proportion had jumped to 60 percent. By 2025, the World Bank estimates that the majority of the world's population will be living in poverty.[29] Migrants may also have problems adjusting to urban areas. Seeking entry into groups for support and friendship in their new surroundings, they may be recruited into groups that espouse violence. Since many of the migrants are young men, generating a much larger demand for education and jobs, they are easily mobilized for political ends.

Deficiencies in public and reproductive health are reinforced by poverty, compounding the challenges faced by urban areas and their populations. Although levels of mortality and infectious disease are generally lower in urban areas relative to rural areas in the developing world, large variations within urban areas remain. The urban poor tend to have far worse health indicators than their wealthy counterparts, reflecting unequal access to health care, an inability to afford it, and generally poor or underdeveloped health systems. Infectious diseases related to poverty and malnutrition may be increasing in urban areas, and the transmission of diseases like cholera and tuberculosis is aided when large, dense, and poor populations live in unsanitary conditions.[30] As noted earlier, HIV/AIDS is a major issue as well, with prevalence rates tending to be higher in urban areas in the developing world, where traditional social patterns and sexual values have broken down.

Despite the plausibility of these interrelations, history reveals relatively few linkages between urbanization and political unrest, although the 1979 Iranian revolution is frequently cited as one example. Before the revolution, urban growth rates were higher than those of rural areas, and despite increasing education among urban residents, they remained poor, leading to frustration and the eventual overthrow of the shah. Likewise, it is thought that urban violence was boosted by poor economic opportunities in developing cities in the 1970s and 1980s and by austerity measures, imposed by debt-ridden governments in the early 1980s under guidance from the World Bank, which removed price controls or subsidies from key goods, such as bread or fuel. The urban poor were particularly disadvantaged, and the removal of subsidies provoked strikes and riots throughout the developing world.[31]

Urban violence, whether it is directed toward the state, takes place between groups (i.e., entails ethnic or religious violence based on perceived differences between groups), is likely to become increasingly common. The current relative quiet of urban populations in the developing world may not last given trends toward increasing poverty, deteriorating economic conditions, and the increased strength and reach of organized crime in cities throughout the developing world. While the risk of conflict could prompt democratization and institutional reform, states frequently respond to crises and unrest with increased repression, which only serves to amplify the likelihood of conflict. The poor, underemployed, or unemployed young provide ready fodder for uprisings, at the same time that the balance of power shifts from the government to other groups, including crime gangs and religious fundamentalist movements. In this way, urban violence is not just a developing-world issue. Following the bombings of London's Tube in July 2005, concerns were voiced not just with unemployment and restlessness among first-generation immigrant youth and their potential for violence against the state, but also with second- and third-generation immigrants who have been economically limited within British society by class and race barriers. Likewise, the U.S. government was concerned with this same group: as British citizens, they would not require a visa when traveling to the United States.

Whether conflict occurs depends partly on the character of the society and the strength of its institutions. Societies that share a history of cooperation will likely be better able to resist conflict. However, in societies that are socially segmented by ethnic, political, or religious rivalries, the likelihood of violence is increased. Numerous examples illustrate this point. Jerusalem, for example, is a city divided between Christians, Muslims, and Jews. The site of frequent and violent clashes between Muslims and Jews, control of the city figures prominently in any peace negotiations between the Israeli state and Palestinians. Similarly, Karachi, Pakistan, is a city deeply divided along ethnic, religious, political, and economic lines, and conflict between groups is frequent.[32] Antigovernment sentiments have simmered near the surface in the Philippine capital and elsewhere in that geographically fragmented country over the past decade, usually motivated by political or economic issues, including widespread poverty, but also related to environmental degradation.[33] Egypt's Muslim Brotherhood has found its greatest strength among the poor in Cairo and other urban areas,[34] illustrating the fact that governments unable to ensure basic services may find themselves increasingly isolated from their electorates, as more conservative or antigovernment groups step in to fill the void. Ultimately, divisions between secular and fundamentalist groups may undermine the legitimacy of the state and government, leading to instability and conflict.

Avoiding urban violence may prove difficult given the complexity and absolute size of the problem. Policies that slow urban growth or address urban problems, for example, have been promoted, including attempts to limit the growth of urban areas by restricting internal migration. China has, for example, vigorously attempted to control internal migration, but it has not succeeded in curbing rural-to-urban migration. Instead, corruption and economic necessity drive "illegal" internal migration despite a degree of social control unknown in most societies. Moreover, migrants are not necessarily the poorest of urban residents, and policies that restrict rural-to-urban migration are typically ineffective and hurt the poor.[35] Similarly, Indonesia's **transmigration** policy encouraged relocation from Java, the most inhabited island. This program, too, has come with its own problems, engendering social segmentation along religious lines and the violence that erupted between Christians and Muslims in 2000 and 2001.[36] National and international governments have also invested in the development of strong urban networks that are interconnected, deflecting some of the development away from the largest or primate cities and reducing the negative consequences for local resources.

If demographic control is not an option, then urban problems may be addressed through other policy routes. Most importantly, economic reform, improved governance, and policies aimed at reducing urban poverty and enhancing the livelihoods of the poor by promoting political and economic equity between groups can build a foundation of cooperation and security. Removal of policies that explicitly favor urban areas and indirectly generate in-migration through the promotion of rural development may also be successful. None will be easy, and all will carry a high price.

EMERGENT THEMES AND ISSUES: GAZING DEEPER INTO THE CRYSTAL BALL

Over the coming decades, the world is likely to witness an increase in conflict at various spatial scales, including interstate conflict, internal civil war or violence, and ethnic violence, much of which will be underlain by issues pertaining to resource scarcity and population growth. Humanity has quite possibly underestimated the dependency of its institutions on the environment and natural systems, with population growth straining these systems, including renewable and nonrenewable resources, in the coming decades. The how's and why's of conflict are not simple questions to answer. Assigning fault or attaching significance to specific issues, such as the environment, group dynamics, elitism, or economic and political power, is frequently too simplistic as the roots of most conflicts are deep and tangled. Although other forces will mediate and contextualize their effects, the environment and resources will be the national-security issues of the twenty-first century, fusing with old ethnic and historical divisions. The combined impacts of an increasing population and increasing consumption of resources will have dire consequences on desertification, deforestation, soil erosion, water depletion, air pollution, and loss of biodiversity. The effect will be magnified in societies that cannot generate or supply sufficient ingenuity or financial resources to moderate or alleviate scarcities. The full impact, however, may not be observable until well into the current century.

In deriding the linkage between population, environmental scarcity, and conflict, critics have argued that environmentally based conflicts are not new. This is true, but the speed and regularity with which they will occur will increase in the future as resources become increasingly scarce and as populations grow. Developing countries dependent on local resources but lacking the ability to mitigate scarcities will likely be affected sooner, facing more regular, more complex, and more severe problems arising from

environmental scarcities. If they do not have the ability, measured by ingenuity or finances, to overcome these problems, scarcities may overwhelm
the country and further erode its ability to overcome the scarcity and sustain the population.

The rewriting of how and why conflicts occur has broad implications.
First, while the traditional concepts of "state," "national borders," and
"territory" will remain important, they will also likely mean relatively
less in the near future. The Western idea of the state, along with its role
and identity, is an inflexible and artificial construct that is increasingly
tenuous in an age of globalization.[37] Imposed on the earth irrespective of
geography, language, religion, or culture, the period of the nation-state may
be ending. Instead, globalization of markets and commerce, transportation
and communications, and the political order will dramatically reshape the
globe and reduce the role of the state in world affairs as flows of capital
and information cross the globe, siphoning power from the state into the
corporate boardroom. Although globalization has the potential to unite
groups, it also comes with the potential to further separate the haves and
have-nots as groups or countries are left behind.

Already, globalization has created winners and losers within the existing
world order. Portions of the developing world have been left behind, victims of poor resources, poor government, or investments that have simply
passed them by.[38] The gap between developed and developing countries,
whether measured by investment, capital, level of education, income, or
productivity, is widening and is expected to continue to grow. World Bank
projections indicate that sub-Saharan Africa and other peripheral areas will
be left even further behind in the coming decade.[39] Perhaps Homer-Dixon
was too quick to dismiss the potential for conflict between the developed
and developing worlds.[40] If pivotal countries such as China or India, countries that are economically strong but may yet be hobbled by population
growth and environmental scarcity, fall on the wrong side of the divide,
the result will invariably be increased political instability on a global scale.
Although the countries of the developing world may not have the military
means and technology to fight the developed world, they have the population. In a world that promotes democracy, numbers count, and technology and advanced military capabilities are not always sufficient. Vietnam,
Afghanistan, and Somalia are lessons: if rebel fighters could defeat the
Soviets in Afghanistan, or ragtag, poorly trained, and poorly equipped
fighters could defeat U.S. troops in Somalia, it can happen elsewhere, and
it could happen again.

Second, while large-scale conflict is possible, environmental scarcity will
generate chronic, diffuse violence, with conflicts increasingly on local or
subnational scales. As a consequence of globalization, governments may
be helpless in the face of environmental stress and escalating poverty,

disease, and social friction. Conflict will instead reflect ideological, cultural, or ethnic issues. For peripheral countries, which already face few economic prospects, population growth, disease, and environmental stress, the future is bleak, and conflict will undoubtedly arise between groups over access to scarce resources. Due to globalization, which has tended to bypass many of the poorest countries, as well as the increased power of warlords, crime gangs, drug cartels, and guerrilla groups, future conflict may be "borderless," failing to conform to existing notions of interstate or intrastate conflict, with influence exerted not by a state (if states continue to exist) but by ethnic groups or clans.[41] At the extreme, territory will not be marked by traditional state borders but instead will be defined by shared ethnicity or some similar construct, such as clan or tribe, resulting in a shifting map as power or allegiances change.[42] Maps may have to be redrawn without clear divisions between groups. While the breakup of the former Republic of Yugoslavia in the 1990s did not result in complete anarchy, and while new states (e.g., Slovenia, Croatia) emerged from the old, the region may yet disintegrate into intractable violence and a fractured series of mini- or city-states,[43] driven by centuries of ethnic and religious rivalries. Bosnia, Kosovo, and Macedonia remain tinderboxes of ethnic violence, with their governments having little control as rival groups struggle for power.[44] Worse off are portions of sub-Saharan Africa, a region described by Paul Knox and Sallie Marston as "wild zones,"[45] where some countries, including Sierra Leone, Liberia, and Somalia, have lost control of their populations or territories due to tribal warfare, banditry, or political insurrection. Somalia, for example, technically no longer exists. After Somalia's military leader fled in 1991, the country disintegrated into a violent and chaotic struggle between clans and warlords that now control shifting areas. The resulting famine killed four hundred thousand people, with U.S. troops intervening in 1992 to provide humanitarian assistance. Just two years later, the U.S. troops withdrew, having been forced out by low-level, low-tech guerrilla warfare.[46] The current situation in Iraq, with its daily sectarian violence, may be little better, with the potential for the country to split along ethnic and religious lines and erupt into broader violence, potentially drawing Iran, Pakistan, and Turkey into the arena.

Central Asia, including Afghanistan and the former Soviet republics of Uzbekistan and Tajikistan, is politically unstable and threatens to split along ethnic lines.[47] It is a patchwork region of ethnic groups that do not fit neatly within existing state boundaries and that are groping for identity in a post-Soviet, post–cold war world. Again, the potential for conflict does not lie between states but between ethnic groups, although the United States facilitated the battle between the Taliban and anti-Taliban forces.[48] Already, Afghanistan is less and less a true state, split along ethnic lines and weakened by two decades of war, first with the former Soviet Union and later between rival ethnic groups; it has most recently been divided by religious ideals. The fundamentalist Taliban movement, which controlled much of the country, including the capital prior to October 2001, when the United States and its allies intervened, is composed of ethnic Pathans and has been heavily influenced by Islamic fundamentalists in Pakistan. Resisting the Taliban, the Northern Alliance comprises ethnic Tajiks and Uzbeks, who have been strengthened by ties to ethnic groups in Tajikistan and Uzbekistan, former Soviet republics that are also politically unstable. Despite moves by the United Nations to craft a new government following the defeat of the Taliban, it is unclear whether any agreement on the form of the government will hold; the fragile peace is largely held in place by the presence of foreign peacekeeping troops, while portions of the country remain under the de facto control of either the Taliban or warlords, raising the possibility that Afghanistan could continue to disintegrate as a meaningful state and could be partitioned along ethnic lines. Such an eventuality would threaten Pakistan's territorial integrity because of that country's minority Pathan population, not to mention the threat that it would engulf other states in the conflict.[49]

Third, internal conflict or the disintegration of most any country would most likely produce large flows of displaced persons and migrants, potentially creating a downward spiral that reinforced environmental degradation and social segmentation, as discussed earlier in chapter 6. While there has been a recent reduction in the number of displaced persons and refugees, we cannot guarantee that the trend will continue given the persistence of old conflicts and the potential for new ones to emerge. Regardless, conflicts create humanitarian emergencies that frequently involve other countries in peacemaking or peacekeeping duties. The United Nations has frequently filled this role but may find its reach limited or usurped in the future as regional militaries, such as that being contemplated by the European Union, step in to fill the role or as it finds it lacks the funds to meet all of the potential needs.[50] Despite calls for a full-time peacekeeping unit under the UN flag, member countries are either unwilling to fund the unit or are not prepared to convert traditional militaries (which are generally not designed for such missions) to permanent peacekeeping roles, fearing that doing so would mean surrendering power to the United Nations.[51] Moreover, subnational conflicts will limit the ability of humanitarian organizations, such as the United Nations High Commission on Refugees, to provide humanitarian assistance, unless specifically requested to do so.

Finally, the developed world is not immune to the consequences of environmental scarcity. In the southwestern United States, for example, states may increasingly compete for scarce water resources in order to sustain the region's population, which has placed a premium on water. In Texas, the state population is nearly twenty-one million, a number expected to double within fifty years. El Paso is already experiencing water shortages, and water in the Rio Grande, which is a primary source of water in the area, is nearly all being used, with only a trickle reaching the ocean. In other areas, the Ogallala Aquifer, which stretches north from Texas to South Dakota, is overpumped and stressed.[52] In Texas, where surface water resources are public, but underground water is private, privatization of underground water rights and "water farms" allow water to be pumped without regard for neighbors, a form of resource capture. Indeed, Texas law recognizes it as the "rule of capture." Widespread public concerns have been generated that water pumped for profit and sold to the highest bidder (i.e., cities or industry) could threaten supply in some areas, marginalizing those who cannot afford it and potentially disrupting or destroying irrigated agriculture in the Southwest,[53] creating a situation reminiscent of the great dust bowl migration portrayed in John Steinbeck's *The Grapes of Wrath*.[54] On a continental scale, the need to quench the thirst of America's southwestern states has several entrepreneurs and Canadian provinces, including Newfoundland, exploring the idea of bulk water shipments.[55] Home to some 9 percent of the world's fresh-water supplies,[56] Canada is unsure where it stands on the idea of exporting bulk water, although it has refused (to date) to sell bulk water shipments, citing safeguards within the North American Free Trade Agreement (NAFTA). Under NAFTA, water is exempted from trade rules that require two-way trade in commodities. If Canada were to start exporting bulk water, however, free trade provisions would be invoked, requiring the trade to continue and restricting the government's ability to limit its flow, allowing provincial and state governments to challenge the federal position.

The developed world also feels the impact of induced migration from developing countries. Much of the migration of rural Mexicans or Haitians into the United States, of Chinese into North America, and of North Africans into Europe can be attributed to resource scarcity in a broadly defined way. Many of these undocumented migrants are poor and leaving economically or ecologically marginal areas. With few options in their homelands, they seek a new future elsewhere. For receiving countries, immigration alters the ethnic balance, with immigrants most likely settling in urban areas. As discussed in chapter 4, governments are forced to react, limiting immigration or quelling anti-immigrant sentiments within the larger society. Similarly, the disintegration or political and economic destabilization of states would surely have implications for regional security and trade patterns and, ultimately, for the developed world. Countries and their governments may be precluded from effectively negotiating agreements, or they may be completely excluded by the international community.

NOTES

1. Robert D. Kaplan, "The Coming Anarchy," *Atlantic Monthly* (February 1994): 44–76. Much of Kaplan's article was based on Thomas Homer-Dixon's work, albeit reinterpreted in a very pessimistic and journalistic manner. While pointing out the potential for conflict, Homer-Dixon also provided an important "out" for humanity by pointing to potential interventions that might alleviate scarcities and reduce the potential for conflict.

2. Much of the discussion in this chapter is derived from Thomas Homer-Dixon, *Environment, Scarcity, and Violence* (Princeton, NJ: Princeton University Press, 1999). For additional insights into population and resource scarcity, see also Nicholas Polunin, *Population and Global Security* (Cambridge: Cambridge University Press, 1998).

3. Homer-Dixon, *Environment*, 1999.

4. Some authors refer to the generation of "environmental refugees," such as Jodi Jacobson, *Environmental Refugees: A Yardstick of Habitability*, Worldwatch Paper 86 (Washington, DC: Worldwatch Institute, 1988); Arthur H. Westing, "Environmental Refugees: A Growing Category of Displaced Persons," *Environmental Conservation* 19, no. 3 (1992): 201–207. However, the term implies that resource scarcity directly caused their displacement within a short time, which is rarely the case. Instead, as the text discusses, the reasons for movement tend to be subtler, and environmental scarcity is more likely to produce migrants than refugees.

5. See Douglas Massey, Joaquin Arango, Graeme Hugo, Ali Kouaouci, Adela Pellegrino, and J. Edward Taylor, "Theories of International Migration: A Review and Appraisal," *Population and Development Review* 19, no. 3 (1993): 431–66; Douglas Massey, Joaquin Arango, Graeme Hugo, Ali Kouaouci, Adela Pellegrino, and J. Edward Taylor, "An Evaluation of International Migration Theory: The North American Case," *Population and Development Review* 20, no. 4 (1994): 699–752.

6. Indonesia and Chiapas, Mexico, provide alternate examples of how these processes operate to produce conflict.

7. The amount of land per capita in Egypt is considered to be below a level suitable for sustainable food production. See Homer-Dixon, *Environment*. I refrain from reporting the amount of land per capita as many authors do since these measures tend to be relatively misleading owing to inequalities in the distribution of land and resources.

8. Roger W. Stump, *Boundaries of Faith* (Lanham, MD: Rowman & Littlefield, 2000).

9. Martin Ira Glassner, *Political Geography*, 2nd ed. (New York: John Wiley, 1996).

10. Homer-Dixon, *Environment*.

11. In addition, other significant factors, including Iraq's claim to Kuwait based on the boundaries of the former Ottoman Empire and access to the Persian Gulf, were used to "justify" the invasion.

12. Clayton Jones, "Paradise Islands or an Asian Powder Keg," *Christian Science Monitor*, December 1, 1993, 14; Daniel Yergin, "Oil: The Strategic Prize," in *The Gulf War Reader*, ed. Micah L. Sifry and Christopher Serf, 145–62 (New York: Times Books, 1991).

13. In fact, Homer-Dixon was interested solely in the role of renewable resources as generators of conflict. It should be noted, however, that states will be just as eager to capture scarce nonrenewable resources through a variety of means, including military options.

14. Alanna Mitchell, "The World's 'Single Biggest Threat,' " *Globe and Mail*, June 4, 2001, 8A–9A.

15. William J. Broad, "With a Push from the UN, Water Reveals Its Secrets," *New York Times*, June 25, 2005, 1S.

16. Ismail Serageldin, "Earth Faces Water Crisis," (press release, World Bank, Washington, DC, August 6, 1995).

17. Terje Tvedt, "The Struggle for Water in the Middle East," *Canadian Journal of Development Studies* 13, no. 1 (1992): 13–33. Egypt ultimately backed away from its offer to provide Israel with water from the Nile, realizing its own tenuous supply.

18. See John Kolars and William Mitchell, *The Euphrates River and the Southeast Anatolia Development Project* (Carbondale: Southern Illinois University Press, 1991); Nurit Kliot, *Water Resources and Conflict in the Middle East* (London: Routledge, 1994).

19. Patrick Laurence, "Pretoria Has Its Way in Lesotho," *Africa Report* 31, no. 2 (1986): 50–51.

20. Michael T. Coe and Jonathan A. Foley, "Human and Natural Impacts on the Water Resources of the Lake Chad Basin," *Journal of Geophysical Research* 106, no. D4 (2001): 3349–56.

21. For a discussion of nationalism and its role in the present-day world, see John Hutchinson and Anthony D. Smith, *Nationalism* (Oxford: Oxford University Press, 1994).

22. Associated Press, "Macedonia to Ask for War Declaration," *New York Times*, May 5, 2001, 5A; Reuters, "Macedonia Attacks Albanian Guerillas," *New York Times*, May 9, 2001, 4A.

23. Sanjib Baruah, *India against Itself: Assam and the Politics of Nationality* (Philadelphia: University of Pennsylvania Press, 1999); Myron Weiner, *Sons of the Soil: Migration and Ethnic Conflict in India* (Delhi: Oxford University Press, 1978).

24. Inheritance practices result in the division of land into smaller plots with each generation. Water-control institutions have also limited agricultural output.

25. Homer-Dixon, *Environment*.

26. Gary Hawes, "Theories of Peasant Revolution: A Critique and Contribution for the Philippines," *World Politics* 42, no. 2 (1990): 261–98; Gregg Jones, *Red Revolution: Inside the Philippine Guerrilla Movement* (Boulder, CO: Westview Press, 1989).

27. For a good review of environmental aspects of urbanization, see Jorge E. Hardoy, Diana Mitlin, and David Satterthwaite, *Environmental Problems in an Urbanizing World* (London: Earthscan, 2004).

28. See, for example, Richard E. Bilsborrow, *Migration, Urbanization, and Development: New Directions and Issues* (New York: UN Population Fund and Kluwer Academic Publishers, 1998); Martin P. Brockerhoff, "An Urbanizing World," *Population Bulletin* 55, no. 3 (September 2000); Gavin W. Jones and Pravin M. Visaria, *Urbanization in Large Developing Countries: China, Indonesia, Brazil and India* (Oxford: Clarendon Press, 1997); Josef Gugler, *The Urban Transformation of the Developing*

World (Oxford: Oxford University Press, 1996); Eugene Linden, "Megacities," *Time*, January 11, 1993, 28–38.

29. Brockerhoff, "An Urbanizing World."

30. S. Jay Olshansky, Bruce Carnes, Richard G. Rogers, and Len Smith, "Infectious Diseases—New and Ancient Threats to World Health," *Population Bulletin* 52, no. 2 (July 1997).

31. John Walton and Charles Ragin, "Global and National Sources of Political Protest: Third World Responses to the Debt Crisis," *American Sociological Review* 55, no. 6 (1999): 876–90.

32. Arif Hasan, "Karachi and the Global Nature of Urban Violence," *Urban Age* 1, no. 4 (1993): 4–12; Farida Shaheed, "The Pathan-Muhajir Conflicts, 1985–6: A National Perspective," in *Mirrors of Violence: Communities, Riots and Survivors in South Asia*, ed. Veena Das, 205–23 (New York: Oxford University Press, 1990).

33. Historical insight into conflict and uprising in the Philippines can be found in Richard Kessler, *Rebellion and Repression in the Philippines* (New Haven, CT: Yale University Press, 1989). For insight into some of the most recent uprisings, see Mark Landler, "Manila Moves Incite Talk of 'Dark Side of People Power,' " *New York Times*, May 3, 2001, 3A; Mark Landler, " 'State of Rebellion' Declared after Siege at Manila Palace," *New York Times*, May 2, 2001, 1A. See also the March 2005 issue of the *Geographical Journal*, which published a special issue on poverty and the environment.

34. Stump, *Boundaries of Faith*.

35. See www.worldbank.org/html/fpd/urban (accessed June 27, 2005). See also Arjan de Haan, "Livelihoods and Poverty: The role of Migration—A Critical Review of the Migration Literature," *Journal of Development Studies* 36, no. 2 (2000): 1–23.

36. Jana Mason, *Shadow Plays: The Crisis of Refugees and IDPs in Indonesia* (Washington, DC: U.S. Committee for Refugees, 2001).

37. See Thomas M. Poulson, *Nations and States: A Geographic Background to World Affairs* (Englewood Cliffs, NJ: Prentice Hall, 1995).

38. Paul Kennedy, *Preparing for the Twenty-First Century* (New York: Random House, 1993). For an abridged version of this book, see Paul Kennedy, "Preparing for the 21st Century: Winners and Losers," *New York Review of Books*, February 11, 1993, 32–44.

39. World Bank, "Workers in an Integrating World," in *World Development Report* (Washington, DC: World Bank, 1995).

40. Although the United States intervened, the conflict in Afghanistan is largely an outcome of the terrorist attacks on September 11, 2001, and cannot be described as a conflict between the haves and have-nots or between the developed and developing worlds, despite its geographical focus (the Middle East) and its origins. Instead, it is a new form of war that is based on ethnic and religious differences, with the United States facilitating conflict between groups.

41. See, for example, Robert D. Kaplan, "Countries without Borders," *New York Times*, October 23, 1996, 8A; Paul L. Knox and Sallie A. Marston, *Human Geography: Places and Regions in Global Context*, 2nd ed. (Upper Saddle River, NJ: Prentice Hall, 2001).

42. I hesitate to use "tribe" as a descriptor because of its negative connotations in North America. However, it still fits social constructs of Africa.

43. See, for example, Kenichi Ohmae, "The Rise of the Region State," *Foreign Affairs* (Spring 1993): 78–87.

44. Steven L. Burg, "Why Yugoslavia Fell Apart," *Current History* (November 1993): 357–63. For a broader discussion of state disintegration, see Robert K. Schaeffer, *Severed States* (Lanham, MD: Rowman & Littlefield, 1999).

45. Knox and Marston, *Human Geography*, 2001.

46. The United Nations also sent troops to Somalia in 1993. They were withdrawn in 1995 when they, too, were no longer able to fulfill their role effectively.

47. Boris Rumer and Eugene Rumer, "Who'll Stop the Next 'Yugoslavia'?" *World Monitor* 44 (November 1992): 36–42.

48. It is important to note that the conflict in Afghanistan is not based on resource scarcity but has roots in ethnic (and religious) divisions.

49. During the initial campaign against the Taliban and al Qaeda in Afghanistan, the Pakistani government was lukewarm to American involvement and the use of military force within the region, fearing for its own hold on power given the high level of support for the Taliban within Pakistan. Later, as the Taliban and al Qaeda were defeated, official Pakistani support for the Taliban diminished, although support remains at the local level.

50. The United States, for instance, has lagged in the payment of its UN dues.

51. Tad Daley, "Can the U.N. Stretch to Fit Its Future?" *Bulletin of the Atomic Scientists* (April 1992): 38–42; Michael T. Klare, "The New Challenges to Global Security," *Current History* (April 1993): 155–61.

52. David E. Kromm, "Low Water in the American High Plains," *The World & I* (February 1992): 312–19.

53. Jim Yardley, "For Texas Now, Water and Not Oil Is Liquid Gold," *New York Times*, April 16, 2001, 2C.

54. John Steinbeck, *The Grapes of Wrath* (New York: Penguin Press, 1993).

55. Mark MacKinnon and Campbell Clark, "Chrétien Lands in Hot Water," *Globe and Mail*, May 15, 2001, 5A.

56. Statistics Canada, *Canada Year Book 1988* (Ottawa: Minister of Supply and Services, 1987).

Conclusion

Five Demographic Forces
That Will Shape the World

A s of 2005, world population was approximately 6.477 billion and continued to grow at a rate of 1.2 percent. Theoretically, at this rate the world's population will double in just fifty-three years, meaning that the world's demographic situation remains critical by almost any measure. In the preceding chapters, this book has explored the major demographic issues that the world now faces. It has discussed current knowledge, as well as emerging themes and issues, such as the effects of population on resources and environmental degradation, the relationship between population growth and conflict, the implications of low fertility and an aging society, the impact of HIV/AIDS. Distilling these ideas into their component parts, we see that the five most compelling demographic forces that the world must still grapple with include population growth, population decline, the HIV/AIDS epidemic, international migration, and refugees and internally displaced persons (IDPs).

POPULATION GROWTH

Despite declines in fertility rates and slowing population growth rates since the 1960s, the optimistic view that the population crisis has passed is premature. Instead, population growth will continue into the near future before leveling off later in this century at between 7.3 and 10.7 billion. The certainty of continued growth is grounded in three assumptions. First, improvements in life expectancy (reduced mortality) will contribute to population growth as individuals survive longer and complete their reproductive years. Second, with a large proportion of the world's population under reproductive age or just entering it, population momentum will ensure continued growth, regardless of the future fertility decisions of this group of young women. Third, fertility rates will remain well above replacement in many regions of the world for the foreseeable future. Although it is reasonable to assume that fertility rates will decline further, the extent of the decline is uncertain, reflecting the complex personal, social, and economic environment that surrounds decisions regarding family size. Given the apparent "stickiness" of fertility rates in Egypt, Bangladesh, India, and Argentina, we cannot assume that fertility rates will eventually become equal to or less than replacement level in all societies.

With the majority of population growth occurring in the developing world, the greatest challenge may be in Africa, where fertility rates remain stubbornly high, and there has been relatively little progress toward fertility transition. Moreover, it is unclear when a sustained reduction in fertility levels will occur and how far fertility will drop. Despite improvements, the structures that maintain high fertility, including high mortality rates for infants and children, gender inequality, and poor health care systems, remain firmly in place. Various family-planning programs have been implemented, but they have met with limited success owing to insufficient funding (both domestically and internationally), inappropriate goals, or a population not yet ready to reduce fertility. More importantly, continued population growth poses deep problems for many African nations. Here, where governments are fiscally strained, state institutions are weak, and health and educational systems are poor, the strain of population growth is already showing as governments are unable to maintain investment in public infrastructure. Population growth and, ultimately, the absolute size of the population will continue to pose challenges to societies and their governments as they deal with growing scarcities of land and water and the provision of infrastructure and social services, including education and health care. The potential for conflict is strong as groups or states seek to capture resources.

POPULATION DECLINE

Paradoxically, the decline of fertility rates to below replacement levels in the developed world has led to population decline and aging. Linked to deep societal and economic changes, including gender equity and rising consumer aspirations, low fertility (the average for the developed world is just 1.6) has reduced growth to just 0.1 percent per year in the developed world, meaning it will take 809 years for the population to double under current conditions. For the developed world, slowing population growth or decline brings its own problems and opportunities. In particular, it is unclear what impacts aging will have, but most commentators assume there will be negative consequences. In the game of democracy, shrinking populations are associated with declining national and international political influence and a feared loss of national identity; the experiences of Quebec's francophone population and the difference in birthrates between Palestinians and Israeli Jews reflect these concerns. Domestically, politics are likely to reflect the increasing political power of an aging population and its political agenda as low fertility rates increase the size proportionally of the elderly population. Low fertility rates are expected to slow economic growth, and the large baby boom generation threatens to overwhelm medical and social security programs, the costs of which will consume an increasing portion of national budgets at the same time as the labor force and economically active population is shrinking.

Fearing the potential demographic and economic problems associated with low fertility, the developed world has searched for ways to diminish its impact. Several countries have promoted pronatalist policies, including tax incentives, cash bonuses, and preferred access to day care. Most, including Quebec's profertility incentives, have met with only modest success. Alternatively, immigration can be used to support population growth, but it too engages thorny issues of national identity and ethnic relations. These issues are particularly relevant in Europe, which has experienced strong anti-immigrant sentiments in the past decade. Although Canada and the United States have been historically more receptive to immigration, with both countries billing themselves as "nations of immigrants," anti-immigrant sentiments have also appeared in legislation, including welfare reform and Proposition 187, which may be indicative of emerging ethnic and national tensions.

THE HIV/AIDS EPIDEMIC

With 40.3 million infected, of which 4.9 million were infected in 2005, HIV, the virus that causes AIDS, has created a global epidemic far more severe than anyone anticipated just ten years ago. Now, midway through its third decade, the HIV/AIDS epidemic is having a significant demographic impact in the developing world, where the large majority of cases are found, and the epidemic continues to grow. Haiti's prevalence rate (5.6 percent in 2004), for example, is the highest national rate outside of sub-Saharan Africa. The number of people living with HIV/AIDS has grown in every region, with some of the steepest increases in East Asia, Central Asia, and Eastern Europe, where transmission is aided by high rates of injected-drug use, a known and significant transmission route.

In sub-Saharan Africa, where the epidemic is most severe, the adult prevalence rate is 7.2 percent. Although this represents a slight decline and stabilization in the prevalence rate, differences across the region are large. In countries like Botswana, Zimbabwe, and South Africa, this rate exceeds 20 percent, and it reaches as high as 38.0 percent in Botswana. In these and other countries in the region, death rates are higher, life expectancies have been reduced, population growth has slowed, and infant mortality rates have increased, reversing hard-won improvements in health that occurred in earlier decades. The economic implications of the epidemic are just as severe: reduced economic growth, lower productivity, loss of labor force members, and increased medical costs. Socially, the epidemic is responsible for a swelling number of orphans, in addition to augmented personal fear and denial, in countries where HIV/AIDS is still seen as a curse and may yet promote conflict as economic growth and institutions are eroded.

There is some hope on the horizon. Reductions in infection rates in a handful of countries have recently been noted, and the infection rate in sub-Saharan Africa has decreased, but these examples remain rare. Likewise, the decision by the major drug companies to reduce prices associated with antiretroviral drugs drastically is significant, as is the production of generic drugs; together they mean that millions who have been denied treatment until recently simply because they could not afford it will have new opportunities. To date, many programs, such as Brazil's, have met with success, although UNAIDS's "3-by-5" program of supplying AIDS drugs to three million by 2005 did not reach its target, leaving millions untreated. While it remains too early to ascertain what effect existing programs will have, they offer the hope of long-term survival and a productive life, reducing the human and economic costs of the disease. Before the first drugs are distributed, however, governments and other groups must overcome the problems associated with distribution, financing, and compliance, which any new programs will entail. The application of new drug programs remains especially daunting in sub-Saharan Africa, where the number of cases is greater, and distribution is more difficult.

The developed world has obviously not been immune to the effect of HIV/AIDS. First diagnosed in the United States in 1981, it was initially concentrated in the male homosexual and injected-drug-user communities. Adult prevalence rates have remained low (less than 1 percent), but the disease has seeped into the larger heterosexual community, where it poses a greater risk. Able to marshal more resources to educate their populations and fund medical research into new anti-AIDS drugs, the developed world has seemingly controlled the epidemic, but vigilance cannot be reduced. The greater prevalence of the disease among African Americans, together with increased high-risk behavior and correspondingly higher infection rates among young gay men, indicates the need for ongoing control efforts over both the short and long terms.

INTERNATIONAL MIGRATION

Over the past hundred years, most states in the developed world have moved to control immigration, limiting the types of immigrants accepted (i.e., those seeking family reunification and economic opportunity), their origins, and the overall number allowed entry. Despite their efforts through both legislation and active enforcement of borders, most countries have found it increasingly difficult to control the entry of immigrants, creating an immigration crisis due to the "gap" between immigration-control policies and their outcomes. The emerging reality is that governments are less able to control immigration now than in the past. Globalization and the increasing flow of labor and capital, the emergence of civil rights and liberalism, and the domestic need for inexpensive labor, which legitimized immigration flows, have contributed to this inability to control legal migration flows.

While not denying past immigration policies that were openly racist and exclusionary, both the United States and Canada have historically been receptive to immigration. South of the forty-ninth parallel, this history may be in danger, illustrated by the fear of demographic "Balkanization," welfare reform, the debate over Proposition 187 in California, and the tightening of immigration and refugee policies in a post–September 11 world. Anti-immigrant sentiments are especially visible in Europe, coloring national political debates and economic opportunities. European countries have only recently shifted from being exporters to importers of labor, a shift that is difficult to digest. Yet, the demographic realities of low fertility and an aging population mean that European countries face a crisis in their labor forces. Increased immigration may be the only option to meet employment requirements, but it remains an option that entails significant political, social, and cultural problems since most Europeans continue to associate the foreign born with unskilled work and unemployment. Most likely, Europe will ultimately need to address its new role as a receiver of immigrants. In addition, both North America and Europe are grappling with increasing flows of illegal immigrants, who impose burdens on local service providers at the same time that they sustain the economy by working for low pay in positions or conditions that few others are willing to tolerate.

It is increasingly apparent that there is relatively little room for states to maneuver with their immigration policies. Attempts to restrict immigration often end up increasing the foreign-born population through loopholes and "backdoor" immigration or illegal entry. Moving to increase immigration flows overtly would be political suicide, particularly in Europe, where political parties promoting reduced immigration are enjoying greater support. As a result of reduced fertility, coupled with economic globalization, developed countries will become increasingly dependent on foreign labor to fill job vacancies. At the same time, globalization and high fertility will produce a surplus labor force in the developing world. In other words, international migration into the developed world will continue. Restricting entry will not solve the problem but will only shift it to one of illegal immigration as the demand for and supply of labor will remain, and illegal immigrants will continue to be attracted by the array of opportunities. The reality may create strange bedfellows as trade unions, which have traditionally resisted immigration, move to embrace immigration as one way of protecting their viability in the new world order.

REFUGEES AND INTERNALLY DISPLACED PERSONS

As the developed world grapples with legal and illegal immigration, refugees and IDPs pose a significant humanitarian challenge around the globe. Making up a population of over thirty million people, the actual number of both refugees and IDPs has declined recently, although this is unlikely to be a long-term trend. With the end of the cold war, the nature of conflict has changed from large-scale confrontations backed by superpowers to smaller, internal struggles. Population growth only compounds the problem, with new conflicts spurred by ideology, desire for land, and a scarcity of resources ultimately leading to population displacement. The human and economic costs associated with displacement are incalculable. What is measurable is the size of the displaced population. Uprooted but unable to leave their states, these people are caught in civil war, criminalized by the state or other groups, and typically ineligible for humanitarian assistance, which poses additional challenges to the international relief community.

While refugees and IDPs remain an important issue, states have moved to restrict their entry, given increased security screening, fears associated with the fiscal and social responsibilities mandated under the UN convention on refugees and the political fallout as refugees clash with the native born in the host country over ideological or ethnic differences. Even the developed world has become increasingly uneasy with large-scale refugee resettlement. U.S. refugee policy has frequently been a tool of foreign policy. Moreover, while Canada and the United States have resettled refugees of a variety of origins, they could do much more, such as increase the number of refugees resettled each year or increase financial assistance and support to agencies such as the UN High Commission on Refugees. Likewise, Europe has moved to close its borders to refugees. The actions of the developed countries have had a ripple effect around the world, with smaller and poorer states refusing to protect refugees.

In light of the September 11 terrorist attacks on America, the developed world revisited immigration and refugee policies, further restricting resettlement. Immigrants and refugees alike are more carefully screened due to security issues arising out of the fear that terrorists may be included in legal immigrant and refugee flows. Countries with more liberal policies, such as Canada, may be forced to place greater restrictions on the movement of individuals into the country, as is illustrated by the Safe Third Country Agreement. Doing so will probably entail some loss of Canadian sovereignty as Canada and the United States adopt common entry controls and strengthen perimeter control while making it easier to move between the two countries.

INTERACTIONS AND OTHER EFFECTS

Independently or together, these five main demographic forces will drive a series of related demographic processes that will shape the global environment in the decades to come. While the debate between neo-Malthusians, distributionists, and economic optimists drags on, the emerging consensus is that population growth slows economic growth. In the process, population growth exacerbates land degradation and resource depletion, promotes violence and conflict, and places pressure on institutions and governments. In effect, there is a causal link between population growth, resource scarcity, social effects (i.e., migration and decreased agricultural or economic output), and conflict. Clearly, population growth is not solely or directly responsible for resource scarcity; likewise, resource scarcity is not the only factor contributing to violence. Rather, both become underlying causes that cannot be discounted.

The not-so-trivial question is whether the world can support *and* sustain a population of six billion with an acceptable standard of living, let alone a future population of seven to ten billion. It is unclear, for example, whether there is sufficient capacity to continue to feed the world's population. While some commentators have recently proclaimed that the crisis of feeding the world's population has passed, others claim that just the opposite is true, that sufficient food supplies are not yet ensured, pointing to declining agricultural production, loss of cropland, increasing demand, and a decreased likelihood of new crop strains that will significantly increase yield as indications. The situation becomes more problematic if the goal of increasing the average standard of living for the world's population, a laudable and just goal, is targeted. Doing so increases consumption by moving people "up the food chain," thereby increasing the consumption (both in quantity and variety) of food. The same logic must also be extended to economic growth. Can a growing population that increasingly demands more resources be sustained in the future? Again, the emerging consensus indicates that population growth reduces economic growth by increasing poverty and underemployment, weakens investment in human and physical assets such as education or other institutions, decreases ingenuity, and degrades resources. Worse, rapid population growth and poor economic growth appear to be self-reinforcing, making it exceedingly difficult for countries to pull themselves out of this spiral, given the lack of well-developed institutions in many of the poorest countries.

The effects of population growth will be clearly visible in urban areas as rural-to-urban migration and natural increase in the developing world fuel the growth of large urban areas. Megacities of ten million or more will not be uncommon. There is, as of yet, no apparent limit to the size of cities before they produce more negative externalities and costs than benefits, and while and we can point to the ability of cities like New York, London, or Tokyo to function, these cites are in the developed world. The majority of the new megacities will be in the developing world, and it is unknown whether the cities themselves or the states will be able to provide sufficient infrastructure and employment opportunities for the burgeoning urban population. More likely, the new megacities will be characterized by high levels of poverty, poor living conditions, poor health, and few employment opportunities—the very types of conditions that can easily breed resentment and insurrection.

In the developing world, population growth and increasing consumption of resources will create scarcities through degradation or depletion of resources. Even renewable resources are now recognized as being finite in situations where population growth exceeds the ability of the resource to regenerate or where the resource has been degraded through pollution or other means. Caused by resource scarcities, social effects including decreased agricultural output, decreased economic output, migration, social segmentation, and the disruption of social institutions will create an environment that promotes conflict. Complicating matters, conflict related to resource scarcity will occur with greater severity, speed, and scale in the future, meaning that its effects will not be confined to a spatially small area. Conflict will not be felt within the developing world alone. Instead, the consequences of resource scarcity and population growth will ripple across the globe, promoting (among other things) international migration and the displacement of populations, destabilizing governments, threatening trade relations or economic development, and inducing further environmental degradation. The effects of global warming, which are not yet fully understood, remain a wildcard but are likely to exacerbate resource scarcities.

Globalization of the world's economy may be touted as the harbinger of a new economic order that can lift nations out of poverty. Yet, it is more likely that large regions of the world will be left out of the new international arrangement. Geography matters. Africa, the Indian subcontinent, and parts of Asia will become marginalized, characterized by a lack of international investment, poor leadership, few resources, and distance from markets. Unless the developed world is prepared to extend aid and investment, reversing the declines in international aid noted over the past few years, these regions are likely to be pulled into a reinforcing cycle of violence and poverty. Conflict will not take the traditional form of state versus state for control of territory. Instead, conflict will be subnational and defined by local resource scarcities, with group-identity conflicts focusing on ideological or ethnic differences—a "we" versus "them" mentality—or local insurgencies and civil strife. Like Somalia, Angola, and Sierra Leone, countries may, for all intents and purposes, cease to exist, defined only by the traditional Western notion of maps and boundaries but torn apart by local conflicts. National governments will cease to operate, replaced by warlords and private armies controlling shifting territories.

Preventing or decreasing the likelihood of resource scarcity and conflict is a challenge. Education, better employment opportunities, and gender equity for women will go a long way toward reducing fertility levels and the risk of HIV infection. To meet these needs, however, there is a need for increased investment in the developing world, something that the developed world has backed away from in recent years. Economic optimists would simply point to the need for functioning institutions and free markets to encourage investment, innovation, and substitution. Yet, the value or applicability of such concepts is frequently limited. Globalization offers little hope for the least-developed countries. If anything, countries may only hope to be suppliers of inexpensive labor, earning income from funds remitted by their emigrant populations. Input substitution does not necessarily offer alternatives, and ingenuity itself is not a costless or ubiquitous good. Instead, it is fostered where resources such as time and capital are abundant, a tangible concept that may be missing from many poor developing countries and that cannot simply be provided through free markets or democracy. Likewise, markets and other institutions, including governments, may be poorly developed or corrupt, short-circuiting any attempt to invest in a society. If the ability to generate ingenuity is missing, countries may face an ingenuity gap, and their ability to respond to resource limits or other threats will be diminished.

Surely, the world of child six billion is in jeopardy.

Glossary of Key Terms
and Acronyms

age pyramid   Representation of a population distributed by age and sex.

aging   An increase in the proportion of population in older age groups.

AIDS   Acquired Immune Deficiency Syndrome.

alien   A person resident in a country who has not acquired citizenship by naturalization.

antinatalist   Positions or policies that discourage fertility and childbearing; disincentives may include reduced child benefits or other, more repressive options.

antiretroviral drugs   The class of drugs that are used to suppress the HIV virus, inhibiting the development of HIV into AIDS; also known as the "triple cocktail."

assimilation   The economic, social, cultural, and political processes of adjustment undergone by immigrants, transforming them into citizens of the host country.

asylees   Individuals forced out of their country of origin who are seeking refuge in the new country in which they are living.

asylum   The act of seeking refuge and protection within a country.

baby boom   The rise in birth rates in many Western countries between 1946 and 1964.

Boomsters   *See* economic optimists.

Bracero Program   Program enabling Mexicans to be admitted legally into the United States for labor between 1942 and 1964.

Border Safety Initiative (BSI)   A program run by the Border Patrol to educate would-be illegal entrants about the dangers of crossing the border and to provide medical assistance if needed.

carrying capacity The maximum number of organisms that can be supported theoretically in a habitat for an indefinite period of time, dependent upon the social, economic, political, and natural systems, as well as upon the level of consumption.

child mortality rate The annual number of deaths of children under five years of age per thousand.

cohort A group of individuals born in the same calendar year or group of years.

demographic transition (DTT) The process whereby a country moves from high to low mortality and fertility rates, accompanied by rapid population growth.

dependency ratio The ratio of people of dependent age (0–14, 65+) to the economically active population (15–64). The young dependency ratio is the ratio of those aged zero to fourteen to those in the labor force and is usually associated with rapid population growth.

developed world Following UN classification, the developed world includes Europe, North America, Australia, Japan, and New Zealand.

developing world All countries and regions outside the developed world.

distributionists Individuals adhering to Marxist thoughts, and assuming that commodities such as food can be more equitably distributed.

Doomsters *See* neo-Malthusian.

doubling time The number of years it will take the population to double, assuming a constant rate of natural increase.

ecological footprint A measure of environmental sustainability, based on past and present demands on the earth's natural resources.

ecological marginalization The forced movement of individuals or groups into ecologically marginal areas.

economic optimists Individuals who believe that population growth stimulates economic development.

emigrant A person who leaves one country to settle in another.

epidemiological transition Shifts in health and disease patterns as mortality moves from high to low rates.

fecundity The physiological ability of individuals to have children.

fertility The ability to reproduce.

fertility rate The annual number of live births per thousand women aged 15–44 or 15–49 years.

fertility transition The shift from high to low fertility.

green revolution The improvement in agricultural productivity in the 1940s and 1950s associated with new, high-yield crop strains, fertilizer, irrigation, and pesticide use.

gross domestic product (GDP) The total value of goods and services produced by a country, not including international trade.

HIV Human immunodeficiency virus, the virus that causes AIDS.

illegal immigrants Individuals entering a country without proper documentation or approval.

immigrant A person who moves into a country where she or he is not a native to take up residence.

immigration gap The differential between states' immigration policies and their outcomes.

infant mortality rate (IMR) Annual number of deaths of infants under one year of age per thousand live births.

INS U.S. Immigration and Naturalization Service.

interdiction The policy of stopping would-be refugee or asylee claimants before they enter a country and initiate the refugee claim process.

internally displaced persons (IDPs) Individuals or groups forced to flee homes to escape armed conflict, violence, human rights abuses, or disaster. Unlike refugees, they are not residing outside their countries of nationality.

IRCA Immigration Reform and Control Act (1986, United States).

least-developed countries Defined by the United Nations, those countries where per capita income is less than US$900 per year.

life expectancy The average number of years beyond age x that an individual can expect to live under current mortality levels; usually expressed as life expectancy at birth.

life span The longest period over which a person may live.

Malthusian Adjective referencing the writings of Malthus, who believed that population grows geometrically, but food supplies grow linearly, resulting in an inadequate food supply and population decline through famine, disease, or war (positive checks).

maquiladora Assembly plant employing Mexicans where parts are shipped to Mexico, assembled, and then reexported for sale, allowing companies to benefit from the cheaper labor.

Marxist An adherent of the theories of Karl Marx.

megacity A city with a population over ten million.

morbidity Sickness.

mortality Deaths. Along with fertility and migration, mortality is a key concept of population size and structure

mortality (death) rate The annual number of deaths per thousand people. This rate is not age-standardized to account for differential death rates across age groups.

natural increase The birth rate minus the death rate, indicating the annual rate of population growth (without migration) expressed as a percentage.

neo-Malthusian An individual who accepts Malthusian principles but believes birth control methods can be used to reduce population growth.

nonrefoulement   The basic tenant of the UN refugee convention that prohibits states from returning refugees against their will to their countries of origin.

nonrenewable resources   Finite resources such as oil or minerals.

overstayers   Individuals who enter a country legally but remain in the country after their permission to do so expires.

points system   The tool used by Citizenship and Immigration Canada to assess the suitability of economic immigrants. Points are awarded for occupational or language skills, age, education, and whether a job has been pre-arranged. Individuals must score a minimum of 67 points (out of 100) to be admitted as an economic immigrant.

population explosion   The rapid growth of the world's population.

population momentum   The potential for population growth present within the age and sex structure of a population, even if fertility rates were to drop to replacement level.

prevalence   The number of people in a population sick with a disease at a particular time, regardless of when the illness began.

pronatalist   Policies that favor a high birth rate; may include tax incentives, cash bonuses for the number of children born in excess of the first, day care provision, or parental leaves.

Proposition 187   Legislation in California meant to limit access to education and health services among illegal immigrants, passed by a majority in 1994 but ruled unconstitutional by a federal judge.

quota system   U.S. immigration policies that imposed quotas on the number of immigrants relative to a defined base (Northern European) population.

refugees   Individuals or groups who, owing to well-founded fears of persecution for reasons of race, religion, nationality, membership in a particular group, or adherence to a political opinion, are outside the country of nationality and unable or unwilling to return.

renewable resource   Resources such as water, croplands, or forests that can be used indefinitely, provided a threshold of sustainability is not exceeded.

replacement fertility level   The fertility rate (2.1) required to replace a generation exactly, accounting for death before completion of childbearing years.

resource capture   Control of a scarce resource through the use of legislation or other means.

rivalrous resources   Resources used by one or more actors, reducing their availability to others.

rural   Areas dominated by open countryside, low population densities, and extensive land use.

social segmentation The division of society, typically along class, ethnic, or religious lines.

STDs Sexually transmitted diseases, including syphilis, gonorrhea, and HIV.

sustainable development The level of human activity that meets present needs without compromising the ability of future generations to meet their own needs, subject to constraints.

total fertility rate (TFR) The average number of children a woman would have, assuming that current age-specific birth rates remain constant through the childbearing years (ages fifteen to forty-nine).

transmigration The relocation of individuals from one area to another; typically refers to the relocation of Indonesians out of Java to other regions or of Russians to other republics or satellite states.

UNAIDS United Nations program on HIV/AIDS.

UNFAO UN Food and Agricultural Organization.

UNHCR United Nations High Commission on Refugees.

UNICEF United Nations Children's Fund.

urban A concentration of people in space whose livelihoods are organized around nonagricultural activities. Different countries will define the urban threshold differently.

urbanization The process of becoming urban.

USAID United States Agency for International Development.

USCIS United States Citizenship and Immigration Services (formally INS)

USCRI United States Committee for Refugees and Immigrants.

WHO World Health Organization.

xenophobia The fear of strangers.

zero population growth (ZPG) The situation in which the population does not change in size from year to year.

Selected Bibliography

Amery, Hussein, and Aaron T. Wolf, eds. *Water in the Middle East: A Geography of Conflict*. Austin: University of Texas Press, 2000.

Beaujot, Roderic, and Don Kerr. *Population Change in Canada*. 2nd ed. Toronto: McClelland Stewart, 2004.

Bender, William, and Margaret Smith. "Population, Food, and Nutrition." *Population Bulletin* 51, no. 4 (February 1997).

Brockerhoff, Martin P. "An Urbanizing World." *Population Bulletin* 55, no. 3 (September 2000).

Brown, Lester R. *Who Will Feed China? Wake-up Call for a Small Planet*. New York: W. W. Norton, 1995.

Clark, William A. V. *The California Cauldron*. New York: Guilford Press, 1998.

Cincotta, Richard P., and Robert Engelman. *Economies and Rapid Change: The Influence of Population Growth*. Washington, DC: Population Action International, 1997.

Cornelius, Wayne A., Takeyuki Tsuda, Philip L. Martin, and James F. Hollifield, eds. *Controlling Immigration: A Global Perspective*. 2nd ed. Palo Alto, CA: Stanford University Press, 2004.

De Souza, Roger-Mark, John S. Williams, and Frederick A. B. Meyerson. "Critical Links: Population, Health, and the Environment." *Population Bulletin* 58, no. 3 (September 2003).

Ehrlich, Paul. *The Population Bomb*. New York: Ballantine Books, 1968.

Ehrlich, Paul, Anne Ehrlich, and Gretchen Daily. "Food Security, Population, and Environment." *Population and Development Review* 19, no. 1 (1993):1–32.

Espenshade, Thomas J., ed. *Keys to Successful Immigration*. Washington, DC: Urban Institute Press, 1997.

Ferrie, Joseph P. *Yankeys Now: Immigrants in the Antebellum U.S., 1840–1860*. New York: Oxford University Press, 1999.

Foot, David. *Boom, Bust and Echo*. Toronto: McFarlane, Walters, and Ross, 1996.

Gelbard, Alene, Carl Haub, and Mary M. Kent. "World Population beyond Six Billion." *Population Bulletin* 54, no. 1 (March 1999).

Gimpel, James. *Separate Destinations*. Ann Arbor: University of Michigan Press, 1999.

Goliber, Thomas J. "Population and Reproductive Health in Sub-Saharan Africa." *Population Bulletin* 52, no. 4 (December 1997).

Gould, Peter. *The Slow Plague: A Geography of the AIDS Pandemic*. Oxford: Blackwell, 1993.

Hirschman, Charles, Philip Kasinitz, and Josh DeWind, eds. *The Handbook of International Migration*. New York: Russell Sage Foundation, 1999.

Homer-Dixon, Thomas F. *Environment, Scarcity, and Violence*. Princeton, NJ: Princeton University Press, 1999.

———. *The Ingenuity Gap*. Toronto: Alfred Knopf, 2000.

Isbister, John. *The Immigrant Debate: Remaking America*. West Hartford, CT: Kumarian Press, 1996.

Kaplan, Robert D. "The Coming Anarchy." *Atlantic Monthly* (February 1994):44–76.

Klare, Michael T. *Resource Wars*. New York: Henry Holt, 2002.

Livernash, Robert, and Eric Rodenburg. "Population Change, Resources, and the Environment." *Population Bulletin* 53, no. 1 (March 1998).

Lutz, Wolfgang, ed. *The Future World Population*. London: Earthscan, 1996.

Malthus, Thomas Robert. *An Essay on the Principle of Population*. Reprinted in Scott W. Menard and Elizabeth W. Moen, eds. *Perspectives on Population*. New York: Oxford University Press, 1987.

Martin, Philip, and Elizabeth Midgley. "Immigration: Shaping and Reshaping America." *Population Bulletin* 58, no. 2 (June 2003).

Massey, Douglas, Joaquin Arango, Graeme Hugo, Ali Kouaouci, Adela Pellegrino, and J. Edward Taylor. "Theories of International Migration: A Review and Appraisal." *Population and Development Review* 19, no. 3 (1993):431–66.

———. "An Evaluation of International Migration Theory: The North American Case." *Population and Development Review* 20, no. 4 (1994):699–752.

McFalls, Joseph A., Jr. "Population: A Lively Introduction." *Population Bulletin* 58, no. 4 (December 2003).

Menard, Scott W., and Elizabeth W. Moen, eds. *Perspectives on Population*. New York: Oxford University Press, 1987.

Moore, Eric G., and Mark W. Rosenberg. *Growing Old in Canada*. Ottawa: Statistics Canada Cat. No. 96-321-MPE, 1997.

Olshansky, S. Jay, Bruce Carnes, Richard G. Rogers, and Len Smith. "Infectious Diseases—New and Ancient Threats to World Health." *Population Bulletin* 52, no. 2 (July 1997).

Owram, Doug. *Born at the Right Time: A History of the Baby Boom Generation*. Toronto: University of Toronto Press, 1996.

Plane, David, and Peter Rogerson. *The Geographical Analysis of Population*. New York: John Wiley and Sons, 1994.

Polunin, Nicholas, ed. *Population and Global Security*. Cambridge: Cambridge University Press, 1998.

Portes, Alejendro, ed. *The Economic Sociology of Immigration.* New York: Russell Sage, 1995.

Portes, Alejendro, and Reuben Rumbaut. *Immigrant America: A Portrait.* Berkeley: University of California Press, 1996.

Simmons, Alan B, ed. *International Migration, Refugee Flows and Human Rights in North America.* New York: Center for Migration Studies, 1996.

Simon, Julian L. *The Ultimate Resource.* Princeton, NJ: Princeton University Press, 1981.

———. *Population and Development in Poor Countries.* Princeton, NJ: Princeton University Press, 1992.

Smith, James P., and Barry Edmonston. *The New Americans.* Washington, DC: National Academy Press, 1997.

Watts, Julie R. *An Unconventional Brotherhood: Union Support for Liberalized Immigration in Europe.* La Jolla, CA: Center for Comparative Immigration Studies, 2000.

Weeks, John R. *Population: An Introduction to Concepts and Issues.* 7th ed. Belmont, CA: Wadsworth, 1999.

Zelinsky, Wilbur. *A Prologue to Population Geography.* Englewood Cliffs, NJ: Prentice Hall, 1966.

Population Websites

Websites are current as of July 2005. Note that Websites are not necessarily permanent, so up-to-date addresses cannot be guaranteed.

GENERAL

www.population.com
Population provides world news related to demography.

www.iom.int
The International Organization for Migration (IOM) is an intergovernmental organization that promotes migration for economic development, understanding of migration issues, and humanitarian programs to assist refugees and displaced persons. Among its publications, IOM publishes *International Migration*, a quarterly peer-reviewed journal.

www.cis.org
The Center for Immigration Studies is a nonprofit organization devoted to research and policy analysis of immigration. The site includes recent numbers, background reports, and news, reflecting a diversity of issues and opinions.

www.populationinstitute.org
The Population Institute provides information about population issues and promotes programs to reduce population growth.

www.populationconnection.org
Population Connection has actively promoted a reduction in population growth. The website includes many topical links, as well as information.

www.npg.org
The Negative Population Growth Council educates the American public on the dangers of population growth. The website provides alternate perspectives to population issues, advocating a smaller U.S. population and reduced immigration levels in order to create a sustainable future. The site provides links to like-minded organizations, such as Californians for a Sustainable Population, along with mainstream agencies or groups such as the U.S. Citizenship and Immigration Services.

www.refugees.org
The United States Committee for Refugees is a private organization that helps refugees. The site includes information on refugees and asylees throughout the world.

www.acf.dhhs.gov/programs/orr
This is the website of the U.S. Office of Refugee Resettlement, providing information on refugee legislation and resettlement within the United States.

www.popcouncil.org
The Population Council is an international, nonprofit organization devoted to biomedical, social science, and public health research related to population issues.

www.psi.org
This nonprofit organization seeks to increase the availability of health and population control products and services in low-income areas of the world.

SOURCES OF DEMOGRAPHIC STATISTICS

www.world-gazetteer.com
World gazetteer provides population statistics for cities, towns, and places, along with related data.

www.aecf.org
The Annie E. Casey Foundation has worked to promote the opportunities and environments of children and families in the United States. The website includes demographic data on children within the United States.

www.prb.org
This is the website for the Population Reference Bureau. It is very useful for both lay and academic interests in population issues, including data,

information, publications, and other services relating to the United States and the world.

www.ciesin.org
The Center for International Earth Science Information Network at Columbia University is a nonprofit, nongovernmental organization. The website includes detailed demographic information, including interactive mapping from the U.S. Census Bureau, census data, and other data sources, including environmental information and social indicators of development.

www.census.gov
The home page for the U.S. Census Bureau, this site includes information on the 2000 census and downloadable information and data on the United States on a variety of spatial scales. It also contains links to international statistical agencies in countries such as Mexico, the United Kingdom, or Germany.

www.census.gov/ipc/www/idbsum.html
The International Data Base section of the U.S. Census Bureau is particularly useful for demographic and socioeconomic data on other countries.

www.statcan.ca/start.html
This is the Statistics Canada home page, available in both French and English, with information and data that is downloadable.

www.cic.gc.ca
Citizenship and Immigration Canada maintains information on immigrant and refugee arrivals in Canada, along with current policy information and some historical records.

http://uscis.gov/graphics/index.htm
The U.S. Citizenship and Immigration Services website includes links to Border Patrol and Management, recent statistics on the origin of immigrants, immigrant class, and the settlement of arrivals.

www.usaid.gov
The United States Agency for International Development website includes information on current programs, missions, and statistics.

www.cdc.gov
The Centers for Disease Control and Prevention is the lead federal agency for the prevention of disease and promotion of health. The site includes information on health topics and statistics for the United States and the world.

www.cdc.gov/nchs
The Centers for Disease Control and Prevention provides links to the National Center for Health Statistics, which includes vital statistics, including

data on births, deaths, and marriages. Links to state health units are provided.

www.worldbank.org
The World Bank has a large amount of comparative world data, including population statistics.

UNITED NATIONS

www.unaids.org
Operated by the United Nations and other health groups, this website contains up-to-date information on the HIV/AIDS epidemic and links to other sources.

www.who.int
This home page for the World Health Organization monitors world health and includes updates on world health and health initiatives. The Statistical Information System provides access to the latest world-health data.

www.unhcr.ch
This website for the UN High Commission on Refugees includes publications and up-to-date statistics.

www.un.org/unrwa
This is the home page of the UN Relief and Works Agency for Palestinian refugees in the Near East.

www.unicef.org
This UN Children's Fund website includes resources and statistics related to children's health.

www.un.org/esa/progareas/pop.html
The UN Population Information Network coordinates population information activities at a variety of scales. Resources include links to other sites, as well as an electronic library.

www.un.org/esa/population
The United Nations runs its own population division, responsible for providing current data on population and development.

www.unfpa.org
The United Nations Population Fund (UNFPA) helps developing countries with population issues. The UNFPA website includes information on recent programs.

www.fao.org
The Food and Agricultural Organization of the UN website includes information and statistics relating to nutrition, food, forestry, fisheries, and agriculture.

BIBLIOGRAPHIC DATABASES

http://canada.metropolis.net
This is the website for the Canadian Metropolis Project, linking researchers at institutions across Canada and throughout the world that focus on immigration issues. The site has a digital library of papers produced by its associates, many of which are downloadable free of charge.

http://db.jhuccp.org/popinform/basic.html
Billed as the world's largest online bibliographic database on population issues, POPLINE is based at Johns Hopkins University.

ACADEMIC SITES

www.ccis-ucsd.org
Center for Comparative Immigration Studies at the University of California, San Diego, includes information on programs, research areas, and links to other sites.

www.cpc.unc.edu
The Carolina Population Center is a community of scholars and professionals collaborating on interdisciplinary research and methods.

www.psc.isr.umich.edu
The Population Studies Center at the University of Michigan focuses on both domestic and international population issues.

www.iussp.org
The International Union for Scientific Study in Population promotes scientific studies of demography and population-related issues.

www.ercomer.org
The European Research Center on Migration and Ethnic Relations focuses upon comparative migration analysis, ethnic relations, and ethnic conflict and is based at Utrecht University in the Netherlands.

http://opr.princeton.edu/archive
The Office of Population Research websites offer links to demographic centers throughout the world, as well as to other statistical resources and organizations.

www.popassoc.org
The Population Association of America is a society of professionals working in the population field. Links include publications.

Index

Page numbers in italics indicate figures or tables.

Aboriginals, 63–64, 69
abortion, 20–21
Afghanistan, 4, 156, 208–9, 144
Africa, 8, 9, 11, 193, 200, 216; conflict in, 198, 200; fertility, 42–43; HIV/AIDS in, 68, 78–86, 93–96; mortality, 43; refugees, 5, 142–43, 145, 147; sub-Saharan, 2, *8*, 9, 43, 52, 78–86, 185, 208
African Americans, 60–61, *62*, 63, 91–92
age pyramids, 31, *32–33*, 83, *84*, 107
aging, 26, 31, 34, 107, 216–27
AIDS. *See* HIV/AIDS
aliens, illegal, 4, 110, 113–14, 116, 127
antiretroviral drugs, 74, 94, 86–89, 218
assimilation, 106–7, 125, 130. *See also* balkanization and nativism
asylees. *See* refugees
asylum, 105, 130, 142. *See also* refugees

baby boom, 30, 217
balkanization debate, 103, 134, 219
Bangladesh, 9, 22, 42, 66, 201, 216
birth control. *See* contraception

Bongaarts, John, 20, 22
boomsters. *See* economic optimists
Border Patrol, 109, 116–18; Border Safety Initiative, 117
Boserup, Ester, 31, 168, 172
Botswana, 58, 79, 81–82, 84
Bracero Program, 102, 110
Brazil, 8–9, 218

Canada: aging, 30–32; illegal immigration to, 127–28; legal immigration to, 121–23, *124*, *126*, 127; Quebec, 35–36, 217; refugees, 151, *152*, 154
carrying capacity, 183
child mortality rate, 2, 20, 29, 37, 59
China, 127, 176, 205; fertility, 7, 18, 24–26; one child policy, 24–26; public health in, 68
Clark, William, 115
conflict, related to resources, 3, 178, 180, 186, 194–201
contraception, use of, 21, 35, 41, 75
Cornelius, Wayne, 102, 104
Cuba, refugees, 142, 148, 153

About the Author

K. Bruce Newbold is a professor of geography at McMaster University, Hamilton, Ontario, where he received his Ph.D. in 1994. He is also the director of the McMaster Institute of Environment and Health, a position he has held since 2004. He taught at the University of Illinois, Urbana-Champaign, between 1994 and 2000 and has held a guest scholar position at the University of California, San Diego. His research interests include internal migration, immigration, population health, and aging. With over forty refereed journal articles or book chapters published, he has received funding from the Canadian Institutes of Health Research, the Social Science and Humanities Research Council of Canada, the National Science Foundation, and the Social Science Research Council.

Breinigsville, PA USA
24 August 2010
244202BV00004B/47/P